OCCUPIER'S LAW

OCCUPIER'S LAW

Israel and the West Bank

by Raja Shehadeh

Prepared for Law in the Service of Man,
the West Bank affiliate of the
International Commission of Jurists

Institute for Palestine Studies

Washington DC

The Institute for Palestine Studies, founded in Beirut in 1963, is an
independent non-profit Arab research and publication center, which is not
affiliated with any political organization or government. The opinions
expressed in its publications do not necessarily reflect those of the Institute.

Library of Congress Cataloging in Publication Data

Shehadeh, Raja
　Occupier's Law
　1. Rule of law — West Bank.　2. Martial law — West Bank.
　3. Rule of law — Gaza Strip.　5. Israel-Arab War, 1967 Occupied Territories.
　I. Title.
　LAW　　　　　340'.11　　　　85-20941
　ISBN 0-88728-149-4
　ISBN 0-88728-150-8 (pbk.)

Designed by Pat Taylor, Inc.　Photograph by Karen Benzian

Edited and typeset by the International Commission of Jurists,
Geneva, Switzerland
Printed in the United States of America
by John D. Lucas Printing Company, Baltimore, Maryland

Contents

i

Acknowledgement

I wish to express my gratitude to my colleagues in Law in the Service of Man, in particular to Jonathan Kuttab, Sami Ayed, Mona Rishmawi, Tim Hillier, Ali Jaradat and Emma Playfair who have contributed to the making of this book by collecting and checking the accuracy of the data used and discussing the contents.

I also wish to thank my friends abroad. In particular, Jay Winter, Hyman Gross and Joe Raz and Patricia Williams, and my friends in Israel, Naomi Eilan and Daniel Amit, who have been strong supporters of my work and a great encouragement to me in the course I am pursuing. They share my depth of feeling against the injustice being inflicted on the Palestinians in the West Bank and the grave consequences this will have for all the inhabitants of the area. Their solidarity in our common fight is of great help.

My thanks to Janice Majors and to Christine Grandjean who typed this manuscript.

My very special thanks to Niall MacDermot, Secretary-General of the International Commission of Jurists, who went over the manuscript and offered his very valuable comments. But he has done more. His dedication to the cause of justice and the rule of law, his honesty and his integrity have been an invaluable moral support for me in all my work. My very special thanks to him.

The contents of this study take account of developments and information available up to November 1984.

Introduction

The occupation by Israel of the West Bank of Jordan is now in its eighteenth year. A wide gap exists between Israel's declared position towards the West Bank and its actual practice. The length of the occupation has accentuated this difference.

In 1980 *The West Bank and the Rule of Law* was published by the International Commission of Jurists and Law in the Service of Man. This study attempted to describe the changes the Israeli military orders[1] had brought about in the Jordanian law in force in the occupied territories.

Lawyers in the military administration of the West Bank prepared a reply to the study, which was published by the Israeli section of the International Commission of Jurists in 1981 under the title *The Rule of Law in the Areas Administered by Israel.* The Israeli publication attempted to justify Israel's activities by referring to international law to prove the consistency of these actions with the law of occupation. It is clear, therefore, that Israel takes the position that its activities in the West Bank are governed by international law, and are consistent with it.

---

1) *The West Bank and the Rule of Law* was the first publication to point out the unavailability of the military orders. Since 1982 the military have reprinted the military orders which are now more readily available. Military regulations made by virtue of these orders and regulations pertaining to the Jewish settlements in the West Bank, however, are still difficult to obtain. Also difficult to obtain are other regulations such as those concerning value added tax which has been amended 18 times and the amendments are not available even for lawyers. Also different military orders continue to be given the same number. This was the case, for example, with two military orders concerning the imposition of tax on imported services and the order amending Order 807 concerning Jewish religious councils. Both these orders were referred to as Order Number 1116.

Israel declares its objective is to remain within the parameters of international law which dictates that all changes in the existing legal system should be made for the benefit of the local population or the security of the occupation forces. This declared policy is irreconcilable with the facts which seem to indicate that the Israeli goal is gradually to drive out the local Palestinian population and to annex the territory. Israel has been astute in the way it has tried and still tries to present all it is doing in terms of the international law of occupation.

Israeli pronouncements have tended to be very legalistic using expedients common to the craft of lawyers. When the Israeli prime minister announced in 1983, for example, that Israel was not confiscating any Arab land in the West Bank, he was legally-speaking strictly correct. While it may have been true that Israel was not actually confiscating Arab land, it was nevertheless taking it by other methods which are described in the first part of this study.

Since 1980, many developments have occurred which clarify the objectives of the policy Israel is pursuing in the West Bank. The need for an analysis of these changes and a description of the new situation has made this sequel to the earlier study (which is now out of print) essential.

It is the thesis of this study that the policy which Israel has been pursuing in the West Bank is intended to drive out the Palestinians, to take over their land, and eventually to annex the occupied territories.

In a lecture given in the Spring of 1980 at Jerusalem's Hebrew University, Aharon Yariv (former chief of Israeli military intelligence) said: 'Some people talk of expelling 700,000 to 800,000 Arabs in the event of a new war, and instruments have been prepared (for the contingency)'[2].

Other pronouncements made by Israeli prime ministers over the years have made their intentions to annex the occupied territories very clear.

Israel is pursuing its West Bank policy by the following means:

— giving inalienable ownership and possession of the land to Jewish settlers and Zionist agencies for the exclusive use of Jews. The most recent figure for West Bank land already so acquired is 2,150,000 dunums (a dunum is 1,000 sq.m.), or 40% of the total area of the

---

2) Reported in *Inquiry* Magazine, Washington D.C., 8 December 1980.

West Bank[3];
— using regional planning schemes and road planning schemes, devised to serve Israeli interests to prevent the Palestinians from developing and using the remaining land;
— conferring on Palestinians in the West Bank a legal status equivalent to that of alien residents with none of the rights, privileges and guarantees normally enjoyed by nationals or permanent residents;
— subjecting the Palestinian population in the occupied territories to repressive laws created by the Israeli military authority without Palestinian participation or consultation;
— pursuing policies of harassment and intimidation of the population and denial of its basic human rights, including the right to self-determination.

This study is divided into three parts. The first part describes the various methods by which the alienation of 40% of the land in the West Bank has been brought about. It also explains the means by which the Palestinians are restricted in their use of the land which has not yet been acquired for Jewish settlement. Recent regional and road plans are described, showing the discrimination in favour of the development of Jewish settlements at the expense of the development of the Palestinians in the area.

As will be seen, the Israeli position is that it is entitled to use for the benefit of its settlers land which it regards as "state" land. Israel regards itself as the legal successor to the government of the British mandate and as such entitled to use "state" land for its own purposes. Even where this designation of the land that is being claimed as "state" land is correct in law, Israel is required to act as a trustee over this "state" land and the only use which Israel is entitled to make of it is one which is either for the benefit of the local population or is necessary for the security of the armed forces. By making the land available for the exclusive use of Jewish settlers neither of these two legal requirements is being fulfilled.

---

3) Meron Benvenisti, who has made a thorough survey of Israel's policies in the West Bank (published in *The West Bank Data Project, a survey of Israel's Policies* by the American Enterprise Institute for Public Policy Research, 1984), to which reference is made here, has said (p. 19) that: "The Israelis are in the process of gaining direct control over 40% of the West Bank land mass and 81% of the Gaza Strip area". He has pointed (on page 30) to the variety of definitions and classifications used to determine land under direct Israeli possession. He quotes the conflicting estimates of the size of the expropriated area, "which varies between a quarter and two-thirds of the total area of the West Bank".

In fact, far from increasing the security of the armed forces, the Israeli settlers put an added strain on them. They constitute foreign islands amidst a hostile population requiring their own system of self-defence and make it necessary for the armed forces to take action against the local population which otherwise would not have been necessary. Registered and unregistered land initially expropriated by the military authorities and which in the future can possibly be expropriated by the Jewish regional and local councils for their benefit, as well as lands declared "state" land, have now been registered in a special secret land registration department at the military headquarters. The land registration procedure according to which land registration under Jordanian law should take place has been discontinued. Registration in the West Bank of unregistered land has been facilitated only for Jews as will be described later.

The process of alienating the land, registering it and making plans for the prosperity of the Jewish settlers has gone so far that all the regional land use plans, including road plans, are designed to serve exclusively the benefit of these settlers.

For example, Israelis working on the West Bank planning schemes operate on the basis that Ramallah is in the Jewish regional council area of Binyamin, rather than that Ofra and other Jewish settlements are in the Ramallah District. The Arab population of the Ramallah District is over 100,000 while the Jewish population of Ofra and the other Jewish settlements in the Ramallah District is less than 5,000. The planning is designed to serve the settlements, not Ramallah.

It is clear even to the most optimistic among the proponents of settlements of Jews in the West Bank that the demographic balance in the West Bank between Palestinian and Jew can not change in favour of Jews for at least several decades, assuming there is not a forceful mass expulsion of Palestinians from the West Bank. Pending this change in the demographic balance, after which the formal annexation of the West Bank can be carried out without endangering the Jewish character of Israel, what will be the status of Palestinians in the West Bank? How will their affairs and those of the Jewish settlers be administered? What laws will apply to each of the two communities and to which courts of law will each be subject? These questions are examined in the second part of this study, which makes clear that the status which Israel has accorded to the Palestinians in the West Bank is that of permanent alien residents. The Israeli settlers on the other hand enjoy full Israeli citizenship and are spared the disadvantages suffered by the Palestinians in being subject to the local law, namely the remnants of Jordanian law as amended by over 1,100 Military Orders now in force.

Israeli residents in the Occupied Territories are subject to Israeli law which has been applied to them by using emergency regulations to extend Israeli legislation to the settlers, by issuing Military Orders which are applicable only to the Jewish settlements, and by distinguishing the local government units of the Jewish settlements, called local and regional councils, from the Palestinians' local government units of village councils and municipal councils. Thus, any Military Order which applies to local and regional councils will only apply to the Jewish residents of the West Bank and orders applicable to village councils and municipal councils will apply only to the Palestinians.

Through a series of Military Orders, the Jewish settlers have also been removed from the jurisdiction of the local court system. They have come to be subject to the Israeli legal system and have also been allowed to establish their own settlement courts. The three systems of justice now operating in the West Bank are described in the second part of this study.

The West Bank and the Rule of Law described in full the condition of the local court system for the Palestinians. Since the publication of that study there has been a marked deterioration in the local system, while the Jewish settlers have been rendered immune from the jurisdiction of this system.

The present state of the courts in this local system of justice has been described as unprecedented by the elder lawyers working in the West Bank, some of whom have been in practice since the time of the British Mandate. There is widespread corruption amongst the judges, who are appointed by the military authorities, and the police refuse to cooperate with the courts in ensuring that the accused or witnesses are brought to court or that the decisions of the courts are executed. Those in the military government who have control over the system have been showing an indifference towards this situation which has led to despair by those concerned for the application and enforcement of the law. An example of this was when the Israeli army officer in charge of the judiciary, who exercises 14 different crucial powers, departed on vacation without delegating these powers to any other official. Among the powers which he exercises is the power of issuing permits to those who wish to take legal proceedings in the West Bank High Court of Justice involving the military authorities or any of the authorities under its control.

Complaints of the lawyers about the state of the courts were brought to the attention of those holding the highest positions in the military administration of the West Bank in several meetings in 1984. It became clear, however, that the authorities had no intention of carrying out any improvements. Their answer was that the situation is not any better in Jordan, which is not in fact true. They also responded by saying that the largest percentage of those who are employed in the judicial system are Palestinians. This is indeed true, but they were appointed by the military authorities without consultation with the local population or legal profession. The military authorities should, therefore, bear the responsibility for their performance. As to the refusal of the police force to perform its duties in protecting the population and assisting the courts in the application of justice, the response was that the police force is composed of local Palestinians. This statement is untrue because although Palestinians are employed in the lower ranks, the police force is officially part of the Israeli police and all the responsible officers are Israelis. The authorities are fully aware of this fact.

A case which occurred in Tulkarim in the spring of 1984 made very clear the course which Israel seems to be following concerning the administration of justice for Palestinians.

A murder had taken place there which under Jordanian law had to be investigated by the police and the accused brought to stand trial before a regular criminal court. However, some members of the village league organisations, which Israel has been nurturing, took it upon themselves to form a tribal court (in accordance with traditional law rules) and imposed certain conditions upon the family of the accused and upon the court. They decreed that the family of the accused should be exiled from Tulkarim and they ordered that the court should not agree to release the accused on bail. This was a clear infringement of the jurisdiction of the court and the rule of law as it has been practised in the West Bank for over a hundred years. It is difficult to find proof that the military instigated the village league to carry out such action. It is clear that they did not discourage it or attempt to prevent it. It is also clear that the policy which the military is carrying out is leading the society towards a situation whereby those of ill-repute, such as Palestinians who join the village leagues, take over the judicial functions in the society. As the Jewish settlers are immune from the jurisdiction of the local courts, the deterioration of these courts is not seen as endangering settlement. By making the day-to-day life of Palestinians intolerable, the breakdown of law and order forces them to leave the Occupied Territories, which is what the military authorities encourage.

Further examples of the deterioration of the local courts are given in Part Two.

Part Three analyses the effects of the occupier's law. As has been stated above, the general policy of the occupation is to drive the Palestinians out. To bring this about, attempts are made to stifle the growth of the Palestinian population by exercising in a discriminatory manner the extensive powers of granting to Palestinians permits necessary for running the day-to-day business of society. The promulgation of the orders which make such permits necessary is justified on the grounds of security which in turn is used as a base for assuming its legality under international law. Israel's use of the concept of security is analysed in Part Three. Israel's reliance on the security justification has been extensive and all pervasive. Israeli propaganda outside and inside Israel has made unfounded use of its security needs. What has come to be accepted is that the PLO is a terrorist organization whose sole aim is the destruction of Israel and that all Palestinians are supporters of the PLO and are bent deep down on destroying Israel. As it is morally and legally justifiable to destroy in self-defence an enemy bent on your destruction, it is legitimate to destroy all Palestinians. The effect of this indoctrination by Israeli propaganda was evident in the Lebanese War when the Israeli army behaved brutally towards civilians as well as those engaged in the fighting.*

Following this argument Israeli authorities have maintained that membership of the PLO is "akin to advocating violence". Amnesty International however does not consider that membership of the PLO alone demonstrates advocacy of violence (see Amnesty International Report 1984, p. 341).

Security is also cited as justifying refusals to register charitable and cooperative organizations as well as interference in and restrictions imposed on their work. An illiteracy programme serving around 8,000 adults was asked by the social welfare department to stop on the grounds that it uses prohibited books. The collection of aid by charitable organizations from philanthropic Palestinians is also restricted to discourage the spirit of volunteerism and caring help by Palestinians.**

---

* A vivid description of the Israeli army's brutalities in the Lebanese War and their refusal to help civilians is in the war diary of Dov Yarimia published (in Arabic) by Arabesque and Anwar, Aker 1980, also available in Hebrew and English.

** This was also the policy in Lebanon. The ship of a Lebanese philanthropist, El Hariri, loaded with food and clothing for the victims of the war was not allowed to land.

Restrictions on the work of cooperatives and charitable organisations are extremely serious in view of the important function which these organisations perform in the West Bank, filling the gap created by the absence of an indigenous government. Since the assumption of joint control in Israel by the Labour and Likud Parties, there has been talk about a change in the policy of the military authority in the West Bank to bring about an improvement in the quality of life there. Although much publicity has been given to this, no basic change has occurred. Despite the promise of the Israeli Prime Minister Shimon Peres to re-open Najah University in the autumn of 1984 this was not done until the order for closure had expired. The cement factory project for which the approval of the authorities has been sought for over three years is still not approved. The reason given for this is that Israeli cement factories are not selling enough. It is clear that no more than a cosmetic change will result from the sharing of power by the Labour Party. The real change is only one of style. Likud was much less concerned about international public opinion than is Labour.

Part Three also describes the manner by which the authorities in the West Bank pursue policies of harassment and intimidation of the Palestinian population and deny it its basic human rights. Several reports describing violations of human rights in the occupied territories, while mentioning individual violations, fail to assess them in the context of the general Israeli policy towards the Palestinian population and therefore reflect an incorrect picture. The denial, for example, of building licences to the universities or other national institutions may not seem particularly grievous. Indigenous authorities elsewhere may do as much. Yet when it is put in the proper context of all the other actions intended to disrupt the growth of national institutions a different picture emerges. Similarly with the treatment of detainees. It is true that physical torture such as that practiced by other oppressive regimes is not as prevalent in the West Bank. However the entire process should be taken into account beginning with the midnight arrest of the detainee, his total physical isolation, the dehumanization and psychological torture to which he is subjected, all of which can be done without physical force. The entire system is carefully worked out to force the detainee to confess whether or not he is guilty. The practice whereby Israel does not allow a delegate of the International Committee of the Red Cross to visit the detainee until the fourteenth day after his arrest creates favourable conditions for this kind of torture. Those who look for physical signs of torture and conclude that because they cannot be found no torture is practiced are using too narrow and outdated a definition of torture and their findings cannot represent the true situation.

The picture which emerges from the study of the situation in the West Bank is that the occupier is pursuing policies which have brought the occupied West Bank close to a situation whereby fragmented Palestinian population centres are trapped between large areas reserved for the exclusive use of Jewish settlers. While the area as a whole is not in theory annexed to Israel the settlements are subject to *de facto* annexation and apply Israeli law and are served by the Israeli infrastructure and administrative structure. The Palestinian areas suffer from severe restrictions of their spatial growth and economic and social development. They also suffer the consequences of a corrupt legal system and of living in a society in which either the village-league-appointed mayors or other surrogates of Israel will ensure that carrying out the day-to-day affairs of the Palestinians becomes worse and worse. Those who cannot tolerate such conditions will have no alternative but to emigrate, thus furthering Israel's eventual goal of annexing the occupied areas (see the Israeli weekly *Kol Ha'ir*, 26 October 1984).

Many of the practices described in Part Three have been mentioned in reports published in Israel, the most comprehensive of which was the report of Yehudit Karp, the assistant to the Israeli Attorney-General. Her report on the behaviour of the settlers in the West Bank catalogues 70 cases of murder, damage to property and vigilante activities allegedly by settlers of which the police investigated only 15. The report was completed in May 1982 but published only in February 1984. Since then little or no action has been taken by the authorities to implement the recommendations of the report or to deal with the abuses documented in it.

There are a few cases in which legal action has been taken against the perpetrators of criminal activities. One such case in which seven Israeli soldiers were tried before an Israeli military court is described in Part Three. There were other cases involving torturers in Al-Fara'a Prison. Captain Ghadir and Moshe Biton were tried for their criminal activities, and convicted. An Israeli District court is at the time of writing hearing a case against the members of a Jewish terrorist group, and a petition is pending in the High Court of Justice against conditions in Al-Fara'a Prison. Such actions by the Israeli judiciary, civil and military, are commendable. However, in those of the above cases where the accused were convicted the sentences were lenient. In the case of Captain Ghadir, against whom a charge of torture was made and proven, the Appeal Court sentenced him to two months actual imprisonment, and two months suspended and reduced his military rank by one degree. Moshe

Biton, convicted of assaulting Mohamad Avada in a Jenin prison in May 1983 by tying him up and beating him, was sentenced to four months in prison by the Tel Aviv District Court. The Court accepted Biton's request not to start serving his sentence until an appeal has been considered (see *Jerusalem Post*, 19 September 1984).

The fact that legal censure is not more frequent and consistent is to be regretted as is the fact that the members of the ruling political groups in Israel do not come out more forthrightly against illegal actions in the Occupied Territories. Once, in its decision in the case of Elon Moreh, which is discussed in Part One, the Israeli High Court did condemn a settlement of Jews in the West Bank as illegal. Although the decision of the court was that in this case the requisitioning of private land was not in accordance with the law, the court left the door open for the use by the authorities of another method of acquisition of land for settlements, namely to declare the land to be "state" land. This has since been widely used with great effect and accounts for the acquisition of the largest proportion of land that has been acquired for Jewish settlement. The Court's decision, as it turned out, did not prevent the Elon Moreh settlement from being established nearby and it continues in existence.

Some Israeli politicians in responsible government positions have not concealed their support for the activities of the Jewish terrorists. The former Minister of Science, Yuval Ne'man, stated that although he believed Jewish terrorists had gone too far, it was not to be denied that their activities have brought positive results.

The legal situation in the West Bank is exceedingly complex. Its complexity was, indeed, used by the Israeli police commander who is head of the Investigation Division to excuse the failure of the police to act in the cases mentioned in the Karp report (supra).

There was no need for Israel to devise such a complex legal structure to administer the West Bank. The inevitable conclusion is that the complexity was intentional and designed to disguise the real policies of the occupation which in a less complex form would be more evident and therefore subject to stronger opposition.

In 1967 Israel occupied an area which had a local but not a central government. It must have been clear from the start that the occupation was going to be a long one. Israel was confronted with two alternatives: either to create a central administration as is proposed in the Camp David accord, or, to establish a military government to take over this role.

In the circumstances, it is understandable that Israel chose the second course as it suits Israel's long-term goals far better.

Israel has claimed that its occupation of the West Bank is the most benevolent in history and has insisted that it be judged by legal principles. When one looks closely at the legal structure which has been created, this proposition becomes untenable and riddled with inconsistencies. Several examples can be given.

The establishment of settlements was justified on security grounds. The High Court then began to consider Jewish settlers in the area as constituting part of the local population. As a consequence, any activity such as the West Bank road plan which is designed for the benefit of the settlers has been justified by the court as being for the benefit of the population. The principle in international law, of course, is that such changes in occupied territories are justifiable if they are for the benefit of the occupied population, not the occupier's. In assessing Israel's claim that certain changes are justified as being for the benefit of the Palestinian population Israel's declared aim of eventually annexing the occupied territories must be kept in mind. This ultimate illegal objective violates the presumption that certain actions are done for the benefit of the population. It cannot be the case that a military authority working for an aim which is detrimental to the national existence of the Palestinian population is seriously serving the interests of the population.

Israel refuses to accept that the West Bank was under Jordanian sovereignty. Yet on the travel documents issued to Palestinians by the Israeli interior ministry, the nationality of the holder is declared as Jordanian. Still, Israel refuses to admit that the land upon which those whom it recognises as Jordanians live, is part of Jordan.

What is to be made of the insistence on the necessity of Jewish settlement for security? Had it been thought that settlement of civilians of the occupier in the occupied territory could conceivably be essential for the security of the occupant, the international conventions would have allowed it; there would not have been such an absolute prohibition on settlement in the Geneva Conventions.

Israel has pursued a determined settlement policy. The link between the Jewish settlements and Israel is so far-reaching that it amounts to annexation in all but name. Nevertheless, Israel has succeeded in concealing from public opinion abroad that this is what is taking place. In the conclusion to *The West Bank and the Rule of Law* the example of the prohibition on picking wild thyme was given to illustrate how comprehensive the military orders dealing with the West Bank were and how irreconcilable they can be with any possible security justification.* It was asked then, "whether the point of issuing it was to protect nature, to safeguard the economic interests of Israeli planters, or perhaps to deprive the Palestinian population of access to a herb which through the many allusions to it in Palestinian literature has come to symbolize the attachment of Palestinians to their land?"

The purpose of analysing the complex legal situation that has arisen in the West Bank since 1967 is not merely to meet the intellectual challenge it provokes. It is hoped that publication of this study can help to serve the cause of justice.

---

* The example of the prohibition on picking wild thyme evoked varying reactions. Many refused to believe that such a prohibition existed. The review of the study in the *Jerusalem Post* insisted that it was introduced by the Israeli society for protection of nature.

Now several years later the real reason has become known. According to *Al Fajr* of 14 September 1984, the Israeli weekly supplement *Kol Ha'ir* revealed on 1 September 1984 that the military order prohibiting picking and marketing *za'atar* (wild thyme) in the West Bank was in fact issued to protect an Israeli family's monopoly over the herb's production from the low prices offered for the herb by Palestinian merchants in the West Bank.

Part One:

The Alienation of the Land
in the West Bank

Part One

Chapter One

The Acquisition of Land

"We are not taking land from anybody. Nothing."

Israeli Prime Minister Yitzhak Shamir
Time, 9 April 1984

The settlement of Jews in the occupied West Bank started with the beginning of the occupation. Different governments in Israel have pursued different settlement policies, and the objectives they have sought to achieve through settlement as well as their policies towards the West Bank have gone through many changes.[1] But settlement has always continued, although the methods for acquiring land have changed and have had to be adapted to the changing policies and realities. For example, when the drive for settlement intensified under the Likud government, new means for acquiring extensive areas of Palestinian land had to be adopted. The methods used to acquire land for settlement is the subject of this chapter.

A primary requirement for the Judaization of the West Bank is the possession of land. Successive Israeli governments have attempted to acquire all the land that it is possible to acquire by the 'legal' methods that have been devised during the 17 years of the occupation. As to the remaining areas, the policy is to prevent, as far as possible, Palestinian development in them. But this is the subject of the next chapter.

From the beginning of the occupation of the West Bank until 1979, the most frequently used method for acquiring land was requisition for military purposes. The decision of the Israeli High Court of Justice in the case of Elon Moreh[2] caused the government to abandon the use of

17

this method and to adopt the method whereby areas are declared to be 'state' land.

This case sheds light on the way in which the government was proceeding to requisition land, as well as on the arguments which the court used against this procedure. The objections the court found led the government to rely, after 1979, on the "state land" method of alienating land. The case is worth examining in some detail.

The Elon Moreh Case

On a hilltop within the boundaries of the lands of the village of Rujeib, 2 kms. east of the Jerusalem-Nablus road, Mustafa Duweikat and 16 other owners of 125 dunums* of land, witnessed on 7 June 1979, a "settlement operation" carried out with the help of the Israeli army. The operation was carried out with the assistance of helicopters and heavy equipment which started to build a road from the Jerusalem-Nablus highway to the hilltop. In the process, olive trees and other vegetation were destroyed. The advantage of the element of surprise, the Israeli High Court later said, was "to ward off the danger of this Court's intervention in the wake of landowners' applications even before work in the field began".

The background to the case was described by Justice Landau in his judgment as follows: On 7 January 1979, in the course of an illegal demonstration of persons from "Gush Emunim"** on a road in the Nablus area, a discussion was held by the Ministerial Defence Committee during which the following resolution was adopted:

---

* A dunum is 1,000 sq. m.

** Gush Emunim (translation: the block of the faithful) was an offshoot of the National Religious Party, founded in February 1974. It expanded rapidly, benefitting from the conservative—religious—annexationist backlash which followed the October War in 1973.

From 1975 Gush Emunim was at the forefront of "unauthorized" settlement bids in the West Bank highlands. The movement gained impetus, with the support of part of the labour government (notably Defense Minister Shimon Peres) and became official policy after the 1977 elections which brought the Likud party to power.

Thereafter, the Gush Emunim became *de facto* the settlement arm, or rather vanguard, of the government. All new settlements in the occupied territories are approved in the final analysis by the government as a whole, but Gush Emunim, the WZO, the Ministry of Housing, and an inter-ministerial committee all play a role in the planning process.

(Cont. p. 19)

"A) The Government views the 'Elon Moreh' settlement nucleus as a candidate for settlement in the near future.

"B) The Government will decide on the date and place of the settlement in accordance with the appropriate considerations.

"C) When determining the area of settlement for Elon Moreh, the Government will, as far as possible, take into consideration the wishes of this nucleus.

"D) The Elon Moreh people must now return to the camp which they left."

Following this resolution, an advance visit was made by representatives of the Ministerial Settlement Committee aimed at finding a suitable area for the settlement of the Elon Moreh nucleus. The Judea and Samaria Region headquarters looked into the possibility of finding some area in the region which was not privately owned, but no such place was found. On 11 April 1979, the Chief of Staff gave his approval to the relevant General Staff department for the requisitioning of the area for military purposes. The Ministerial Defence Committee decided to authorise the requisition order. The Deputy Prime Minister appealed against the decision of the Ministerial Defence Committee to the Cabinet Plenum, and, on 3 June 1979 the Cabinet rejected his appeal and by a majority vote approved the decisions of the Ministerial Committee. On 5 June 1979, Brig. General Ben-Eliezer (the Military Commander of the West Bank) signed the requisition Order entitled "Order Concerning Seizure of Land, 16/79". The text of the Order opens with the statement that "on the basis of my authority as Commander of the area and being of the opinion that the measure is required for security needs, I hereby command: . . .". In the main text of the Order, he declared an area of approximately seven hundred dunums, designated on a map affixed to the Order, as "seized for military purposes". According to paragraph five of the Order, "an announcement of the contents of the Order shall be delivered to the owner or the possessor of the lands

---

(Cont. from p. 18)

The ideological leaders of Gush Emunim profess a "whole land of Israel" dogma which stresses the Messianic redemption of the Jews through settlement of the biblical heartland. Their "religious" message in fact seems to have a secular purpose: settling the occupied territories and in effect annexing them.

Their best-known leader, Rabbi Moshe Levinger, expressed their vision of relations with Arabs: they are to be treated as the Old Testament orders the treatment of minorities: if they do not abide by the rules imposed upon them they are to be removed from "Eretz Israel".

in the area". "With respect to the conveying of the required announcement to the landowners", the High Court found, "it emerges that it was
only on the actual day of settlement, at 8 p.m. close on the commence-
ment of work in the field, that an announcement of the Order was
made to the *mukhtars*** of the village of Rujeib, who were summoned
to the office of the Nablus Military Governor. The *mukhtars* were
handed written announcements — in order to pass them on to the landowners — only on 10 June 1979", i.e. three days *after* the settlement
operation had started.

Mustafa Duweikat and the other landowners whose land was requisitioned, applied to the Israeli High Court on 14 June 1979. On 20
June 1979 an Order *nisi* was issued against the respondents — the
Government of Israel, the Minister of Defence, the Military Commander
of the West Bank and the Commander of the Nablus District — ordering them to show cause why the seizure orders should not be declared
null and void, and why the site should not be cleared of the instruments
and the structures erected on it, and the establishment there of a
civilian settlement stopped. In the ensuing proceedings, the Court
decided to make the Order *nisi* absolute, and to declare seizure Order
16/79 null and void with respect to the lands owned by the petitioners,
and to require the respondents to evacuate the civilian settlers from the
petitioners' lands together with every structure raised upon them and
any object introduced therein.

The Elon Moreh settlers refused to rely on the argument that their
settlement was being made on grounds of military security. They
sought to claim the right to settle on the land on ideological and,
indeed, religious grounds. In reaching its decision, the court rejected
these arguments, and the attitude of the settlers convinced the court
that the decision to establish the settlement was not made on security
grounds. In his judgment, Justice Landau found that "both the Ministerial Committee and the Cabinet majority were decisively influenced
by reasons stemming from the Zionist world view of the settlement of
the whole land of Israel".

The view concerning the right of the Jewish people to settle in 'Judea
and Samaria', Justice Landau said in his judgment, was based on the
fundamentals of the Zionist doctrine. But the question before the court
in the petition was whether this view justifies taking private property in

---

* Village elders — under Jordanian law this head of the village is elected. Most of those serving
as *mukhtars* at present have been appointed by the military authority.

an area subject to military government. He asked: "Would the decision at the political level to establish the settlement at that site have been taken had it not been for the pressure of Gush Emunim and the political/ideological reasons which were before the political level"? "I have been convinced", Justice Landau said, "that had it not been for these reasons, the decision would not have been taken in the circumstances which prevailed at the time".

The final legal ground for the decision in the Elon Moreh case was that the decision to establish a permanent settlement intended from the outset to remain in its place forever — even beyond the duration of the military government, which was established in Judea and Samaria — encounters a legal obstacle which is unsurmountable, because the military government cannot create in its area facts for its military needs which are designed *ab initio* to exist even after the end of the military rule in that area, when the fate of the area after the termination of military rule is still not known. This contains a *prima facie* contradiction which shows also, according to the evidence before us in this petition, that the decisive consideration that led the political level to decide on the establishment of the settlement under discussion was not the military consideration. "In these circumstances", Justice Landau concluded his judgment, "the legal form of seizing possession only, without confiscating ownership, cannot change the situation . . .".

By ruling that international law prohibits the taking of *private* property, the court suggested to the government that it would hold differently if the property seized were not private property.

The Court imposed two limitations on any future recourse to the High Court in cases of land requisition or possession by military authorities:

1) Only seizures of privately owned land could be prevented or reversed by recourse to the High Court,

2) The High Court was not prepared to intervene in any disputes over ownership status of land.

In order, therefore, for the military authorities to prevent the possibility of the resort by Palestinian landowners to the High Court they had to find property which they could claim was not private property, and they had to establish a tribunal which would hear disputes over ownership status of the land. The High Court would then be unwilling to hear petitions against the acquisition of such property.

21

The Elon Moreh case has been given extensive publicity by Israel. It is repeatedly referred to as proof of the effectiveness of the High Court in keeping the military within the parameters of the law. In fact, the Elon Moreh case did not prevent the eventual establishment of the Elon Moreh settlement. The settlement was later built on 'state land', a short distance from the original site. Nor did the case effectively obstruct the process of massive land acquisition in the West Bank. All it did was to pave the way for a new and (in the Court's opinion) sounder legal course for the military authorities to pursue. Since the Elon Moreh case, therefore, the main method for the acquisition of land in the West Bank has been taking place by declaring land to be 'state' land.[3]

Acquisition of Land by Declaring it to be 'State' Land

The two obstacles imposed by the High Court against petitioners challenging the take-over of their land cannnot be overcome when the land is being taken through declaring it to be 'state' land. Use by the authorities of this method of land acquisition, therefore, became the more convenient and certain course after the Elon Moreh case. The ground for the use of this method was already prepared. Order 59[4] was already on the books. Order 364[5] had already amended it to render a mere declaration by the authorities that land is state land sufficient proof that the land is to be considered as such 'until the opposite is proven'. This meant that contrary to normal procedure, proof lay not on the party making the claim, but on the party contesting it. The tribunal competent to hear the challenge is a Military Objection Committee established by Order 172. Where, therefore, such seizures were not of privately owned land but of 'state' land and the dispute was over ownership status, the two obstacles imposed by the High Court pertained, and the Palestinian whose land was being acquired could not resort to that Court.

Before going further into the discussion of how land is acquired using this method, it is necessary to describe the theoretical basis of the land law applicable in the West Bank.

The theoretical basis of the land law

When the occupation of the West Bank by Israel began in June 1967, only one-third of all West Bank land had been registered under the operation of the "Settlement of Disputes over Land and Water Law".[6]

22

Registration had been introduced by the British Mandate Government.[7] The Jordanian government continued it, but it was a slow, protracted process. Little land beyond this one-third has been registered since 1967 because the Israeli authorities suspended all operations of the Settlement of Disputes Law.[8] Ownership of the remaining two-thirds is attested by possession of a Turkish or British certificate of registration, or through registration in the tax registers. Title under Jordanian law is also proven through purchase and use.

The law which continues to govern land holdings in the West Bank is the Ottoman Land Code[9] as amended and developed by legislation passed during the British and Jordanian regimes, and the Military Orders issued by the Israeli Military Authority since the occupation. The theoretical basis of the Ottoman Land Code, however, continues to apply.

According to the Land Code, all lands in the West Bank are classified into the following categories:

(i)   Wakf lands, which are lands that are dedicated to pious purposes,

(ii)   Mulk land, which are the lands that were initially given out by the Ottoman conquerer of the area (who considered himself the owner, by conquest, of all the lands he occupied) to the Muslim residents and the Khuraj lands handed over to non-Muslims,

(iii) Miri, matruke, and mawat land, which are all considered by the Israeli authorities to be 'state' lands. Miri lands are lands which the Ottoman Emir (or Sultan) did not allow to be dedicated as wakf or given out to be possessed as mulk. It is land whose raqabeh (or ultimate ownership) continues to reside with the Emir, but whose use he has granted to the public under certain conditions.

The theoretical basis of the land law conforms to the theoretical basis of other systems of land law, such as, for example, English land law. There also, all the land came into the ownership of the Crown with the Norman invasion when it was acquired by conquest. The Crown has given out land to the people to use in accordance with different tenures. But the maxim "no land is without a lord" has always applied, and the ultimate lord is the Crown. However, this provides only the theoretical basis. In practice, the only lands which are in the actual ownership and possession of the Crown in England are those areas which are classified as crownhold. The rest are in the actual ownership and possession of their registered owner or user, as the case may be.

23

Similarly, the theoretical basis of the Palestinian land law was never altered, but the actual implications of the law have been subjected to several amendments during the Turkish, British and Jordanian regimes. Jordanian Law No. 49 of 1953,[10] for example, removed all the restrictions previously existing on the extent of the use which the possessor of miri land could make of the land, thus removing any practical difference that existed between the powers of the owner of mulk land and the owner of miri land. Similarly, a Jordanian law of 1953[11] declared all miri lands falling within the municipal areas as transferred to mulk land. Some differences, however, continue to exist in the way each category of land devolves upon the death of its owner. The present Israeli policy, however, is to consider miri land as 'state' land.

Another category of land which is considered to be 'state' land by the military authorities is matruke land. This is land which has been left for public purposes, such as the building of roads, cemeteries, etc. The third category is mawat land which is considered dead land because it lay further from the village "than the human voice could be heard" (in the words of the Ottoman Land Code).

The Ottoman system and all later governments until 1967 acknowledged that the land surrounding the village was for the use of the villagers either as common pastures or for the future development of the village. The inhabitants of the village did not have any need or opportunity to register their lands. They knew amongst themselves which of the village lands belonged to which families and which were owned in common (mashaa).

The land which has been registered under the operation of the law for settlement of disputes includes lands which fall under each of the above categories with the exception of some types of wakf land which, having been inalienably dedicated to the Almighty, cannot be registered in the name of a private owner.

Although according to the Ottoman Land Code there was no category of public or state land, the Government of the British Mandate introduced this category through the 1922 Order-in-Council[12]. Article 2 of the Order-in-Council defined "public lands" as "all lands in Palestine which are subject to the control of the government of Palestine by virtue of Treaty, Convention, Agreement or Succession and all lands which are or shall be acquired for the public service or otherwise."

It is apparent from the definition that public lands were restricted to lands subject to the control of the government and used in execution of its purposes, such as the erection of government houses, etc. They did

24

not include land which was not the subject of a grant to the public, and, therefore, did not include miri, mawat, and matruke lands whose raqabeh remained with the Sultan, but upon which no actual control was exercised by the Sultan. The definition includes lands which are to be acquired for the public service, by expropriation, for example. The High Commissioner was vested with all rights in or in relation to such public lands in trust for the government of Palestine. The position of the Sultan as the ultimate owner of the land (the holder of the raqabeh) was necessarily transferred to the High Commissioner who replaced him and who inherited the Sultan's ultimate theoretical ownership of all the lands of Palestine.

Inspection of the records of land registered before 1967 shows that approximately 13 percent of the land in the West Bank was in fact registered in the name of the state. This includes land which the Jordanian government expropriated under the "Law of Expropriation for Public Purposes"[13] and land which was acquired under the 1939 Emergency (Defence) Regulations.[14]

It was never the practice under the Jordanian government before 1967, nor is it now the practice of the present government in Jordan, to consider all lands except land falling in the wakf and mulk categories as state land. It is, therefore, correct to conclude that in June 1967 state lands comprised those lands which were already registered in the name of the Jordanian government by the operation of one or another of the laws in force in Jordan which allowed the state to acquire land for public or for military purposes. That category of state land, though, was not a closed one. Other lands were liable to be included in it in accordance with Articles 8(3) and 8(4) of the Settlement of Disputes Law mentioned above. However, that could not occur after 1967 because Order 291 issued by the West Bank Area Commander suspended all the operations of the Settlement of Disputes over Land Law.*

---

* When the author wrote to the Area Commander asking that settlement of disputes over land be resumed to enable land registration to continue, he received a reply from the legal adviser of the military government. In his reply on 27 December 1983, the legal adviser said that the authorities could not allow registration because this would jeopardise the interests of the absent landowners. In the case of François Albina (16/82), the custodian of Absentee Property took possession of his land and transferred it to the settlers while Mr. Albina had been in the area and had never left it. The Objection Committee, to which an appeal was made against this "error" by the Custodian upheld the Custodian's decision and the settlers retained possession of the lands. It must also be pointed out that registration in the names of Jewish settlers of unregistered land is in fact allowed to continue in the secret land department at the military headquarters where "special" transactions in land are registered.

Similarly, the courts during the British mandate did not interpret lands falling into the miri category as state land. In Israel the land was divided into the same categories as in the West Bank today. The Ottoman land code was still applicable until 1969. According to article 153 of Israel's Land Law of 1969: 'The ownership of property which immediately before the coming into force of this law belonged to the miri category shall be full ownership in accordance with the provisions of this law.' It is difficult to understand how Israel can interpret the same law to imply one thing in the West Bank and another in Israel, but this is in practice the case.

The procedure used to declare land 'state property'

This was the condition of the land law and registration when Military Order Number 59 was issued by the Area Commander on 31 July 1967. The Order defined state property as:

(i) All property which on the specified date (i.e., 6 June 1967) pertained to one of the following:
  (a) the enemy state,
  (b) a juridical body in which the enemy state possessed any right, whether directly or indirectly, and whether this right referred to control or not;

(ii) Property which was registered on the specified day in the name of one of the above two;

(iii) Property in which one of the above two was a partner on the specified date;

(iv) Property in respect of which on the specified date one of the two mentioned in (i) above was either an owner in partnership, or a registered owner, or was in possession.

Order 59 provided that the "person appointed to implement the Order may assume possession over state property and carry out whatever action he deems necessary for this".

It is not difficult to appreciate the justification behind passing Order 59 so shortly after the occupation. During the first days of occupation, many Military Orders were passed relating to assumption of power and control over various aspects of life in the occupied territory (as will be discussed in Part Two). It is not, therefore, surprising that an Order

26

should be passed concerning the assumption of control over state property. In 1967 Military Order No. 58[15] concerning assumption of possession of another category of property (absentee property, which will be discussed later), and Order 25[16] requiring licences to be obtained for all land transactions, were issued. Order 59 was amended to serve an entirely different purpose which does not seem to have been foreseen when the Order was issued.

It is by virtue of Order 59 that hundreds of thousands of dunums — which constitute the majority of land used for settlement — have been declared 'state' land and transferred to the Jewish settlers.

A careful reading of Order 59 in its original unamended form reveals that it was intended to enable the Custodian of Government Property (which office was created by Order 59) to assume control over and to manage the property of the Jordanian government for the duration of the occupation.

Pursuant to this objective, the order empowers the Area Commander to make arrangements concerning the means of supervising the government property. The assumption of such powers over government property is to enable the custodian whom the Area Commander appoints to fulfill his duties and exercise his powers under the order of managing the properties of the Jordanian government pending the termination of the occupation. The present use to which this Order is put, namely to declare non-registered property state land and to transfer it to the exclusive use of Jewish settlers, is clearly an improper and illegal extension of the original intention of the Order. It is also inconsistent with Article 2 of the Order which empowers the custodian to assume possession of state property and to take whatever action he deems necessary for this. It cannot possibly be deemed necessary for the fulfillment of the intention of the Order to transfer the use and ownership of government property to private individuals to use for private purposes as owners for long periods — as is now the case with land used for establishing a permanent Jewish presence in the occupied territory.

The present use of Order 59, to declare areas of land state property according to an enlarged definition, began in 1979. It coincided with the decision of the Likud government of Israel to intensify its settlement activities in the West Bank.

Before 1979, smaller areas of land were being acquired for the Jewish settlement of the West Bank. The methods which were used to acquire them will be described later. None of them sufficed to facilitate the transfer of the areas of land required by the Likud government to fulfill its large-scale plans for Jewish settlement of the West Bank. To assess the availability of legal methods which the military authorities could employ to acquire the areas of land required, a comprehensive survey of the ownership and registration status of all West Bank lands was begun in December 1979 by the Office of the Custodian of Absentee Property (which is under the control of the Israel Land Authority) under the supervision of Mrs. Plia Albeck, a legal expert working with the Israeli Ministry of Justice.

Palestinian employees of the Land Department, the Survey Department and the Office of the Custodian of Absentee Property were put to work to investigate the land records and make reports. Experts in the local land law, such as Mr. Yusuf Atallah, the then Director of Lands, were encouraged to make available their knowledge about the Land Law.[17]

The comprehensive survey revealed that the majority of land in the West Bank was not registered and fell into the categories of miri, matruke and mawat lands. The government, therefore, decided to consider all unregistered lands falling into one of these categories to be state land. Declarations of land as state land began to be made. Under the alterations that were carried out in the judicial system, which will be described in Part Two, the only tribunal competent to hear appeals against such decisions is the Objection Committee, which is controlled and administered by the military authorities who make the declarations. The Israeli High Court of Justice had already decided in the Elon Moreh case (as has been mentioned above) that it was not prepared to intervene in any disputes concerning the ownership of land and that it will only hear appeals concerning seizure of *privately* owned land. It is clear then that the military authorities have found the means to have full control over the process of land acquisition for Jewish settlement, as well as over appeals submitted against any decisions made pursuant to it, since the decisions of the Objection Committee are no more than recommendations which are submitted to the Area Commander who may accept or refuse them.

Following these changes, the acquisition of hundreds of thousands of dunums of land proceeded at a very fast pace and is continuing at the time of writing.

This method is the one most commonly used to acquire possession of lands in the West Bank for Jewish settlements. Before proceeding to discuss the other methods that are used, it is necessary to describe fully the steps by which land in the West Bank is acquired using this method.

When the Ministerial Settlement Committee decides to establish a new settlement in the West Bank or to enlarge an already existing one, the area of land required is considered by the legal experts at the Israeli Ministry of Justice. Their decision is passed to the Israeli Land Authority, of which the office of the Custodian of Absentee and State Lands in the West Bank is a department. This main office passes the decision to the regional office of the Custodian of Absentee and State Lands in the area where the land in question is situated. The Custodian usually summons the mukhtar (village elder) and takes him to the area that has been declared state land and points it out to him. It then becomes the responsibility of the mukhtar to inform those members of his village whom he believes own plots within this area. They are informed that if they wish to appeal against the decision they should apply to the Military Objection Committee.

With such a vague reference to the land that is the subject of the declaration, confusion as to the exact boundaries and area of the land so declared often occurs. In practice, the first indication to landowners that their land has been the subject of a state land declaration is often the sight of bulldozers working the land to prepare it for the construction of a Jewish settlement. This is because many of the mukhtars are appointed by the military authorities and are not on good terms with the residents of the village.

If, however, the landowners are served with a written declaration, a photocopy of a map may be appended to it. But in practice it is not. In appeal number 7/84, the map of the area (the subject of the declaration) was made available only five months after the owners of the land submitted their objections against the declaration. The map was a fiscal map where the area, the subject of the declaration, was delineated with a thick marking pen. In the declaration, the description given of the land referred to the name by which the "site" is commonly called and its number. In areas where no registration has taken place, reference to an area by giving the name and number of the "site" without giving the boundaries will not be sufficient to identify the land, because each "site" can comprise thousands of dunums. With such a confusing description of the area to be the subject of the declaration, the owners cannot be sure whether and which part of their land is included in the area declared state property. They may as a result submit the wrong documents. The representative of the Custodian of state property then uses the confusion against the appellants, as happened in the case referred to above, where he claimed that the confusion indicates that the appellants were not in fact the owners of the land, the subject of the declaration.

The first task, therefore, is to ascertain the exact location of the area in question. The Office of the Custodian is rarely cooperative in this regard. Since 1983, it has been the practice not to attach a map at all. The only identification of the area declared "state" property is obtained from the Custodian of state property, who points the area out by hand on the site. In case no. 7/84, the Custodian pointed out several hills, which amounted to 3,000 dunums. The appellant had to prepare survey maps of all 3,000 dunums at very great expense. The area actually declared turned out, in fact, to be much smaller. But the Palestinian appellant was not compensated for his expenses in preparing survey maps of the larger area pointed out by the Custodian.

After overcoming the initial difficulty of discovering the exact location and area of land the subject of the declaration, those claiming ownership can choose to submit an appeal against the declaration to the Objection Committee. However, in deciding whether or not to resort to the Objection Committee, they must take into consideration the fact that the declaration that the land is state land is declarative and not constitutive. A decision by the tribunal in favour of the military authority can only add legal weight to the authority's decision.

According to the rules provided by Order Number 172 concerning appeals against a declaration of state land, an appellant (upon whom falls the burden of proving that the land in question is not state land) must submit with his appeal a survey map of the whole area in dispute, prepared by a licensed surveyor, which shows the exact boundaries of all the plots claimed by the various appellants.

The area of land involved in such cases is often more than two thousand dunums. The expense involved in preparing a survey map of such a large area of land can be exorbitant. The rules also require that each appellant submit with the appeal a sworn statement declaring the basis on which he claims ownership of the land, as well as copies of all documents upon which his claim is based. All these must be submitted forty-five days after the declaration is made. The Custodian then submits his reply to this appeal and the case is heard by the Objection Committee. Although, according to the rules of procedure followed by the Committee, it is empowered to make interim injunctions to stop all further work on the land pending the end of the proceedings, the Committee, in practice, refuses to make such orders. In case no. 17/83, the settlers began constructing two roads and building houses on the land while the Committee was hearing the case. The case has not been decided at the time of this writing, but the fact that the roads will by then have been completed and the houses constructed is bound to prejudice the outcome of the case.

The Committee is unwilling to accept receipts for payment of tax on the land or registration in the tax department as sufficient proof of ownership. If use is the basis of the ownership claim, the appellant must prove "continuous use," that is, cultivation for the preceding ten years.

The Custodian has available to him the aerial photographs of the West Bank, which have been taken periodically. These are often presented to the Committee as proof that the land has not been continuously cultivated. As the authorities have refused to grant permits to Palestinian farmers for the drilling of artesian wells, agriculture, in most cases, is dependent upon the irregular and often insufficient rainwater. Some years the rainfall is so slight as not to make it worthwhile to cultivate the land. Also, since the occupation, West Bank residents have been attracted by the availability of work in Israeli factories and leave their lands and work instead for the more secure wages provided by Israeli employers. These circumstances, together with the conditions that the Objection Committee places upon the appellants, have resulted in a low success rate for such appeals. In addition, the expenses involved, including payment for the professional services of the surveyor and lawyer, are often much higher than those an average villager in the West Bank can afford.

Even if an appellant succeeds in meeting the high standard of proof required by the Objection Committee, the Committee may still decide against him. Article 5 of Order Number 59 provides that "every transaction made in good faith between the Custodian and another person concerning property which the Custodian considered, at the time of making the transaction, to be state property, shall not be cancelled and shall continue to be binding even if it is proven that the property in question was not state property at the time when the transaction was made". The standard of proof required to satisfy the Committee that the transaction was entered into by the Custodian in good faith is not high.

Five years after this method of taking possession of land in the West Bank had started, most lands that would be acquired using this method have already been declared "state" land. The military have now reverted to the use of expropriation to acquire more land.

In 1983, several thousand dunums of land were seized in Ramallah on grounds of security. Some of these lands fall within the municipal areas of Ramallah and all are registered lands. The Army Camp for which the military claim they need the land is situated far away from the area seized. This area borders on the industrial zone of the town. Its seizure will restrict the town's development and the growth of its industrial zone. The military made this seizure order knowing that the High Court of Justice would be unwilling to accept a challenge to the military order because of the Court's reluctance to question the military claim that land is required on grounds of security. The Elon Moreh case (see above) was in this respect quite exceptional.

Lands that are expropriated are now defined as "state" property and can be registered as such. Military Order Number 59 concerning "state" property has been amended[18] to include in the definition of state property land that was or will be the subject of an expropriation order.

In December 1974, Military Order 569[19] established a department for the registration of special transactions in land. Article 2 states that transactions involving lands which have been declared state land or which have been acquired for military purposes or were the subject of an expropriation order, should be registered. Inspection of the register has been restricted. Article 7 states that registration under this Order shall be considered as proper registration for the purposes of any law requiring the registration of transactions in land.*

Unregistered land in the West Bank can be registered using a special procedure under Jordanian law.[20] This law was amended by special military regulations published on 24/8/84, whereby it has become possible for the Custodian of government property to submit applications for the registration of "state" property. When the Custodian is the applicant, different requirements are made than is the case for any other applicant. The Custodian is required to submit with his application only the following documents: (1) a certificate made by virtue of Order 59 concerning state property that the land to be registered is "state" property; (2) a copy of the map that was attached to the order; (3) a report that the mukhtar (village elder) was notified of the declaration; and (4) a certificate from the Custodian that no objections were made to the declaration, or, if they were, the recommendations of the Objection Committee. As to publication of the request for registration, the regulations empower the officer in charge of immovable property to carry out publication in the village or town where the property lies either through the mukhtar or a representative of the military governor who will certify in writing that publication has taken place.

It is noteworthy that in cases where the applicant is the Custodian

---

* Under Jordanian law *no* transaction in land is considered legal unless it is registered at the Land Registration Department established by the government.

32

the Committee does not require a succession order to prove the legal heirs of immovable property the subject of the application, as is mandatory according to the law in force in the West Bank. It can accept in place of a succession order a declaration from the applicant, declarations from two witnesses and a certificate of the mukhtar giving details of the names of the relatives of the testator and of the shares of the heirs.

Disputes over unregistered land for which an application for registration has been submitted have also been removed from the jurisdiction of the local courts. After the promulgation of Order 1060,[21] even those cases that were being heard by the local courts were transferred to the special military committee constituted under the Order to hear such land cases. In one case,[22] the decision was final as regards one of the appellants, yet the Court of Appeal decided that it was obliged under Order 1060 to transfer the whole case to the special committee. This case had been in the local courts since 1980. The settlers were fighting a losing case because they had obtained the land through an illegal purchase, and there was strong evidence to that effect. When they despaired of success in the local courts, Military Order 1060 was invoked whereby their case was transferred from the local court to the military tribunal.

Because of the secrecy of the operations and records of the Special Land Registration Department,[23] it has not been possible to discover the extent of the area of land which has already been registered in the West Bank in the names of Jews. But it is clear that Israel is not wasting any time in acquiring and registering the largest possible area of land in the West Bank in the names of Jewish individuals and corporations. No doubt it hopes through this to jeopardise any future possibility of the return of this area to Jordan or to any other Arab government, should pressure be exerted on it to end its military occupation.

Before concluding this discussion of how the land laws in force in the West Bank in 1967 have been misinterpreted to enable large areas to be acquired as "state" lands, it must be mentioned that even if the definition Israel is using for the lands it is claiming as state land is correct, the Hague Regulations, in Article 55, state that an occupying power shall be regarded only as the usufructor and administrator of state property. It must safeguard the capital of the property and administer it in accordance with the rules of usufruct. A usufructor may enjoy the use of the property but may not impair its substance or alter its character. The policy of the Israeli authorities towards the lands in the occupied West Bank is clearly a distortion of existing law and of Israel's duty as an occupier.[24]

Acquisition of Property by Declaring it 'Abandoned'

The concept of 'abandoned' property has its origins in the thinking of the early Zionists at the beginning of this century, prior to the establishment of the State of Israel. Consistent with their belief that the Palestinians did not have a strong tie to their land, Zionist activists were inclined to believe that many Palestinians would be willing to abandon their property if offered property elsewhere in the Arab world. Those Arab landowners who lived outside Palestine before 1948, the feudal lords, were the first target.

After the establishment of the State of Israel in 1948, the Palestinians, who were driven or fled from the territory of pre-1967 Israel, left behind immovable property with an estimated value of 100,383,784 Palestinian pounds. This property included extensive stone quarries, 40,000 dunums of vineyards, 95 percent of Israel's present olive groves, nearly 100,000 dunums of citrus groves, and 10,000 shops, businesses and stores.[25] They also left behind 19,100,000 Palestinian pounds' worth of movable property.

Many of the Palestinians who stayed were termed "internal absentees" because they left or were forced out of their original place of residence although they remained within the boundaries of the State of Israel, and 40 percent of the lands of those remaining Palestinians was also confiscated as 'abandoned' property.[26]

Islamic wakf land (land which is dedicated for a pious purpose), amounting to hundreds of thousands of dunums in Israel, was also considered to be abandoned land.

In 1950, the Israeli Knesset passed the Absentee Property Law[27] by virtue of which a custodian was appointed to manage this property. The Development Authority (Transfer of Property) Law, also of 1950,[28] established a Development Authority in Israel, which was permitted to buy the lands placed by the earlier law under the control of the Custodian of Absentee Property. The Development Authority has eight members from the Jewish National Fund* and seven representatives of the State of Israel.

---

* A semi-governmental corporation, which holds in its name approximately 93.3% of the lands in Israel, pre-1967. See article by Walter Lehn on the activities of the Fund in purchasing land in the West Bank, *"And the Fund Still Lives"*, in the Journal of Palestine Studies, Summer 1978, pp. 3-33.

The Israeli Absentee Property Law of 1950 defined an absentee as, *inter alia*, someone who left to go to a country which is in a state of war with Israel. The Military Order of 1967,[29] however, defines an absentee as someone who has left the area of the West Bank before, during, or after the time of the 1967 war. This definition in the 1967 Order would make even a Palestinian who was resident in June 1967 in a country not in a state of war with Israel, for example, in the U.S., an absentee. This strict application of the definition in the Order, however, has not so far been applied in the West Bank.

The control of the military authorities over the land registers and their successful penetration of Palestinian society in the West Bank helped them to identify which property is (according to the Order) 'abandoned' property. However, even when the owner of the property has not left the area (and, therefore, his property does not qualify as abandoned property) and a Jewish settlement is in need of land, the Custodian can still acquire possession of it and enter into transactions with third parties who are either individuals or Israeli development companies. In one such case[30] involving land registered in the name of a Palestinian who lives in the area, the Custodian leased for 49 years over 70 dunums of land to the Zionist Agency for the use of private Israelis who were living in the Jewish settlement of Beit Horon and who wanted to enlarge their settlement. When the owner objected, the Custodian invoked Article 5 of Order 58, which states that "any transaction carried out in good faith between the Custodian of Absentee Property and any other person, concerning property which the Custodian believed when he entered into the transaction to be abandoned property, will not be void and will continue to be valid even if it were proved that the property was not at that time abandoned property". The Military Objections Committee found that "there is no doubt in our eyes that the appellant is the legal owner of the land in question". Even so, the Committee decided that the transaction which the Custodian had made with the Zionist Agency to lease the land for a period of 49 years for the purpose of establishing a settlement "is in fact standard, strong and binding and this in spite of the fact that we concluded in our opinion that the ownership of the said land belongs to the appellant". In his summing up, the attorney for the appellant in this case had stated that: "If the Article 5 on good faith is not interpreted strictly and the Custodian then believes that whatever action he takes (even if based on improper legal considerations) will be retroactively validated by imputing to it good faith, without using strict criteria to ascertain whether or not it in

35

fact existed, the Custodian will in effect be given a free hand to act arbitrarily and take less care to act according to proper legal principles and in accordance with the facts of each case. If this happens, a mockery would have been made of the law."

The response of the legal advisor to the military government that the Area Commander cannot allow the resumption of land registration under Jordanian law (as mentioned in the footnote on page 25 above), on the grounds that the resumption of such registration would prejudice the rights of absent Palestinians, can only be regarded as cynical in view of the above case.

The head office of the Custodian of Absentee Property is in West Jerusalem. The office is called "The State of Israel Lands Authority, Custodian of Absentee and Government Property in the districts of Judea and Samaria". As the title implies, the office of the Custodian of Absentee Lands in the West Bank is administered by the Israel Lands Authority (whose director is the Israeli Minister of Agriculture, *ex officio*). This authority supervises the use of 93 percent of the land in pre-1967 Israel and has effective responsibility for the supervision of land acquisition and use in the West Bank.

The Jerusalem head office acts through offices in each of the major West Bank towns. Those employed in these offices (Palestinians and Israelis) are constantly on the lookout for more land to acquire under the pretext that it is abandoned property. They are helped in this by the legal and administrative changes that have rendered the approval of the Custodian necessary for all transactions involving land. This includes all sales and the re-registration of land, even when it does not involve any alienation of land. It also includes registration of land in the name of the heirs of a deceased owner. The obvious objective here is to identify any share in the land which devolves upon a non-resident which the Custodian will be able to take.

It is clear both from the working of Military Order 58 (in particular the provision on transactions made in good faith) and from the practice of Israeli governments in the past and in the West Bank at present, that it is not the intention of Israel to hold the property of absentees in trust and in accordance with the rules of usufruct pending the resolution of the conflict. The Custodian is handling 'abandoned' property as if he were an absolute owner and transferring it, usually through 49-year leases, to third parties to use to establish Jewish settlements. According to one estimate, the Custodian of Absentee Property has seized a total area of 430,000 dunums.[31]

Land Requisitioned for Military Purposes

Privately owned land can be seized by unnumbered Military Orders which proclaim that the land is needed for "vital and immediate military requirements". Such lands remain theoretically under private ownership. Many settlements have in fact been built on these lands. The total area thus seized is estimated at 35,000 dunums.[32]

Land Closed for Military Purposes

Military Orders have been issued declaring certain areas in the West Bank to be closed areas. Although the power to make such declarations is wide and can be used for many reasons (including, for example, to prevent reporters visiting a place where there is a demonstration which the military authorities do not wish to have reported), this power is more often used to close areas on the grounds that they are "security zones" claimed to be needed by the army as training grounds, firing ranges, etc. Closed lands later tend to be requisitioned, as was the case of the land on which the Jewish settlement near Hebron, the largest settlement in the West Bank, Kiryat Arba, was established. Restricted military areas cover 1.11 million dunums or 53% of the total area seized for Israeli purposes in the West Bank.[33]

Land Expropriated for Public Purposes

According to Jordanian Law No. 2, Expropriation of Land for Public Purposes, of 1953,[34] an authority or corporate body wanting to expropriate land must first publish in the Official Gazette its intention to submit to the Council of Ministers the application for expropriation of the land specified in detail in the Gazette. If no objections are submitted within 15 days, the approval of the Council of Ministers is applied for. When this approval is obtained, it must be endorsed by the King. It is then published in the Official Gazette. Thereafter, the person, authority or body interested in making the expropriation submits to the Registrar of Lands in the area where the land is situated the list of names of the owners of the land in question, as well as a copy of the decision of the Council of Ministers endorsed by the King. The body requesting the order must then compensate the owners of the land with an amount equal to the market value of the property on the date of expropriation. The competent court to which any of the above decisions may be appealed is the Court of First Instance in whose area of jurisdiction the land falls.

The Military Orders amending this law have brought about the following changes:

A military authority appointed by the Area Commander has been given all the powers and privileges which, according to the expropriation law, were vested in the Jordanian government. The requirement to publish the intention to carry out an expropriation, the need to obtain the approval of the Council of Ministers and the endorsement of the King, the necessity to publish again the approval, and the requirement to submit the pertinent documents to the land registrar are not applicable when the body seeking the expropriation order is one appointed by the Military Commander.

The right of the owner of the land to appeal against the expropriation or the compensation to be paid for the land has been transferred from the Court of First Instance to the Objections Committee.

A new article has been added to the law whereby the Area Commander may order that force be used to evacuate the owner of the land if he refuses to vacate it within the period decided upon by the Area Commander. Anyone resisting such an order may be imprisoned for a period of five years or fined or made to suffer both punishments.

The effect of the above changes is to make it possible for sponsors of Israeli settlements and any other body of which the military government approves to expropriate land quietly without having to go through the requirements of announcing his intention or obtaining permissions from non-military bodies. It also removes from the local courts the power to review decisions as to expropriation or as to the compensation to be paid for the expropriated land. The aggrieved party is left with the remedy only of appealing to the Objections Committee which, as explained earlier, is composed entirely of military personnel. Finally, in many cases it has imposed a heavy punishment on any owner resisting the execution of the Order.

The Expropriation Law as amended has been used by the military authorities to acquire land for the settlements as well as for roads, including arterial and access roads to serve the Israeli settlements. The possibility of registering expropriated property in a special Land Department at the military headquarters has already been mentioned (see *supra*).

38

The use of this method of acquiring land has been on the increase since the amendment of the regional plan, RJ5, which will be discussed in the next chapter.

Acquisition of Land for Jewish Settlement by Purchase

It is not possible to estimate the area of land that has been sold to Jews in the West Bank because such lands are registered in a special Land Registration Department at the military headquarters. But it is estimated that it constitutes a small percentage of the land used for settlement.

Most of the properties bought by Jews during the period of the British Mandate, before 1948, were kept under the trusteeship of the Custodian of Enemy Property appointed by the Jordanian government. When the occupation of the West Bank took place in 1967, the area of land which the Custodian had been administering was estimated at 30,000 dunums.[35]

Jordanian law imposed restrictions on the sale of land to non-Jordanians.* Such sales were only possible after special permission was granted by the Council of Ministers. The Jewish National Fund registered several branches in the West Bank. Of particular importance was Hamanuta which, being a local company, was able to register land in its name in the West Bank without restriction. After 1979, the Military Commander of the West Bank, who assumed all the legislative and governmental powers under Jordanian law, removed the restrictions on the purchase of land in the West Bank by individual Jews.

Sale of land by Palestinians to Jews in the West Bank has always been considered an act of treason by the community. In Jordan it has been made a crime (carrying the death penalty) for a Jordanian citizen — which all West Bankers are — to sell land to Jews.[36] The reason for this

---

* Article 5(1) of the Law Concerning the Possession of Immovable Property by Juridical Bodies, of 1953, prohibits foreign juridical bodies from acquiring ownership or possession of property except with the permission of the Council of Ministers. Three conditions must exist:

(i)   that the immovable property is within the towns and villages;
(ii) that it does not exceed what the organisation needs for its purposes; and
(iii) that the acquisition is not for the purposes of mere possession or for trading.

Article 8(3) allows such bodies to acquire immovable property outside the towns and villages if public interest requires it, provided the other conditions above are complied with.

is the belief that since the interest of Israel is to annex the West Bank and prevent Palestinians from having a state of their own, the sale of land is tantamount to assisting a policy of denying the society the opportunity to exercise its basic right of self-determination. Being aware of this, the military authorities have attempted to acquire all the powers of control over matters of land in the West Bank, and to make whatever changes in the law that are needed to enable those desirous of transferring their lands to Jews to do so in secret without needing to resort to any public department.

In addition to the establishment of the secret Land Registration Department at the military headquarters, which has already been mentioned, the following changes that have bearing on the purchase of land by Jews have been made:

(i) Order 25 had made it mandatory to obtain the consent of the Israeli military officer in charge of land for any transaction involving immovable property. Similarly, Orders 450 and 451 declared that all the powers by virtue of the Jordanian law vested in the Director of the Land and Survey Departments are transferred to the Israeli military officer in charge of the judiciary and, as far as the survey law is concerned, to the officer in charge of survey matters;

(ii) Under Jordanian law an irrevocable power of attorney valid for five years could be given to an attorney to sell land to a purchaser named in the instrument. Military Orders Numbers 811 and 847 prolonged the period of validity of such instruments from 5 to 10 years and later to 15 years. Israeli notaries public were permitted to authenticate the signatures appearing on these instruments and Israeli consulates were declared the only authority outside the West Bank with power to validate powers of attorney. The Officer in charge of the Judiciary was given the authority to validate the signatures of the Israeli consuls.

(iii) Military Order Number 1025 granted a general permission to the juridical bodies which are chosen by the Military Commander to acquire immovable property in the West Bank despite the restrictions under Jordanian law on such acquisition by foreign bodies. It has not been made public who these juridical bodies are.

(iv) Public inspection of the Land Registration Department has been completely restricted as far as the local Palestinian population is concerned, as has been mentioned above. Only an owner or one who holds a power of attorney from him may acquire an extract of the deed of registration of his or his principal's property. If an extract is required for starting litigation in court, the court to which the case is submitted must grant permission to obtain the extract, and the Registration Department will provide the extract of the deed only after receiving the court's written order.

(v) The condition of the local courts, the lack of independence of the judiciary, and the power under Military Order Number 841 of the Officer in charge of the Judiciary to withdraw and inspect files of cases being heard by the courts make it possible to present to the courts cases where one party has agreed with another to start a case concerning land in which the defendant either has a limited or no interest. The parties decide before the court to settle their apparent dispute and register the settlement in court. Later, by virtue of this court settlement, the land is registered in the name of the plaintiff.

Israel's Defence of its Land Acquisition Policy

The process is in accordance with the law

It has been consistently claimed (often self-righteously) by Israel in defence of its policy of land acquisition that the process is being carried out in accordance with the law in force in the West Bank. It is argued that when illegal practices are discovered the government is quick to condemn them and to take measures to prevent their recurrence. On 15 March 1982 and in May 1983, the forging of proofs of title to land and of instruments for its transfer was reported in the local newspapers.[37] The condemnation by the Israeli authorities was strong and attempts were made to stop the practice. This, at least, was the public position of the office of the Attorney-General in Israel.

In practice, illegal transactions continue. Lawyers in the West Bank have evidence that forgeries have taken place at the office of the Public Notary of the Court in Salfit. The signatures of landowners have been forged on irrevocable authorisations for the sale of land. The Officer in charge of the Judiciary failed to take action when evidence was brought to him of such forgeries being carried out by court employees for whom he is responsible.

41

In the village of Bidia, near Nablus, illegal practices for land acquisition have been numerous. Lawyers have raised before local courts actions involving land acquired through illegal means. After encountering great difficulties, the Nablus Court of First Instance finally did make interim orders to stop the settlers from working on the land pending the end of the proceedings. The settlers refused to obey the orders and the police refused to enforce them. The lawyers involved in these cases then petitioned the Israeli High Court of Justice, asking why the police should not be forced to execute the orders of the Court. At the time of writing, the petition had not been heard by the Court. However, similar situations are not likely to arise in the future because the jurisdiction of the local courts over disputes involving unregistered lands has been removed altogether. A special military tribunal has now acquired their jurisdiction. The settlers are less likely to be obstructed in their illegal efforts in the future.

However, it remains the preference of all Israeli authorities that land acquisition be carried out by "legal" means. The determination of the legality or illegality of an action can be arrived at only in relation to a legal framework.

Most countries of the world consider Israel to be a belligerent occupant of the West Bank and consequently expect that the laws regarding belligerent occupation be observed. The United Nations and the U.S. hold the position that the Fourth Geneva Convention applies to Israel's governance of the occupied territories.[38] As a general rule, according to the laws of belligerent occupation, the occupying state must preserve the laws which were previously in force in the area occupied. International law and the relevant conventions concerning the take-over of land and the transfer of citizens of the occupying state into the occupied areas are very clear: "Everyone has the right to own property", declares Article 17 of the Universal Declaration of Human Rights. "No-one shall be arbitrarily deprived of his property", it continues. Article 23(g) of the Hague Regulations forbids the occupying country "to destroy or seize the enemy's property, unless such destruction or seizure be imperatively demanded by the necessities of war". Article 49 of the Fourth Geneva Convention declares that "the occupying power shall not deport or transfer parts of its own civilian population into the territory it occupies".

According to international law, therefore, what Israel is doing in the West Bank with regard to the take-over of land and the settlement of Jews in the occupied territories is illegal.

42

But Israel takes a different view.

Except for the first five months of the occupation, Israel's official position as to the legal status of the occupied territories has been that it does not consider itself to be an occupying state. This being so, it has not felt bound to apply the Geneva Conventions but agrees to apply "the humanitarian standards laid down in these conventions". What this statement exactly means in practice has not been, nor can it be, explained conclusively.*

Pursuant to its stated legal position, Israel has since the beginning of the occupation in 1967 been amending the laws in force in the West Bank. Discussion of the amendments in some areas other than land will be made in Part II of this study. Here the discussion is limited to the changes made in the law relating to land and in the legal system affecting the settlement of disputes over land.

Despite the dubious international legality of the changes made to the laws in force in the West Bank, it is these laws which Israel utilises to transfer ownership of land from Palestinian to Jewish hands. When the legality of Israeli practices in this sphere is challenged, the legality or illegality is determined according to the legal order imposed by Israel since it has been occupying the West Bank.

The historical claim

In an article in the *Jerusalem Post* of June 29, 1979, Meir Merhav, a member of the Post's editorial staff, referred to this frequently made historical justification of the settlements of Jews in the West Bank and responded to it. He wrote, "If (the settlements) are not accepted, the heartland of historical Eretz Israel will become the only place on earth from which Jews are banned. (This defence of settlement) is false, because nowhere in the world can Jews settle *by force* (his emphasis) and

---

* Article 35 of Military Proclamation no. 3 of 7 June 1967 stated that the military forces and their officers must apply the terms of the Geneva Conventions of 12 August 1949 concerning the protection of civilians during times of war and concerning everything that affects legal proceedings and that if there should be any contradiction between this Proclamation and the said Convention, the terms of the Convention must be followed. This article was repealed by Military Order No. 144 of 22 October 1967 and has not since been restored.

For analysis of Israel's legal status in the West Bank, see article by Prof. Yehuda Blum, "The Missing Reversioner: Reflections on the Status of Judea and Samaria", in Israel Law Review, Vol. 3, No. 2, 1968, pp. 279-301, where the argument put forward is that the Geneva Conventions do not apply.

For a different view, arguing the applicability of the Geneva Conventions, see article by Prof. Yoram Dinstein, "The International Law of Belligerent Occupation and Human Rights", in Israel Yearbook on Human Rights, Vol. 8 (1978), p. 105.

because, if peace comes one day, there will be no reason why Jews who for religious or sentimental reasons want to live in Hebron, will necessarily be barred from doing so. It is false also because the aim is not so much to settle Israelis on that land as to deny it to the Palestinians." Many of those who settle in the West Bank consider that their right over the area they call Judea and Samaria is not derived from man-made law but from a "higher" law. The area, they claim, was promised to them by God. And this is a sufficient basis for their reclaiming title to it and using it to build their settlements.

In an affidavit submitted to the High Court of Israel in the case of the settlement at Elon Moreh (supra), Mr. Menachem Reuven Felix explained that those who settled at Elon Moreh had the right to do so because of the Divine commandment to inherit the land which was given to (our) forefathers and that "the two elements, therefore, of our sovereignty and our settlement are intertwined", and that "it is the settlement action of the people of Israel in the Land of Israel which is the concrete, the most effective and the truest security action. But the settlement itself . . . does not stem from security reasons or physical needs but from the force of destiny and from the force of the Jewish people's return to its land". He goes on to declare: "Elon Moreh is the very heart of Eretz-Israel in the profound sense of the word — also, it is true, from the geographical and the strategic points of view, but first and foremost it is the place where this land was first proclaimed to our first father, and it is the place where the first property was of the father of the nation after whom this land is named — Eretz-Israel" . . . "This being the case, the security reason, with all due deference and about whose genuineness there is no doubt, to us makes no difference". He then goes on to cite Numbers 33 to 53 — "And you shall take possession of the land and settle in it, for I have given the land to you to possess it". Mr. Felix continues by saying: "Whether or not the Elon Moreh settlers are integrated into the regional defence system according to the IDF's (Israeli Defence Forces') plan, settlement of Eretz-Israel, which is the mission of the Jewish people and of the State of Israel, is *eo ipso* the security, the well-being and the welfare of the nation and the state".

The justices of the Israeli High Court of Justice ruled out such arguments. Justice Landau said in his judgment: "This petition contains a decisive reply to the argument whose aim is to interpret the historical right promised to the Jewish people in the Book of Books as abrogating property rights according to the laws of private property". Justice

Vitkon said: "And let one thing be clear: without the slightest reservations with respect to the statements of my colleague, Justice Landau, I myself see no need to argue with the settlers over their religious or national outlook. It is not our concern to enter into a political or ideological debate." In any event, as has been shown, this case proved to be a turning point in the legal methods employed to acquire land for Jewish settlement in the West Bank, though not because the settlers realised that dependence on the higher law alone would not convince the worldly court of law.

Much can be said about the various justifications of the settlement of Jews in the West Bank, offered by Israelis of different political and religious points of view. However, discussion of these must not divert attention from the basic and overriding objective of the settlement of Jews in the West Bank, which is to drive out Palestinians and annex the area when the demographic balance has changed. Instrumental to this objective is the break-up of the demographic continuity of the land inhabited by West Bank Palestinians in order to render unfeasible the establishment there of a Palestinian state.

Jewish settlement is necessary for the security of Israel

The most common justification of Jewish settlement in the West Bank is that it is necessary for Israel's security. When the Israeli cabinet discussed the importance of the settlement of Elon Moreh, there was disagreement as to the security purpose served by the settlement of civilians in the West Bank. The Israeli High Court of Justice, which heard the appeal in this case, was presented by the appellants' lawyers with sworn statements from Israeli military personnel who argued that in fact civilian settlement in the West Bank would be detrimental to security and not an asset in the event of a war. Lt. General (Reserves) Haim Bar-Lev (the present Minister of Police) expressed his professional assessment that Elon Moreh makes no contribution to Israel's security, neither in the war against hostile terrorist activity during times of tranquillity, nor in the event of a war on the eastern front, because a civilian settlement, situated on a hill some 2 kms. from the Nablus-Jerusalem road, cannot facilitate the safeguarding of this traffic axis; the more so since close to this road itself is located a large Israeli army camp which dominates the traffic lines southward and eastward. In fact, says Bar-Lev, because of hostile terrorist activity in time of war, Israeli troops will be tied down in guarding the civilian settlement rather than engaging in the war against the enemy's army.

General (Reserves) Mattityahu Peled, in his affidavit presented to the court in the same case, quoted from a discussion held by the Institute for Strategic Studies at Tel Aviv University on 26 April 1979. Professor Moshe Arens, who was at the time Chairman of the Knesset Foreign Affairs and Security Committee, then said that it is ridiculous to suppose that a civilian settlement could fulfill a military role in the event of a battle in the area where it is situated. The experience of the Yom Kippur war on the Golan Heights, continued General Peled, confirms this conclusion as, in fact, all the settlements that were on the Heights were speedily evacuated and this task constituted an unnecessary burden on the security forces while they were faced with the difficult mission of blocking the enemy penetration. Professor Arens was Israel's Defence Minister with ultimate responsibility over the occupied territories, under the Likud government, when more settlements were established than at any time before, all in the name of Israel's security.

The retention of a strip of land as small as the West Bank is a poor guarantee of security from attack. Certainly, stronger guarantees can be obtained if a comprehensive peace agreement is reached which will better guarantee Israel's security. But clearly logistics are not the primary consideration of those who put forward the security benefit of the retention of the West Bank. The majority of Israelis consider the mere establishment of a Palestinian state next to Israel — even if it is a de-militarised state — to be the real threat. In the article in The Jerusalem Post quoted above, Mr. Merhav wrote: "The recent years of occupation, however, began to turn the colonizers into colonialists. We had subdued another nation and began to use it as a source of cheap labour and as a market for our wares... Then came Premier Begin, bringing peace with Egypt. But the peace he pursues reveals itself as a ruse to perpetuate our rule over the Palestinians. The land on which they live is to be carved up by a grid of roads, settlements and strongholds into a score of little bantustans so that they shall never coalesce again into a contiguous area that can support autonomous, let alone independent, existence.

Thus, colonisalism is to be formalized and made permanent in the guise of autonomy. Resistance is to be crushed by force. The Abraham who divided the land with Lot for peace, who at Beersheba paid Abimalech to establish his right to a well he had dug, and who at Hebron paid Ephron for the cave of the Machpelah, is to become an Ahab who forcibly takes Naboth's vineyard." (The reference in Merhav's article concerning Naboth's vineyard is from I Kings 21. Elijah tells Ahab who acquired Naboth's vineyard after killing him, "Have you killed, and also take possession?".)

Land Martyrs

The acquisition of land by Jews in the West Bank has not always proceeded without opposition. Many Palestinians use the legal methods available to them — even though the standards and procedures imposed are unfair, and successful cases have been very rare. Others do not become aware that their land is being seized — through one or other of the methods described above — until they see the bulldozer working on their land. There have been instances where the landowner, in an attempt to protect his land, has prostrated himself before the bulldozer, thereby losing his life.

The following incident was described in a statement under oath made to Law in the Service of Man by Zainab, the wife of the land martyr, Ibrahim Ahmad, from the village of Bidia near Tulkarim:

We were surprised, Zainab said, to find on 27 April 1983, at about ten in the morning, four Israeli bulldozers which were intending to dig up our land, which is of an area of 40 dunums. They spoke to the driver of one and asked him why he was digging here. "This land is ours", they told him. The family were able to hold off the work until the next day when a person claiming to be the Chairman of the company which he claimed had bought the land from the village mukhtar came. A jeep of border guards also came with him. One soldier asked the husband why he was obstructing the work. The man replied that the land was his and he had the documents to prove it and that naturally any owner of property would try to prevent others from working on it.

This is how the widow described what took place afterwards:

". . . one of the soldiers struck my husband on the face with a very strong blow which was followed by three blows directed at his stomach and by another with his boot. This led to my husband falling to the ground, unconscious. When I saw this, I brought water to sprinkle it on my husband's face and immediately one of the soldiers who were waiting said after my husband regained consciousness: get off the land. But my husband said to the soldiers: This is my land. At this point, one of the soldiers drew a gun and fired two shots at my husband.

The first hit him in his chest and the other in the abdomen. My husband was martyred on the soil of his country."

Questions of Morality

Many sectors of Israeli society are involved in the process of land acquisition: employees in the military government, the Jewish Agency and the various ministries in Israel. Also involved are many independent professionals — legal experts, land surveyors, lawyers who sit as judges on the Objections Committee and military experts who give expert testimony in favour of the Custodian of State Property.

Many of them do not consider the significance of their participation and consider that they are carrying out their duty as part of their job or in the course of their compulsory reserve army service. Some have considered the matter and have convinced themselves of the legality of the method of acquisition of land through declaring it "state" property. Self-deception is a common and convenient assurance against the agony of confronting moral dilemmas.

A common justification of the morality of forms of land acquisition other than declaring the land "state" land is that Israel offers compensation to those whose land it acquires. As has already been argued, the acquisition of land by an occupying state for its own nationals is contrary to international law. The offer to pay compensation for the land acquired does not legalise the practice. However, the conscience of many is eased when they know that the owner has been offered compensation for land of which he has been deprived.

It is true, compensation is offered for the forms of land acquisition other than "state" land, but the offer is almost never accepted. Does the offer exonerate the authorities and are the Palestinians wrong not to accept the compensation?

Jordanian law makes it a crime to sell land to Jews. However, apart from the state of the law and from the personal sacrifices involved in losing one's land (often the only source of livelihood) without accepting any compensation, the refusal to accept the offer of compensation is due to a common, deeply held morality which all Palestinians share.

One could rationalise this attitude by pointing to the principle in civil law that compensation should correspond to the damage caused. Of course, the matter here is not one of a simple civil wrong, but the same principle should apply. The damage Israel is causing the Palestinian by taking his land is not damage that can be calculated or compensated for in monetary terms. By depriving the Palestinian of his land (with or without payment of compensation — although, in fact, much less is offered than the land's real value), Israel is depriving him, as a member of the Palestinian nation, of his future. The Palestinian nation is being deprived of its basic right which it shares with all other nations, the right to self-determination. Its people are deprived of the opportunity to express themselves as a community with their own traditions and character and to live out their hopes and aspirations in creating the kind of society they have dreamed of, a fair and equitable state which every human being would like to be a recognised member of, and would like the chance to take part in creating.

This is what the takeover of the land is depriving the Palestinians of. Can this be compensated for in money?

The constitutions of most countries of the world define an act whereby the life of the nation is jeopardised as treason. And with the Palestinians (though they do not have a constitution) it is the common morality by which everyone abides, that accepting compensation for one's land is tantamount to treason.

In conclusion, this policy which Israel is pursuing, whereby land to which the local Palestinian inhabitants cannot prove their title through certificates of registration (which everyone knows do not exist through no fault of the Palestinians) is declared Jewish land, the exclusive use of which any person of the Jewish faith from anywhere in the world may come and enjoy, is simply racist.

Chapter Two

Restrictions on the Use of
Land by Palestinians

In the first chapter, the methods by which land in the West Bank is being acquired have been described. The aim of this chapter is to describe the land use plans that have been drawn up and promulgated for the West Bank in order to show how restrictions are being imposed on the use of land that has not yet been acquired.

The declared objective of the master plan of the World Zionist Organisation, 1983-1986,* is "to disperse maximally large Jewish populations in areas of high settlement priority, using small national inputs and in a relatively short period by using the settlement potential of the West Bank and to achieve the incorporation (of the West Bank) into the (Israeli) national system."

Meron Benvenisti, in his study of the plan, writes that the criteria established to determine priorities of settlement regions are "interconnection between existing Jewish areas for the creation of settlement continuity" and "separation to restrict uncontrolled Arab settlement and the prevention of Arab settlement blocs"; "scarcity refers to areas devoid of Jewish settlement". In these criteria "pure planning and political planning elements are included" (sic).

Meron Benvenisti has observed from his study of the plan that the Israeli planners do not pretend to use professional, objective planning criteria. They are proud of their partisan approach. He writes: "A quantitative point system was introduced to identify priority areas. The high

---

* Benvenisti, Meron: "The West Bank Data Base Project: A Survey of Israel's Policies", American Enterprise Institute for Public Policy Research, Washington DC and London, 1984.

priority areas encompass the central massif of the West Bank in such a way as to encircle the populated Arab areas... The extension of the high priority Jewish settlement area to the Northwest of the West Bank as far as the armistice line is explained thus (in the master plan): 'An area along the Green line from Reihan to east of Tul Karm and east of Elkanah [is] liable to become an Arab settlement block, therefore separation through settlement activity and legislation (to restrict Arab building) is necessary and imperative'. Arab populated areas are considered 'problematic' for settlement because 'the chances for land acquisition are small and there is continuous Arab settlement or intensive agricultural cultivation...'!"

Palestinian population and Palestinian land use are regarded as constraints. Palestinian areas are encircled in the first stage and are then penetrated and fragmented.

The plan is based on the work of high-level officials of the Israeli government and the West Bank military government and of planning experts. It bears the official stamp of the Israeli government. According to Benvenisti, "it cannot be viewed as other than the official land use plan for the West Bank". This is confirmed by the fact that regional and road plans (which will be described below) made by the planning departments in the West Bank apply the principles contained in the World Zionist Organisation's master plan.

The Israeli military authorities, having amended the Jordanian planning law, now have a free hand to draw up and implement regional and road plans for the West Bank.

The Jordanian planning law of 1966 contains procedures for the participation of various local institutions, such as the Engineers' Union, in its operations. It imposed a hierarchical structure of local district and national planning committees. Military Order 418 abolished all local participation in the planning operations. All planning powers were vested in the Higher Planning Committee composed of Israeli officers only and appointed by the Area Commander. The Order also restricted the licensing powers of municipalities. In place of the village planning committee there is now a military committee, the Higher Planning Committee, which was given extensive powers to suspend any plan or licence, to assume all power vested in any local committee and to exempt any person from the need to obtain a planning licence.

Thus, all the powers for land use planning in the West Bank are in the hands of officers appointed by the military authorities. Examination of their plans reveals clearly that the objectives which they serve are not to benefit the Palestinian population or to ensure the security of the army.

51

They follow the principles laid down in the master plan referred to above. As such, they exceed Israel's powers as an occupier under international law.

Two plans have already been published by the military Planning Department. They are Plan 1/82 known as the RJ5 (Region Jerusalem 5) of 1982 and the road plan for the entire West Bank referred to as road plan Number 50, of 1983.

Plan No. 1/82

The outline plan No. 1/82 is a statutory outline scheme for an area of 275,000 dunums bordering on Jerusalem, including the towns of Bethlehem and Ramallah. This plan determines the use of the land outside the municipalities and villages within the area it covers. The boundaries of these population centres have been fixed by the plan. Some villages have been left out altogether. The areas surrounding the Palestinian towns and villages are designated either as agricultural areas in which building is almost entirely prohibited or special areas comprising approximately 35% of the area which are not defined by the plan but which are implicitly for the expansion of Jewish settlements. Natural reserves and areas for future planning are also designated.

Although the plan is said to be an amendment to a British mandate plan, that plan had no statutory effect. In any event it cannot be used as the basis for planning the region, 50 years later, without fully taking into consideration the natural expansion of the Palestinian population in the area.

As it now stands there are many legal objections that can be made to the plan. Contrary to the planning law, the local population was not consulted at any stage of the preparation of the plan. The articles of the law which require the planning department to take several steps and make specific surveys to determine the best interest of the population when preparing a plan were not complied with. The Israeli officials justify their failure to consult the local population and not to comply with the law by claiming that plan 1/82 is merely an amendment of an earlier mandate plan, the RJ5. Such a claim is unfounded.

According to the regulations published with the plan, no building licence may be given until the applicant submits final proof of his ownership of the land for which a licence is requested. Such a request is not in accordance with the planning law.

The plan restricts building in areas designated as agricultural areas which surround the Palestinian population centres. Building on agricultural land is greatly restricted to one house per plot provided that the area for building is not more than 150 square meters. An owner of a large plot intending to construct more than one house may not partition the land. Article 8 in Chapter 3 of the Regulations appended to the plan prohibits partition of land in an agricultural area if the partition is intended to alter the rights to build in the area. The Higher Town Planning Council, however, has retained discretion for itself to allow use of agricultural land for non-agricultural purposes. In view of the constitution of this council such authorization is more likely to be given to the Jewish settlers than to the Palestinian population.

Article 10 in Chapter 4 imposes a general prohibition on building except if authorization is given by the Higher Town Planning Council until an outline scheme is approved for the area in which licence to build is sought.

Two new kinds of land are introduced by this plan: "land for future development" and "special areas". The first is described in Article 3 Chapter 4 as lands which are either for use as agricultural land or for any other use which the Higher Town Planning Council approves. "Special areas" are described as areas of land "the use of which shall be determined by the Higher Town Planning Council."

It is quite clear that the plan imposes great restrictions on land use leaving wide discretionary powers with the Higher Town Planning Council which it is likely the Council will exercise in a manner that is prejudicial to the development of the Palestinians and more favourable to the development of the settlements. As it is, large areas have been marked out on the plan as pertaining to Jewish settlement and this is out of proportion with the number of settlers inhabiting the area as compared to the Palestinians there.

The legal steps that were followed to produce and publish the plan are not in accordance with the Jordanian planning law. After its publication in 1982 the public was invited to submit objections to the plan to a special military committee that was set up for this purpose. No decisions have yet been given concerning these objections but the plan has already been put into effect and licences are being granted in accordance with it.

Road Plan No. 50

The roads that existed in the West Bank in 1967 ran from the north to the south along the centre of the region with access roads running laterally away from this central backbone. Some 93% of these roads were paved. In 1970, the Israeli government started creating east-west links with the Jordan valley. The trans-Judea and trans-Samaria roads were created for which thousands of dunums of Palestinian land were expropriated. The Likud government abandoned the north-south strategy and stressed integration of the West Bank road system into the Israeli system. Many roads connecting the settlements to each other and to Israel were built, but road plan number 50 is the first comprehensive road plan to be published since 1967.

The apparent objectives of this plan are:

— to connect the settlements to each other and to Israel,

— to avoid Arab towns and villages,

— to create access roads for the Jewish settlements to the main Israeli metropolitan areas of Tel Aviv and Jerusalem.

The plan is clearly designed to serve Israel's local, regional and national interests while Palestinian transportation needs are ignored or are served as a by-product of Israeli interests. The plan is also intended to restrict Arab development by restricting building along a width of 100-150 metres on each side of the road. Care has not been taken with regard to the amount of damage the path the roads will take will cause to existing agricultural land, irrigation schemes and other Palestinian installations.

The loss and damage, for example, which the proposed 80 km. road No. 57, extending from the Palestinian town of Tulkarim to the Jiftlic will cause is estimated as follows:

— 3,500 dunums of vegetable farms, 1,200 dunums of olive groves and 350 dunums of citrus groves will be destroyed.

— the Fara'a irrigation scheme which is 14 kms. long will also be destroyed. The scheme irrigates an area of 25,000 dunums.

— 15 artesian wells, 15 irrigation ponds, four tree nurseries and three vegetable nurseries will have to be re-located. Amongst these is the biggest nursery in the area.

When the High Court of Justice heard a petition against the road scheme, the military authorities justified the scheme on the grounds that it is designed to benefit the local population.

The military considerations, by virtue of which the authorities had defended the scheme in an earlier case before the same court, were not argued. The Court expressed its surprise at this. Justice Barak said in his judgment: "It was expected that also in this case before us, the emphasis would be on the defence consideration which completes the civilian consideration. Yet, this military consideration was not mentioned before us. This is a strange situation." Still, Justice Barak found that the scheme was, in fact, for the benefit of the local population. The Court decided unanimously not to accept the petition challenging the road scheme.

Such a finding is unusual in view of the fact that a road network already exists in the area. The existing roads run through the villages. The level of traffic does not justify the erection of a parallel network of roads especially in view of the damage the network will cause.*

Town Planning

The road and regional plans relate to land use outside the towns and villages. Within the municipal boundaries the Palestinians have not been allowed to carry out their own planning.

The dismissal of Palestinian mayors and their replacement by Israeli mayors in most of the major towns was explained as being due to political causes. In fact, there are convincing indications that the appointment of Israeli mayors was intended primarily to serve the interests of Israeli planning within Palestinian towns.

In Hebron, for example, where a Jewish settlement has been established, the existence of an Israeli mayor is a great asset to the development of the settlement. Before his dismissal, the Palestinian mayor, Mustafa Natshe, had taken proceedings in the High Court of Justice to challenge the expansionist activities of the Jewish settlement inside his town. When the Israeli mayor took over, he promptly withdrew the case from the Court. On 21 May 1984, the boundaries of the town were

---

* For a full analysis of the legality of the road plan and its probable effects see "Israeli Proposed Road Plan for the West Bank — A Question for the International Court of Justice" by Aziz Shehadeh, Fuad Shehadeh and Raja Shehadeh, reprinted by Law in the Service of Man, Ramallah, 1984.

changed to allow more areas to be given to the nearby settlement of Kiryat Arba. The Israeli mayor has also been granting licences for the settlers inside the town to proceed with the enlargement of their settlement and, in some cases, has withdrawn licences that had been granted to Arab residents by the previous mayor. In one case,* he even took criminal proceedings against a Palestinian who had built a house on the basis of a licence given to him by the previous mayor. These proceedings were not successful, but, as a result of other administrative proceedings taken against him, the Palestinian was compelled to pull down the house.

On 5 May 1983, the Israeli mayor moved the bus station and transferred the old site to the Jewish settlers. In the other West Bank towns, town plans are being designed by Israeli planners while the Palestinian planning boards are presided over by Israeli officials. The Jewish Council's planning committee members are elected by the settlers.

The situation then is that the planning authority composed of Israeli officials has created regional plans for the use of land outside the municipal boundaries and Israeli mayors of Arab towns are proceeding to create town plans to suit the purpose of Jewish settlement.

Discriminatory Practices by the Planning Department

The discrimination by the planning authority against the Palestinians is not only in the general planning of the use of the land in the West Bank. Discrimination is also evident in the areas which are designated within the plans as Palestinian zones. When a Palestinian institution applies for building permits within an area zoned for the purposes of the applying institute, the planning authority uses its wide powers to discriminate against the institution.

Birzeit University, for example, is in the course of expanding its new campus within the area which has been designated since 1975 as a University zone. In November 1983, it applied for a licence to build a Fine Arts Building. At the date of writing, September 1984, the permit has still not been granted. In February, it applied for approval of its enlarged University zone and again no licence has been granted. Licences are, however, granted for other Palestinians more favoured by the authorities and whose building conflicts with that planned by the university.

---

* Criminal case No. 1351/83.

When a Palestinian farmer in May 1984 constructed a fence illegally within the approved university zone of Birzeit University, causing a public nuisance, no action was taken for five months to remove the fence despite repeated complaints and appeals by the University. However, action is taken promptly against Palestinians who violate the planning law if the illegal structure lies in the area of the expansion of a Jewish settlement.

The restrictions that have been placed on land use are clearly intended to complement and bring to fruition the process of acquisition of land described in Chapter One.

The concentration of the Palestinians in the West Bank in restricted isolated ghettos seems to be the over-riding aim. What is apparent is that no provision has been made to take into account the natural increase of the local population in the West Bank. The Palestinians will just have to suffer the consequences of over-crowding in the areas to which they have been restricted.

References

(1) See W.W. Harris, "Taking Root — Israeli Settlement in the West Bank, the Golan and Gaza-Sinai, 1967-1980", London, 1980 and also see Benvenisti, Meron, The West Bank Data Base Project: A Survey of Israel's Policies, American Enterprise Institute for Public Policy Research, Washington and London, 1984.

(2) *Izat Mohammad Mustafa Dwaikat and Others v. Government of Israel and Others*, HCJ 390/79 (1980, 34 P. D. (1) 1).

(3) See Ian Lustick "Israel and the West Bank after Elon Moreh: the mechanics of *de facto* annexation", Middle East Journal, Autumn 1981, p. 557 for a discussion of the effect of the Elon Moreh decision on settlement.

(4) Military Order 59, Order Concerning Government Properties, 31 July 1967.

(5) Military Order 364, Order Concerning Government Properties (Amendment No. 4), 29 December 1969.

(6) Settlement of Disputes over Land and Water, Law Number 40 of 1952, Official Gazette 1113, 16 June 1952.

(7) This was done using The Land Settlement Ordinance, 1928-1933.

(8) Military Order 291, Order Concerning Settlement of Disputes over Land and Water, 19 December 1968.

(9) Ottoman Land Code, 1858, in Tute, RC. *The Ottoman Land Laws*, Jerusalem 1927.

(10) Law Concerning the Use of Real Property, Number 49, of 1953, Official Gazette 1135, 1 March 1953.

(11) Law to Transfer the Land from Miri to Mulk, Number 41, of 1953, Official Gazette, 1131, 16 February 1953.

(12) 1922, Order-in-Council. Laws of Palestine, London 1933, Vol. III, p. 2569.

(13) Law of Land Expropriation for Public Purpose, Number 2, of 1953, Official Gazette, 1130, 1 January 1953.

(14) 1935 East Jordan Defence Regulations, Official Gazette, 473, p. 158.

(15) Military Order 58, Order Concerning Abandoned Property (Private Property), 23 July 1967.

(16) Military Order 25, Order Concerning Transactions in Real Property, 18 June 1967, which makes it illegal to conduct any business transactions involving real property without a permit from the military authorities.

(17) The Israeli officer in charge of the judiciary published a work by Mr Yusuf Atallah in 1979, entitled "The Collection of Land Laws".

(18) By Military Order 1091 of 20 January 1984 (Amendment No. 7 to Order 59).

(19) Military Order 569, Order Concerning the Registration of Special Transactions in Land, 17 December 1974.

(20) Law of Registration of Unregistered Immovable Property, No. 6, 21 September 1964.

(21) Military Order 1060, Order Concerning Law on Registration of Unregistered Immovable Property (Amendment No. 2), 28 June 1983.

(22) Civil case 127/80, Appeal Case No. 265/83. No. of file before Special Committee under Order 1060 is 53/84.

(23) Inspection of the register established under Order 569 has been restricted by Order 605 to those empowered to make transactions concerning state land.

(24) See Allan Gerson, "Israel, The West Bank and International Law", Frank Cass, 1978, p. 161.

(25) Don Peretz, "Problems of Arab Refugee Compensation", Middle East Journal 8 No. 4 (Autumn 1954), pp. 404-8.

(26) Don Peretz, "Israel and the Palestine Arabs", Washington DC, Middle East Institute, 1958, p. 160.

(27) Absentees Property Law No. 28, 5710-1950, Laws of the State of Israel, Vol. 4., p. 68.

(28) Development Authority (Transfer of Property) Law No. 62, 5710-1950, Laws of the State of Israel, Vol. 4, p. 151.

(29) Military Order 58, Order Concerning Abandoned Property, 23 July 1967.

(30) *Francois Albina v. Custodian of State and Absentee Property* Case No. 16/82 before the Objections Committee.

(31) Benvenisti, op. cit., p. 30.

(32) Same source, p. 31.

(33) Same source, p. 23.

(34) Law of Land Expropriation for Public Purposes, Number 2, of 1953, Official Gazette, 1130, 1 January 1953.

(35) Benvenisti, op. cit., p. 31.

(36) By virtue of Jordanian law prohibiting the sale of Immovable Property to the Enemy, No. 3, of 1973, Official Gazette 2429, of 1 July 1973.

(37) See *El Quds* Arabic daily, of 15 March 1982, *Jerusalem Post* of 29 May 1983 and 17 June 1983 and 30 May 1983.

(38) U.S. State Department Report on Human Rights, 1982, p. 1165.

Part Two:

The Operation of De Facto Annexation

Chapter Three

Administrative Structures in the West Bank

The previous chapters described Israel's policy of acquiring the land, the aim of which, as has been explained, is to annex the West Bank without its Palestinian inhabitants.

Even according to the most optimistic projections, it is not expected that the Jewish inhabitants in the West Bank will equal or outnumber the Palestinians for several decades. Therefore, barring the possibility of forceful mass expulsion, Israel must create a legal relationship with the West Bank pending full *de jure* annexation.

Among the legal problems that arise in this interim period are the following:

— How to apply Israeli law to the Jewish settlements in the West Bank while the area has not been annexed and is not under Israeli sovereignty. Related to this problem are the problems of which courts are to apply this law and which government departments are to execute it, and how to ensure that only the Jewish settlers will be subject to these laws, courts and government departments.

— How to avoid applying the Israeli law and legal system to the Palestinian inhabitants.

— How to reconcile this peculiar legal state of affairs with the requirements of international law.

In this chapter, the solution which Israel has worked out for these problems in the course of its administration of the West Bank over the past 17 years will be discussed in relation to the executive. The next chapter will examine the changes in the judicial system.

The Executive

The law that applied to the West Bank when Israel occupied it in 1967 was Jordanian law. The Jordanian courts had sole jurisdiction over all residents of the West Bank in civil and criminal matters. This Jordanian law has undergone many changes in the course of the occupation through the military orders which amended and added to it.

Although Jewish settlement of the West Bank started in 1968, by 1979 the number of Jews living in the West Bank was only 10,000[1]. These settlers were all Israeli citizens (or were entitled to be so under the Israeli law of return). Therefore, in terms of the law in force in the West Bank, they were considered as foreigners. When civil disputes arose in the West Bank, the courts which had jurisdiction (with few exceptions) were the local courts which apply the Jordanian law as amended by the Military Orders. In criminal matters, the Military Orders stated that the military courts should have concurrent jurisdiction with the local Jordanian courts to hear any criminal matter. The choice as to which court a criminal suit should be heard in, was reserved to the Area Commander. The Jewish settlers were therefore immune from the local courts in criminal matters but not in civil suits.

The practice of the government towards the Jewish settlers was preferential and violations of the law were overlooked to facilitate the settler's life in a legal situation which did not always work to their best interest. As long as the status quo was continuing, the Israeli settlement policy could continue without the need to define the legal situation more clearly. With the prospect of negotiations for the Camp David plan, this need became urgent, not because settlement in the West Bank was being prejudiced, but because Israel wanted to prejudice the outcome of the proposed negotiations with the Palestinians.

What had been implied, but not stated, was now being declared publicly. In March 1979, Prime Minister Begin said: "The Jewish inhabitants of Judea and Samaria and Gaza will be subject to the laws of Israel".*

Between 1979 and 1981, simultaneously with the autonomy talks, the following legal and physical measures were taken by the military government in the West Bank to forestall the outcome of the talks: survey of unregistered lands, the approval of the new definition of state land, and the first declarations by Military Order of land as "state" land; massive deployment of Israeli forces and construction of infrastructures; massive settlement; transfer of responsibility over water resources from the military government to the national water company, Mekorot; re-organisation of the function of the military government administration; cancellation of development budgets and interconnection of utility grids (water, electricity, roads); creation of Jewish regional and local councils; and creation of a civilian administration.

But how was the Begin government proposing to overcome the legal difficulty of applying Israeli law to the Jewish settlers in the West Bank without exposing itself to the charge of annexing the settlements?

The answer to this was found in the use of two legal devices:

The first was for Israel to extend some of its laws outside its own territories extra-territorially, and the second was to distinguish Jewish settlements from Palestinian population centres by giving them a different and distinct legal status so that legislation which applies to the local government units under the Jordanian law will not apply to them.

As to the extra-territoriality, this was achieved through applying to the Jewish settlers emergency and regular laws passed by the Israeli parliament (the Knesset) either directly or by way of Military Orders.

Under the Israeli Law and Administration Ordinance of 1948, the Prime Minister or any other Minister has the power to make emergency regulations "as may be expedient in the interests of the defence of the state, public security and the maintenance of supplies and essential services" (section 9(a)) following a public declaration that a state of emergency exists.

Immediately following the 1967 war, the Minister of Justice introduced regulations entitled Emergency Regulations (Areas held by the Defence Army of Israel — Criminal Jurisdiction and Legal Assistance), 1967. The validity of these Regulations has been extended annually and later bi-annually by the Israeli Knesset.

---

* Prime Minister Begin's autonomy proposals quoted in "The West Bank Data Base Project: A Survey of Israel's Policies", Meron Benvenisti, 1984, p. 39.

65

These Regulations enable a court in Israel to try any person for any act or omission which occurred in any region (defined in Regulation 1 as "any of the areas held by the Defence Army of Israel") and which would constitute an offence under Israeli law if it were committed in Israel. But Regulation 2(c) excluded from this provision persons who at the time of the act or omission were residents of the region.

Most of the West Bank settlers are residents of Israel, as well as having another residence in the West Bank. So, in practice, an Israeli West Bank settler could under these Regulations be tried for his criminal action in Israeli courts. However, as to those who reside only in the occupied territory, the High Court of Justice ruled in 1972 that Israeli courts have no jurisdiction over acts committed by such settlers in the occupied territories since, as residents of the region, they were specifically excluded from the effect of the provision by Regulation 2. In 1975, an amendment was introduced to extend the jurisdiction of the Israeli courts to these settlers.

An amendment to the Israeli Income Tax Ordinance in 1980 provided that any income of settlers produced or received in the West Bank was to be treated as though its source were Israel, and an amendment to the Emergency Regulations in 1984 extended the power of the taxing authorities to collect the taxes in the 'region'[2], thus avoiding an explicit reference to the settlements.

Similarly, under Emergency Regulations 6B of 1984, a list of nine Israeli laws (which can be added to by an Administrative Order) were made applicable to settlers by extending the meaning of 'Israeli resident' to include 'any person whose place of residence is in the region and who is an Israeli citizen or entitled to acquire Israeli citizenship pursuant to the Law of Return, 1950'.

The nine Israeli laws are:

Entry into Israel Law, 1952
Defence Services Law, 1959
Chamber of Advocates Law, 1961
Income Tax Ordinance
Population Register Law, 1965
Emergency Labour Services Law, 1967
National Insurance Law (Consolidated Version), 1968
Psychologists Law, 1968
Emergency Regulations Extension (Registration of Equipment) Law, 1981[3]

The second device was to establish by Military Orders a separate administration for the settlements.

At first, the status of the settlements was ambiguous. Strictly speaking, if the settlers were within the jurisdiction of a Palestinian municipal council, they were subject to it. In practice, of course, they were not.

As from 1974, 'Religious Councils' were established by Military Orders. Their responsibility was to administer certain named settlements, for example, Kiryat Arba, by Military Order 561 of 1974, which provided that the settlement was to be administered "in accordance with administrative principles which the Military Commander shall declare by internal regulations".

In 1979, only six days before the signing of the Peace Treaty between Israel and Egypt, Military Order 783 established five regional councils in the West Bank and in March 1981, Military Order 892 established local councils for the administration of particular settlements. The jurisdiction of the regional councils covered the whole of the land under Israeli ownership or control, not merely the built-up areas of the settlements.

There are, in fact, three kinds of council:

(i) Local councils, whose jurisdiction is limited to the planned (not existing) areas of the urban settlements. One council, Kiryat Arba, has a non-contiguous jurisdictional area which corresponds to all "requisitioned" areas in the vicinity;

(ii) Regional councils with contiguous areas: the Jordan valley and the Megillot (Dead Sea foreshore) councils. Most of the land has been expropriated, requisitioned or closed or belongs to "absentees". 'Islands' of Arab villages and the town limits of Jericho are left out. The Hof Azza (Gaza) is also a contiguous council;

(iii) Regional councils with non-contiguous areas. The highlands of the West Bank were divided into four general areas (from north to south: Shomron, Matei Binyamin, Etzion, and Har Hebron). Within three general areas non-contiguous patches of jurisdictional areas were delineated. These irregular tracts correspond to the "state" land areas and are composed of all "uncultivable and unregistered lands". Most of the areas are inaccessible and are not useful for settlement or for any other land use. Nevertheless, they have been painstakingly demarcated. The map-makers undoubtedly felt that they were defining the areas annexed *de facto* to Israel. Although non-contiguous jurisdictional areas are scattered and meaningless, the overall planning responsibility of the regional councils encompasses the whole of the 'general areas' allotted to them. In those areas there are Palestinian towns and villages with twenty times the inhabitants of the Jewish settlements. The size of this Palestinian population does not hinder the regional councils from defining planning principles and from implementing them with the assistance of the military government. In fact, the general areas of the regional councils are to all intents and purposes a Jewish administrative division of the West Bank, unrelated and separate from the Palestinian sub-district administrative division.[4]

The power and responsibilities of the local councils as defined in the Military Order are identical with those of ordinary Israeli municipalities.[5]

The Jewish regional and local councils enjoy under the law a greater measure of autonomy than the Palestinian village and municipal councils. The Jewish councils are permitted to elect their own leaders, while the mayors heading Palestinian towns are appointed by the Area Commander and many of them are Israelis.[6]

Jewish councils have also been empowered to exercise wider functions and have more latitude to impose taxes than is the case with the Palestinian councils.

The most significant restriction which only the Palestinian councils suffer from is the need to request permission from the military authorities to borrow money and to accept money that is offered as a gift or a loan. The power to refuse or grant such permits is used as a punishment or reward by the authorities against the municipalities and villages.

Jewish councils, on the other hand, receive state services. The budgetary allocations for such services are incorporated in the general budgets of the Israeli civilian ministries. "Standards are identical with those applied in Israel", writes Meron Benvenisti.[7] "In education, welfare and religious services, the standards applied to the Jewish councils are more generous than in Israel, especially as far as employment of teachers and officials is concerned".[8]

The Military

The heads of the Jewish councils in the West Bank are well connected with the Israeli centres of power. They form a strong lobby through the Council of Jewish settlements in Judea and Samaria. They are involved in all high-level decisions on infrastructure and on legal, economic, security and land and water matters in the West Bank. They have responsibility over the planning schemes of the West Bank. In fact, the main office of the West Bank Planning Department is located in the Jewish settlement Maaleh Adumim.

Both the fact that the Jewish councils do not rely on the military for their budgets and that they have better contacts with the Israeli power centres gives them powers independent of the military government. "No wonder", writes Benvenisti[9], "the military government has abdicated its powers and authority not only on matters concerning the life of the settlements but also on all matters pertaining to the territories except military, political, administrative and development control of the Arab population".

The military government in the West Bank which exercises absolute control over the Palestinians is set up in the following manner:

"Each branch is headed by an army officer who is responsible for the activity of the civilian offices functioning under him. The number and titles of the offices correspond basically to those of the Israeli government ministries. Each office is headed by a staff officer who is a civilian representative of the relevant Israeli ministry."[10]

The following principle agreed by the Israeli government on 11 October 1968 continues to apply:

"The Area Commander is the exclusive formal authority within the area. He is the legislator, he is the head of the executive and he appoints local officials and local judges."[11]

There have been internal administrative changes within the military government during the 17 years of the occupation. The most important of these changes was the introduction of the civilian administration by Military Order 947 in November 1981.

The Civilian Administration

Overview of Military Order No. 947

Military Order No. 947[12] declares the establishment of a civilian administration to be headed by a person whose nationality is not specified, who holds the title "Head of the Civilian Administration", and who is appointed by the Area Commander.

Military Order No. 947 has two main and closely related effects. The first is to institutionalise the already existing separation of the civilian from the military functions in the military government of the West Bank by formally establishing a new structure of civilian government which is empowered to function within the limits determined by the Order. The second is to make it possible to elevate the status of a large number of Military Orders and other legislative enactments promulgated by the Area Commander from the status of temporary security enactments to the level of permanent laws. This is achieved in the following ways:

Section 2 of the Order states that the Civilian Administration is established to "administer the civilian affairs in the region in accordance with the directives of this Order, for the well-being and good of the population, and in order to supply and implement the public services and taking into consideration the need to maintain an orderly administration and public order in the region".

To enable the Head of the Civilian Administration to carry out his duties, Article 3 of the Order states that he shall be delegated with the following powers:

— all powers determined by the law except those specified by the laws listed in schedule 1 of the Order.

— all powers determined by the Security (also called Military) Orders listed in schedule 2 of the Order,

Sub-section (b) of the same article, literally translated, states that "with respect to this article, acts of legislation that were issued by virtue of the law after the determining date (which was defined in earlier orders as 6 June 1967) shall be regarded as part of the law and not as security legislation".

Article 4 empowers the Head of the Civilian Administration to proclaim subsidiary legislation based upon the laws and Security Orders according to which he is empowered to act. He is also empowered by Article 5 to delegate his authority and appoint officials within the Civilian Administration to execute the law and Security Orders. Article 5(c) further authorises him to delegate his powers to issue subsidiary legislation to such appointees.

Relationship between Israeli Civilian
and Military Administrations

The Civilian Administration was established by the Military Commander of the West Bank. It was created by a Military Order and its Head is appointed by the Area Commander. All the powers the Head of the Civilian Administration enjoys are delegated to him by the Area Commander and he exercises them in his name and on his behalf. They can be increased or decreased as the Commander wishes. Baruch Hollander, the legal advisor to the Military Government at the time of issuance of the Order, confirms the above in his explanatory memorandum attached to the Order. Hollander writes in paragraph five of his memorandum that the Commander still legislates in civil and military matters. The entire Civilian Administration structure is, therefore, subsidiary to the Area Commander and accountable to him. Effective authority and the source of power remains with the Area Commander. This is later confirmed by Military Order No. 950 promulgated on 16 January 1982, which adds a paragraph to Order No. 947 stating that "in order to remove any doubt, there is nothing in the provisions of this Order (Order No. 947) which restricts or abrogates any of the privileges or rights vested in the Commander of the Israeli army in the Area or in any of those appointed by him". This relationship between the Civilian Administration and the Military Command is consistent with the present Israeli government's interpretations of its obligations under the Camp David Accords, which in its view calls only for the "withdrawal" but not the "abolition" of the military government. The Military Command, in that view, continues to be the direct source of authority for any "self-governing administrative council" in the Area. The "Civilian" administration is situated within the military headquarters at Beit Eil. Entrance to this military zone is restricted. Only Palestinians who are summoned or succeed in getting an appointment may enter into the compound. Strict security measures and searches are carried out at the door.

Powers retained by the Military Commander

By virtue of Article 3(a) of the Order, the Area Commander transferred to the Head of the Civilian Administration those powers and authorities acquired by virtue of the Military Orders listed in Schedule 2 of the Order and retained all powers not specifically transferred to the Civilian Administration. These residual powers continue to be held by the Area Commander in his own right (and not merely in his capacity as the source for all powers exercised by the Civilian Administration). They include the following:

(i)   Powers acquired by virtue of the laws and regulations listed in Schedule 1 of the Order, most notably the extensive powers granted under the Jordanian and British Defence Emergency Regulations of 1935 and 1945 respectively.

(ii) The powers in all the Military Orders not listed in Schedule 1 of the Order and not amending Jordanian law.

(iii) The legislative power to issue new Military Orders and create new laws.

By specifying the limits of the power delegated to the Head of the Civilian Administration, however, the Order implies that all powers not transferred to the Civilian Administration are non-civilian and are, therefore, military and security related. It is worth noting that Israel has always insisted that it continues to handle matters relating to "security" in the West Bank and that such "security" matters are from its standpoint not negotiable. The significance of Order No. 947 is that it provides more insight into what Israel means by security. Are all the residual powers and authority not given to the Civilian Administration to remain with Israel and should the autonomy negotiations be restricted only to the authority given to the Civilian Administration under Military Order No. 947? If so, then the scope of the negotiable powers has been determined in advance. In addition, the mechanism has been created to implement any concessions (unilateral or negotiated) Israel is willing to make, without necessitating any fundamental alterations in the system of government in the West Bank as a result of implementing the Camp David autonomy scheme. This impression is reinforced by the official release and publication of "Israel's Proposals in the Autonomy Negotiations" by the Prime Minister's Office on 31 January 1982. In fact, the Military Government's Civilian Administration established by Order No. 947 possesses broader powers in certain spheres, such as residence and identity card matters, than those proposed to be delegated to a Palestinian self-governing authority. Of course, it might be argued that Israeli autonomy proposals to date represent only a negotiating position, but the passage of time and repeated government declarations that no more concessions can be made and unilateral actions like Order No. 947 make this view less and less tenable.*

---

* For the text of "Israel's Proposals in the Autonomy Negotiations", see the *Jerusalem Post,* 1 February 1983, pp. 1 and 2.

Powers of the Civilian Administration

The Head of the Civilian Administration is empowered to administer a corpus of laws and Military Orders through the making of appointments and the issuing of licences and permits. The requirement to obtain some of these licences existed in Jordanian law. Other requirements were added by means of Military Orders issued by Israel to enhance its regulatory power in the Area.

One hundred and seventy Military Orders appear in Schedule 2 of the Order which the Head of the Civilian Administration is charged with administering. Some of these Orders enable the regulation and control of economic life in the West Bank, including imports, exports, prices, finance and banks; others regulate taxes, customs and duties; others regulate control over land and water, as well as electricity, telephone and postal services; some deal with specific areas that have come to be totally incorporated into the Israel system, such as tourism, roads and insurance; others deal with licensing of professionals and regulating civil service appointments; a number concern supervision of plays, films, publications, and textbooks. The Military Orders establishing Objection Committees and delegating judicial powers appear in that schedule, as well as the Military Orders establishing regional councils for Jewish settlements.

A few Military Orders in Schedule 2 deal with quasi-police functions, such as regulating the use of explosives, the carrying of identity cards, the guarding of holy places, and the forcing of shops or businesses to remain open. The rest treat a variety of other subjects, such as parks, game protection, animal diseases, and littering.

Many of these Military Orders were used in the past to set up the legislative structure consistent with Israeli policy objectives in the West Bank. It should be noted that the Head of the Civilian Administration or his delegates will have no power to alter or amend that structure but merely to administer it. He and his delegates will, however, have substantial latitude to exercise their discretion in granting or withholding licences or permits by virtue of these laws and Military Orders. Thus, a clear distinction is created between legislative powers to create structures and set broad policies (which remain within the exclusive domain of the military government) and the administrative authority to dispense patronage selectively within that framework. This latter authority may be delegated to a greater or lesser degree to local Palestinians willing to work within that structure.

Delegability of powers

Article 5 of the Order authorises the Head of the Civilian Administration:

(i) to make appointments in the Civilian Administration,

(ii) to delegate to such appointees the authorities given to him by virtue of the law or the security regulations, and

(iii) to delegate to others the authority to create secondary legislation (rules and regulations) based on the law and the Military Orders he is charged with administering.

This last power, to delegate rule-making authority, is ordinarily not implicit in grants of power. The fact that it was given to the Head of the Civilian Administration would favour the decentralisation of Israeli administration in the West Bank.

This right to delegate secondary legislative powers applies to all the powers falling within the Civilian Administrator's jurisdiction, whether they are given to him by virtue of Jordanian law or Military Orders. It must be remembered, however, that under the Order in question, the Head of the Civilian Administration has no primary legislative power at all and that he may pass only secondary legislation within the strict framework of existing laws and Military Orders within his jurisdiction. He has only the limited power of transferring a selected number of the Civilian Administration functions to appointed* representatives of the local Palestinians. In doing so, he will not be transferring to them any primary legislative or policy-making functions.

This arrangement also enables the military government to delegate to those among the local population who are willing to cooperate, patronage powers to issue or withhold permits and licences required by the laws or the Military Orders administered by the Civilian Administration. For example, officers of the Civilian Administration have begun to require the local population to obtain the endorsement of "Village League" functionaries before requests for certain permits or applications for public sector jobs can be considered. The Village Leagues, whose officers are appointed by the Military government, have been set up as an alternative to the elected municipality councils. They presently hold no legal power in the spheres mentioned above

---

* or, under the Camp David autonomy plan, elected.

and merely act as intermediaries. If, under this Order, the Head of the Civilian Administration delegates to them some of his powers, they will become the direct authority to which local Palestinians must turn.

Chapter Four

The Judicial Systems

The First System of Justice: The Local Courts

The condition of the local courts which serve the Palestinians in the West Bank is very bad. The present state of the courts will be described in the second section. The unsuccessful attempts made by lawyers in the West Bank to persuade the military authorities to carry out basic changes and improvements in the system will also be discussed.

To understand why the military authorities persist in their refusal to exercise their power in a proper manner and to carry out basic changes and improvements to the system, it is necessary to remember that the local courts have been usurped of many of their powers. Their jurisdiction has been restricted to West Bank Palestinians and their internal affairs. The Jewish settlers (with very few exceptions) are not subject to the jurisdiction of local courts and activities of the military cannot be reviewed there. The adverse effects of a corrupt legal system are, therefore, suffered only by the Palestinians. They do not hamper the activities of the military authorities, nor the establishment or development of the Jewish settlements, or life within the settlements.

The assumption of control by the military

The single most influential officer in the military government of the West Bank as regards the local courts is the officer in charge of the judiciary. He has been vested with all the powers and privileges of the Minister of Justice under Jordanian law,[13] who had been granted powers by virtue of the law on the independence of the judiciary.[14]

76

Other powers he exercises include the powers of the lawyers' Bar Association,[15] the Registrar of Companies,[16] and the Registrar of Trademarks,[17] Tradenames and Patents.[18]

When approached by lawyers and judges and urged to improve the system and to carry out improvements in the organisation of local courts, his response was that he is helpless to effect any changes.* "Appointments nowadays", he said, "are decided on political grounds".

For a judicial system to function properly, the judiciary must be independent. Otherwise it will tend to serve the interests of those making the appointments, paying the salaries and deciding on promotions. The independence of the West Bank judicial system (safeguarded under Jordanian law) has been undermined by the Israeli authorities. A Committee composed of military officers makes the appointments, decides on transfers, promotions and salaries of judges and all other court employees.**

---

* The author of this study personally made several complaints and was present at other meetings where complaints were made. On 29 February 1984 he testified before the State Controller's committee of the Israeli Knesset on the condition of the law and the administration of justice in the West Bank. Several articles were published in local newspapers criticising the conditions of the courts. See, for example, the article in *Al Fajr* (an Arab daily paper) on 22 April 1984.

** In article 97 of the Jordanian constitution, it is stated that the judiciary shall be independent and subject to no other authority than that of the law. All matters of appointment of judges, promotions, salaries and transfers are determined by a judicial council established by virtue of the law on the Independence of the Judiciary (published in the Jordanian Official Gazette, no. 1224, on 16 April 1955). This council is composed of:
- The President of the Court of Cassation as President;
- Two Members of the Court of Cassation, chosen according to seniority;
- The President of the Court of Appeal of Amman;
- The President of the Court of Appeal of Jerusalem; and
- The Attorney-General.

The above law has been significantly amended by Military Order no. 310 of 16 February 1969, which has effected the following alterations:
- The powers vested in the Minister of Justice according to the law have been transferred to 'the person responsible' who is defined in the preamble as 'whoever the Military Commander of the West Bank area appoints for the purposes of the Order';
- The Judicial Council constituted by Jordanian law in accordance with Section 1 has been replaced by a Committee appointed by the Area Commander. Although the Order states that the composition of this Committee shall be announced, it was only 12 years later, on 17 March 1981, that notice of the members of the Committee for the Appointment of Judges, according to Order 310, was published. In *The Rule of Law in the Areas Administered by Israel*, published by the Israeli section of the International Commission of Jurists, in response to *The West Bank and the Rule of Law*, it was alleged, on page 23, that this announcement was made in October 1967. This is not so. The reference to the earlier date is to an earlier Order, No. 129, which was repealed and

(continued on next page)

Similarly, the system of inspection of courts (required under the Jordanian system of law) has not been functioning.* The military authorities have made it known lately that they intend to appoint an

(continued from preceding page)

replaced by Order 310, dated 16 February 1969. The composition of the Committee was not stated there in any case. The Members of the Committee are all military officers. Similarly, the powers of transfer, promotion, etc., and the disciplinary powers have also all been vested in military officers.

On 3 November 1981, the Officer in charge of the Judiciary declared the establishment of a Committee which he called 'The Committee for the appointment of lawyers to judicial functions'. He appointed himself as President of this Committee and the four other Members were the President of the Court of Appeal, the President of the Nablus Court of First Instance and two well-known lawyers.

In the letter of appointment, the officer declared the constitution of the Committee and informed the Members that he would call the Committee to meet from time to time whenever the need arose to make a new appointment in the judicial system, and that their role would be advisory. The establishment of this Committee occurred at the same time as the creation of the civilian administration. The invitation to these judges and lawyers to participate in the Committee was interpreted as a step in the direction towards implementing the autonomy plan proposed by the Israeli government and publicly opposed by the Palestinians. Furthermore, the Constitution and powers of the Committee were not in conformity with Jordanian law with regard to the appointment of judges. Accordingly, those appointed by the Officer in charge of the Judiciary as Members of the Committee declined to accept the appointments and the matter ended there. As this was going to print, it was reported in the *Jerusalem Post* on 23 October 1984 that, "The President of the appeals court (in Ramallah) yesterday became the first local Arab judge to join the Judea and Samaria judicial appointments committee. Ghalib Haj Mahmoud was appointed by the Civil Administration to the committee which until now has consisted only of Jewish civilian officials and Israel Defence Forces officers. The Committee appoints judges to magistrates courts, district courts and courts of appeal in Ramallah."

* The relevant Jordanian legislation relating to the inspection of courts are the Law of the Constitution of Regular Courts and Regulation No. 105 of 1965 on Inspection of Regular Courts (published in the Jordanian Gazette, No 1877 in 1965). According to these laws, inspectors are appointed by the Minister of Justice with the duty of inspecting the work of the civil and criminal courts, as well as the functioning of the staff of all judicial departments. The duties of the Inspector include the following:
 — inspection of all court records, summonses, judgments, files of the Notary Public;
 — investigation of the reasons for adjournment to see whether such adjournments were warranted or not;
 — inspection of cases before the Execution Department in order to check whether or not judgments have been properly executed;
 — investigation of the functioning of the Prosecution Department, and checking of the files of criminal cases in order to see whether or not the accused has been properly defended and tried and whether the decision taken has been properly executed and any appeal properly heard;
 — Inspection of prisons and remand centres.
 Not less than 15 percent of all the work carried out by the person whose work is being examined has to be reviewed (article 12 of the Regulations). In practice, the Inspector, prior to 1967, chose files at random and inspected their contents. He then submitted annual reports to the Minister of Justice. Complaints were heard before a Special Committee.

Inspector of Courts. But on 2 October 1984, the Officer in Charge of the Judiciary appointed an Inspector of Courts. At the time of writing it is too early to comment on his work.

The necessity for strict control over the courts became more essential because of the reduction of the stages of appeal from three to two by the abolition, in 1967, of the Court of Cassation, the Highest Court of Appeal in the Jordanian system.*

The functioning of the courts

In the early years of the occupation, because of the general strike of lawyers and judges,[19] confusion in the legal system could be justified. Now, 17 years later, inefficiency and corruption continue to characterise the state of the local courts.**

In a meeting held on 26 January 1983 at the Ramallah Court of Appeal between judges, lawyers and the officer in the military government in charge of the judiciary, the following problems concerning the courts were raised. The officer has failed to act on most of the complaints expressed in that meeting.

---

* For the significance of this Court and the effect of its abolition, see *West Bank and the Rule of Law*, International Commission of Jurists and Law in the Service of Man, 1980, pp. 18-19. In *The Rule of Law in the Areas Administered by Israel*, by the Israeli Section of the International Commission of Jurists, 1982, it was claimed that it is incorrect to say that the military government abolished the Court of Cassation since its seat was in Amman only. However, the authorities did not restrain themselves from transferring most of the other Courts in the West Bank. The Courts of Appeal and the Jerusalem Court of First Instance, for example, were transferred from Jerusalem to Ramallah.

Following the same logic, these courts, being within the jurisdiction of Israel (since Jerusalem was annexed immediately after the 1967 war, before the courts were transferred) should have been abolished also. The other arguments made to justify the abolition of this Court, namely the comparison with the Israeli system and the absence of suitably qualified appointees for judges due to the lawyers' strike, are not convincing because, unlike the Israeli system, the Jordanian one is not based on the Anglo-Saxon system as far as structure of the courts is concerned. In the Jordanian system, the Court of Cassation is vital. As to the strike by the lawyers, there are now more than 150 lawyers in practice, so there can be no lack of legally trained people to appoint as judges to this Court.

** In their meeting on 19 October 1984, the lawyers in the West Bank decided to establish a regional bar association. It was not clear at the time of writing whether the military authorities would allow the lawyers to form a regional bar association in accordance with the Jordanian Lawyer's Law in force in the West Bank. At present the powers of the Bar Association are being exercised by the Officer in Charge of the Judiciary.

Court services

Despite the substantial increase in court fees[20] collected by the military (a five-fold increase over the pre-1967 fees), the salaries of judges and court officials continue to be very low. This means that the standards of those attracted to work in the courts are also low, and this, of course, is reflected in the quality of their work. The number of people employed is less than the number needed to carry out the work. This causes delays in the hearing of cases which often result in serious perversions of justice.

Forms for submitting applications to the offices of the Registrar of trademarks and land, for example, were unavailable for six months in 1982. In Nablus, the two Magistrates' Courts and three Courts of First Instance suffered from lack of stationery, including writing paper and files, for several months during the summer of 1982.

Similarly, many transactions were refused or delayed in the various court offices and judicial departments for such reasons as lack of stationary and unavailability of employees to do the work. Very often a lawyer is asked to type out his own blank forms or to make photocopies of them at his expense because the Court is unwilling to part with the last copy in its possession. The Court's judicial departments continue to suffer from unavailability of forms.

Reducing access to the local courts

In the meeting referred to above, the lawyers expressed their concern about the continued enforcement of Military Order No 164, by virtue of which permission is required from the military before proceedings can be taken against, or testimony can be accepted concerning, any of the following:

— the State of Israel, its branches and employees;

— the Israeli Forces and their Members;

— the authorities that have been appointed by the Area Commander or those that have been delegated by him to work in the area;

— persons employed by such authorities;

— whoever works in the service of the Israeli army or who is empowered by it.

According to the interpretation of the legal adviser of the military government, a permit cannot be given to a local court to hear cases against those in the first four categories. The effect of this order has been to render a sizeable segment of the population immune from legal action. The order also makes it possible for those who have an interest in delaying legal proceedings to do so by requesting an employee of a military authority to testify. A permit, if given, for such a witness will take three months to be issued.

The lawyers and judges also expressed their concern about the general dwindling jurisdiction of the Court. The transfer of the jurisdiction to military tribunals will be described fully later.

The withdrawing of cases under the power allowed by Military Order No. 841 has also been of concern to lawyers. The lawyer goes to the Court on the day fixed to proceed with a case and finds that the Court cannot hear his case because the case has been withdrawn by the officer in charge of the judiciary. Usually, when the case is returned the attitude of the judge changes radically, giving the impression that he has been instructed on how to proceed with the case.

Absence of inspection

There is no effective inspection of courts at present in the West Bank.* The deterioration in conditions and standards to which the absence of inspection can give rise is not difficult to imagine in any system. When conditions exist such as those under which the West Bank judiciary functions, inspection is essential. The judges are appointed by the military. They are paid low salaries and have no immunities or independence. At any time while travelling to court, for example, they may be stopped and humiliated — as all other members of society are likely to be. In 1981, there was one case where judges were asked to leave their cars as they were driving to court and remove stones placed in the street. Under such difficult circumstances and with low salaries, lack of inspection leads to even worse conditions than would normally be the case.

The effects of the lack of inspection have been numerous. The courts very often do not follow their own precedents. Cases are rejected for the simplest reasons. In appeal case 49/82, for example, the court decided against one of the parties on the grounds that the lawyer who pleaded the case did not have a power of attorney which "gave him the

---

* *Supra.*

right to submit a statement of claim; the power only authorised the attorney with the power to act on behalf of the principal and stand in his stead".

Delays and adjournments occur often and are not always justified. In the second week of August 1982, in the experience of the present author, five cases in which he was involved in Ramallah, Bethlehem, Jericho and Tulkarim, were all adjourned because of the judge's absence. There was no legitimate reason for the judge to have been absent, nor were the lawyers concerned notified, nor any explanation given for his absence. That particular week was neither outstanding nor atypical. Many judges during the past year, amongst them the President of the Courts of First Instance in Ramallah and Hebron, were absent for periods sometimes lasting a whole month, during which time they were sent to study Hebrew at an *ulpan* in Natanya. No arrangements were made beforehand. No substitutes were found to take over in their absence. The lawyers just had to wait and the litigants had to support the consequences of the delay.

Other causes of delay are the difficulty in summoning Israeli witnesses to testify before the court when their testimony is required. In criminal case number 106/80, the Ramallah Court of First Instance adjourned 15 times because an Israeli witness refused to comply with the Court's summons to appear before it. The Court then decided to order the police to bring the witness before it. The case had to be adjourned another 14 times before the witness finally submitted to the order of the Court and the police. The period over which these adjournments extended was one and a half years.

Delays as long as these due to lack of cooperation by the police are not uncommon. Often they cause the accused to suffer for years in prison awaiting the end of their trials. Accused persons not in custody are often not brought to trial by the police until many months have passed, despite the fact that they have been served with summons, their addresses are known and they are not fugitives.

Delay caused by lack of cooperation of the police is also felt in simple cases involving, for example, a bounced cheque. When a complaint is submitted to the police, it is served by the police on the person complained against. If then he fails to respond, the police refuse to take action to bring him to court. The police in practice are more willing, however, to take effective action when the complaint is submitted by Israelis against Palestinians. In the case of complaints of violations of the planning law, if the complaint concerns land which is either state

82

land or which Jewish settlers are interested in for the establishment or development of a settlement, prompt and effective action is assured.

The following examples are good illustrations of this. In the summer and autumn of 1984, the police refused to take action against violators of the planning law concerning lands within the area where Birzeit University is building its new campus. In the same period prompt and effective action was taken against farmers in the Jiftlic area in the Jordan valley, whom the military claimed were living in structures without planning permits. The military assisted the police in serving and implementing notices to force the Palestinian farmers from these lands on which they have lived and which they have been farming for many decades. The military was interested in vacating the land of Palestinian farmers to dedicate it exclusively for Jewish settlers.

The delays* are not only in criminal cases. In one civil case before the magistrate's court in Bethlehem (civil case no. 65/82), an ex-parte injunction to stop all work was given to the plaintiff. The defendant claimed that the decision was not based on proper legal grounds and that the document presented to guarantee payment of all damages caused by the delay was legally improper. From 14 June 1982 until 2 December 1982, 12 sessions were scheduled in which the defendant attempted to have the Court reverse its decision. No progress whatsoever was achieved. Many of these sessions were not held because of the unexcused absences of the judge. Sometimes, as happened on Monday, 7 November 1982, the delay was because the Officer in Charge of the Judiciary had invited all the judges to visit the morgue in Israel, without making the necessary arrangements with lawyers who had cases set for that day. Delays for similar reasons also occur in the Court of Appeal. Although the length of the delay in arriving at decisions in that Court has now been reduced, there has been no change in the quality of the decisions of this Court or in the consistency with which it follows its precedents. Decisions delivered by this Court relating, for example, to the adjustment of rent payable in the Israeli currency (which is constantly being devalued) to the Jordanian dinar (which is a more stable currency) have not followed a consistent line. Since most members of the community are either landlords or tenants, clarifying the law as to the possibility of adjustment of rent in certain cases is of vital importance. Unfortunately, the Court has not used the opportunity

---

* Under the Jordanian law of inspection, the Inspector appointed by the Minister of Justice had to investigate reasons for all adjournments to see whether or not they were warranted.

given by the cases brought before it to bring clarity to the law or to adjust rents to the changing exchange rates. When the Court did make new precedents it failed to follow them later on.

The lawyers, in the meeting referred to earlier, also requested that a separate magistrate be appointed to sit in Jericho because the number of cases heard there is equal to that of cases heard in the Bethlehem Court, which has its own Magistrates' Court. The magistrate who sits in Jericho hears cases only two days a week, as he also occupies the post of public prosecutor for both Bethlehem and Jericho.

None of the matters raised in the meeting were dealt with effectively by the Officer in Charge of the Judiciary. The local courts continue to be in a bad state. It is worth noting that the Officer in Charge of the courts is not ineffective in all cases. For example, on 20 October 1984 he warned all notaries public to charge all transactions for car transfers (which according to law must be done before the notary public) a fee proportionate to the market price of the car and not the stated price. He said that he will "observe this with care and will take very strict legal measures against the violators." When the issue concerns collection of money for the treasury of the military government, there is no leniency.

On 5 October 1970, the Area Commander declared in Military Order 412 that henceforth "all judicial proceedings shall be carried out and judgments made in the name of law and justice, all provisions in the law contrary to this shall be annulled." The military has been very astute in putting into force all its military decrees. Order 412 is amongst the first of those Military Orders that remain without implementation.

The Second System of Justice:
The Military Courts and Tribunals

Unlike the situation of the administration of the first system of justice, the military authorities exhibit great administrative efficiency in running the second system of justice — the military court system — which does not suffer from many of the problems which plague the local court system.

There is rarely any delay in hearing cases which come before the military courts or other military tribunals. The witness and the accused are always summoned and the cooperation of the police is assured. Parties before the Objections Committee are always served with notice

84

of the dates of the proceedings and cases are heard and decided without hindrance or obstruction.

It is of no surprise that this should be so because the military has every interest in making sure that those accused of "security" offences are tried without delay. As to cases involving objections against declarations of land declared as "state" land, a quick decision by the Objections Committee is required so as not to hinder the progress of the settlement in need of that land.[21]

The differences between the administration of the two systems of justice indicate that the military is able to administer efficiently when it is in its interest to do so. The military occupier who has assumed all the powers of the central government has done nothing to prevent the deterioration of the administration of the first system of justice.

The Military Courts

The emergence of the military courts

Under international law an occupying power is authorised to establish military courts to try cases of those charged with actions that endanger the security of the occupying power. On 8 June 1967, Israel established military courts to deal with security offences in the West Bank.[22] With the passage of years, other tribunals were established also under the authority of the military. The matters over which military courts exercised jurisdiction increased as those of the local courts were decreased.

Military courts have been established in five main towns in the West Bank. They convene in the military headquarters of the respective military governors of these towns.

The courts have acquired concurrent jurisdiction over all criminal matters under the Jordanian Criminal Code.[23] The decision whether a criminal case involving an offence under the Jordanian Criminal Code should be heard by a military court is reserved for the Area Commander. The military courts have tried cases of murder committed by Palestinians against other Palestinians. The decision to transfer such cases to a military court often appears to be due to the fact that the accused is a collaborator whom the military is interested in protecting. The military court also hears cases involving traffic and drug offences and recently offences against the new military order No. 1121 involving price fixing.

In times of general unrest the court convenes in a makeshift court room (sometimes close to a refugee camp) and holds what have come to be referred to as "quick trials". In such trials, scores of offenders are tried together usually without legal representation.

Detention and legal counsel
_____

The Military Orders in force empower the police to detain offenders without trial for a period of 18 days. After this period the detention must be renewed by a military court judge. In practice, the judge comes to the prison, and the detainee is brought, without his lawyer, before him. The decision to renew the detention is usually based on the information supplied by the military prosecutor. Applications for release on bail are almost never accepted. The court has also made it clear that it will not accept applications for habeas corpus.*

Offenders before military courts have no absolute right of legal representation. This fact has often been misrepresented. It has been falsely claimed[24] that Military Order 29 (concerning prisons) does in fact grant an offender this right. However, the right to legal representation under this Order is subject to the discretion of the Prison Commander. When legal representation is allowed, the lawyer is not permitted to visit his client until the interrogation has been completed. Clearance to make such visits must be obtained from the legal advisor to the military government. The delegates of the International Committee of the Red Cross (according to their agreement with the authorities) are entitled to see each detainee not later than 14 days after his arrest, but in practice the visit will be allowed only at the end of this period unless a confession has been made. A detainee is, therefore, in complete isolation from the outside world during this period and, apart from the ICRC visit, remains so until interrogation is completed or a confession is obtained from him. The agreement with the ICRC also contains a clause prohibiting the delegates from advising the detainee that he can see a lawyer or from passing on information to a lawyer should the detainee wish to instruct one.

Over the years, Military Order 378 (which deals with security offences

_____

* Law in the Service of Man has written to the Legal Advisor of the military government seeking clarification of the legal basis for the court's refusal to accept applications for habeas corpus. In his reply, the Legal Advisor did not address the question as to whether habeas corpus applied but confirmed that the detainee can apply for bail at any time. In practice, bail is given in very few cases.

and the military courts) has been amended 46 times. In the few cases where the defences made by lawyers on legal points have been successful, the Order has been changed to prevent future successes.

Judgments and the right of appeal

In a large percentage of the cases that come before the military courts, the judgment is based on a confession from the accused. The confession is almost invariably written in Hebrew — a language few Palestinians can speak or read.

Judgments of the military courts are not subject to appeal.[25] The only recourse under the Military Orders is to make a plea for mercy to the Military Governor of the area in which the convicted person resides. Such a plea will not suspend execution of the sentence whether it be imprisonment or a fine. If it is a fine, and it is not paid immediately, an increment of 100% has to be paid. In addition, the court may decide to imprison the convicted person if the fine is not paid promptly.[26]

Other Military Tribunals

Although the establishment of military courts to look into security offences is in accordance with international law, the creation of other military tribunals to hear civil matters is not. Yet, the military authorities in the occupied West Bank have established other military tribunals which will be discussed here.

The Objections Committee

Military Order 172 has declared the establishment of a military Objections Committee. This Committee began as a tribunal to hear appeals against decisions of the Custodian of absentee and state property. Since its inception in 1967, the jurisdiction of this Committee has been extended to give it jurisdiction to hear cases involving 28 different matters.

Some of the matters which the Objections Committee hears are concerned with appeals against decisions of the military government. However, not all of them are. Other matters which were previously within the jurisdiction of the local courts were later transferred to the Objections Committee. One example is of appeals against tax assessments. Military Order Number 28 made the Court of First Instance the competent court to hear such appeals and the Court of Appeal competent to hear appeals from the first court. By Military Order Number 406, the matter was taken from the local court and the power to hear such cases was transferred to the Objections Committee. This transfer of jurisdiction over matters involving taxes and custom duties is consistent with the policy of the occupation authorities to acquire and exercise full control over the collection of taxes and appeals against assessments.

The replacement of Palestinian employees by Israelis in local tax departments is also in line with this policy.

The decisions of the Objections Committee are in the form of recommendations which the Area Commander may accept or refuse and which cannot be appealed. The functions of this Committee have recently been increased. It now has a fixed secretariat in the military headquarters at Ramallah. Unlike their behaviour regarding the local courts, the police cooperate with this Committee. Military Order Number 164 which requires permission to be granted for certain witnesses to be heard (as has already been discussed) does not apply to proceedings before this Committee. Proceedings take place without delay. Generally, however, cases are heard before this Committee in an orderly and fair manner. The only problem is in the substance of the law which this Committee applies.

The following are some of the matters over which the Objections Committee exercises jurisdiction:

1. Decisions to expropriate land in accordance with the Jordanian law on expropriation, which has been amended so as to abolish the need to publish the intention for expropriation in the local newspapers and the Official Gazette if the authority wishing to expropriate is the military authority. The law has also been amended to vest in the Objections Committee the power to hear any challenges to the expropriation and to assess the compensation payable to the owner. These powers were previously within the jurisdiction of the regular courts.

2. Decisions by the Custodian of Absentee Property declaring any property to be absentee property, as well as decisions concerning property which the Custodian of government property considers to be property of the Jordanian government.

3. Decisions concerning declaration of land to be public land under Military Order Number 59.

88

4. Decisions concerning the use of natural resources.

5. Decisions concerning the registration of land that was previously unregistered. These decisions were previously appealable to the civilian courts.

6. Disputes concerning unregistered land.

7. Decisions concerning the regulations on natural resources.

8. Decisions concerning the registration of "special transactions" in immovable property, Order Number 569.

9. Violations of the Order against planting certain decorative flowers without permission — Order Number 818.

10. Decisions relating to the regulation of the planting of fruit trees — Order Number 1015, which prohibits the planting of fruit trees without first obtaining the permission of the military authorities.

11. Assessments made by the Income Tax Officer for the purposes of payment of taxes.

12. Decisions concerning assessment of goods for custom duties.

13. Decisions concerning assessment for Value Added Tax.

14. Decisions concerning the registration of companies.

15. Decisions concerning pensions for civil servants.

16. Decisions concerning pensions for local police employees.

17. Decisions concerning the prohibition of stocking goods and the refusal to sell goods and provide services.

18. Decisions concerning the appointment of civil servants.

19. Decisions concerning the registration of patents.

20. Decisions concerning the provision of licences for public vehicles.

21. Decisions concerning work insurance.

22. Decisions concerning bringing money into the West Bank.

23. Decisions concerning the control of public legal bodies.

24. Appeals against the Income Tax Inspector.

25. Classification and assessment of goods for customs purposes.

26. Classification and assessment of goods for Value Added Tax purposes.

The Claims Committee under Order 271

This Committee was empowered under Order 271 to hear applications for compensation against damage caused by an operation of the Israeli army or any other group or resident working for the army.

By way of an amendment to Order 271,[27] it has become necessary to obtain a certificate from the Area Commander that the damage was due to a military operation carried out "because of security needs" before cases can be heard by the Committee.

The Civil Pensions Committee

This Committee was established by virtue of Military Order No. 514 (Order concerning the pension law, of 8 May 1971). Article 2 of this Order vested in the Committee all powers and privileges under the Jordanian Pensions Law. The Members of this Committee are appointed by the Area Commander. The decisions of this Committee are appealable to the Objections Committee constituted by Military Order 172 whose decisions are recommendations which can be accepted or rejected by the Area Commander.

The Objections Committee under Order 56
concerning vehicle licensing

By virtue of Article 8 (as amended) of Military Order No. 56 (Order concerning the law of transport over roads, of 19 July 1967), an Objections Committee, constituted of three military officers, specified in the Article, is empowered to look into all objections submitted concerning the traffic authority's decisions to cancel licences, suspend, or refuse to renew them, if the objection is submitted to the military headquarters in the area within seven days of the decision being made. This Committee is empowered to determine its place of meeting and procedure.

The Committee to look into appeals
against regional and road planning schemes

It was declared in the regional and road planning schemes discussed in Part One that objections against the scheme will be heard by a special appeal committee constituted by the military for the purpose of hearing these objections. Those who decide on the objections are the officials who were involved in the creation of these schemes.

The Special Committee under Order 1060
concerning disputes over unregistered land

This Order has been discussed in Part I.

The Third System of Justice: The Israeli
Civilian Courts in The West Bank

There are at present about a hundred Jewish settlements in the Occupied West Bank, excluding Jerusalem, and about 32,000 Jewish Israelis live in these settlements.

Israeli propagandists sometimes defend their settlement policy by blandly saying that there is no reason why Israelis should not be able to live in the West Bank just as Arabs are able to live in Israel. The implication is that Israeli settlers have the same status as Arab inhabitants of the West Bank, and are subject to the same laws and to the jurisdiction of the same courts.* Nothing could be further from the truth. The Israeli settlements in the West Bank are *de facto* extensions of Israel. Their inhabitants are not tried before the local courts in any criminal matters nor, with a few exceptions, in civil matters.

Criminal Courts

There are three types of courts which may try Israeli settlers in criminal matters.

Firstly, they may be tried by criminal courts in Israel. In December 1967 a law was passed by the Israeli Knesset[28] providing that "a court in Israel shall be competent to try under Israeli law any person who is in Israel for an act or omission which occurred in any region and which would constitute an offence if it had occurred in the area of the jurisdiction of the courts in Israel."[29] **

Secondly, the Israeli settlers may be tried before the military courts in the West Bank, which have jurisdiction over all offences committed

---

* It is not suggested that Arabs in Israel are subject to the same laws as Israelis. The British Emergency Regulations theoretically remain in force for all inhabitants of Israel, but in practice they are applied only as a means of repression of the Arab inhabitants.

** Compare the article by Professor Yoram Dinstein criticising the same principle of extending jurisdiction to criminal offences committed outside the court's jurisdiction introduced in Israel by a 1972 amendment to the criminal law, in a Hebrew Law Journal, *"Enoneh Mishpatim"* Part B, December 1972.

there.[30]

Thirdly, they may be tried for certain offences before settlement courts which the Military Commander was empowered to establish in March 1981.[31] These courts were initially called municipal courts but a recent Military Order (No. 1057) has changed their name to "courts for local affairs". The jurisdiction of these courts was specified in regulations made in the same month and includes:

(a) offences committed contrary to any of the Regulations made by the military authorities, for the administration of local councils, with the exception of the rules for the election of the councils;

(b) jurisdiction to try offences against any regulation made by the Council, or any offence committed within the area of the Council against any law or Military Order mentioned in the appendix to the Regulations; and

(c) any other matters which shall be determined in the Regulations or in any other Military Order.

When Military Order No. 783 was published, the military authorities justified the establishment of courts on the grounds that they are only municipal courts with limited jurisdiction. Later their jurisdiction was extended and their name was changed by Military Order No. 1057 on 22 June 1983. This process of giving one justification for an action when it is introduced and later when the action is no longer the subject of public discussion, making changes that render the initial justification inapplicable is commonplace.

Settlement courts are competent to impose the punishments determined in Regulations and in laws or Military Orders mentioned in the Appendix to the Regulations. As these Regulations are not published, and the request for copies by the author have not met with any response, it is not possible to say what the extent of this jurisdiction is, or what penalties these courts may impose. It is, however, clear from paragraph (c) above that their jurisdiction can be extended indefinitely, simply by issuing secret Regulations or Orders.

The judges of these courts and the public prosecutor are appointed by the Area Commander. Judges of the courts of First Instance are appointed from among the Israeli magistrates. There is also a Settlement Appeal Court, whose judges are chosen from among the judges of the Israeli District Courts. The Appeal Court can sit wherever the Area Commander designates.

The procedure and rules of evidence of settlement courts are those of the Israeli courts, and the courts have the same powers as an Israeli magistrates' court to subpoena witnesses and in other matters related to a criminal hearing. The court also has the same powers as the military courts when it looks into violations of the law and of orders.

Fines imposed by settlement courts are to be paid to the Treasury of the local Council. If a fine is not paid, the court may sentence the offender to up to one month's imprisonment.

In Kiryat Arba (an Israeli settlement near the Arab town of Hebron), the first settlement court has been established. The judge is a magistrate judge from Jerusalem. Appeals are heard by three judges from the Israeli District Court in Jerusalem.[32]

There is no law or Military Order which states in terms that Israeli citizens may not be tried before the local criminal courts, but in practice it never happens. They are tried either before a military court, a settlement court, or an Israeli regular court.* In addition, a recent circular (No 49/1350), dated 6 December 1984 and signed by the Officer in Charge of the Judiciary, adds to the difficulty of having West Bank courts hear cases against Israelis. Addressed to all prosecutors and courts in the West Bank, it states as follows: "Reference is made to document No 3/63 dated 11 January 1979, in which the legal advisor has interpreted the law on the West Bank whereby it is not possible to execute judgments from West Bank courts made against holders of Israeli identity cards who are living inside Israel (to include Jerusalem and its suburbs). ... Therefore, and to avoid problems in this respect, West Bank courts should not register any criminal case (to include traffic cases) against holders of Israeli identity cards unless written authorization is obtained from me."

Civil Courts

Civil claims by or against Israeli settlers may be tried before Israeli courts or settlement courts or, in rare cases, the local courts.

In contractual matters the parties may agree in the contract which court shall be competent to hear disputes. If the parties choose Israeli

---

* The group of Jewish people accused of committing serious terrorist offences in the West Bank and Jerusalem and of being members of a Jewish terrorist group (some of whom are Israeli civilians living in West Bank settlements, while others are officers in the Israeli army) are being tried at the time of writing in the District Court in Jerusalem. Both the West Bank local courts and the military courts have jurisdiction to try them.

courts, no permit is required from the court for the purpose of serving process on the party residing in the West Bank outside the jurisdiction of the Israeli courts.*

A special execution department has been established in the West Bank by virtue of Military Order No. 348 to execute decisions reached by Israeli courts concerning property in the West Bank.

In contractual disputes where the parties have not agreed upon the forum, settlement courts or local courts may have jurisdiction. There are some matters which may arise between Palestinian and Jewish inhabitants of the West Bank over which the local courts continue to have jurisdiction. For example, in cases of civil wrongs such as torts the local courts continue to have jurisdiction. However, in practice it is not possible to start legal proceedings against a Jewish settler whatever the subject of the case. Jewish settlements are surrounded by barbed wire. Entry to them is through a guarded door. A Palestinian entering there, whatever may be the purpose of his visit, will be looked upon with suspicion. The settlers are armed and enjoy extensive powers under the defence of settlement Orders. If the Palestinian should announce that his purpose for entering is to serve court papers, he is not likely to be permitted to enter. He is likely to be harassed and perhaps even detained.**

It should be noted that Israeli norms have been introduced in the West Bank on a personal, not a territorial, basis. That is, they relate to the Israeli population in the whole region and are not restricted to the Israeli settlements. This (as has already been described in full above) has been done in two ways:

(i) by enacting Israeli legislation which extended territorial laws of the state to the Israeli population residing outside the borders of Israel;

(ii) through Military Orders.[33]

---

* This is due to a 1969 amendment of the civil procedure (service of documents to the Administered Territories) Regulations and to an Israeli court ruling that a permit from the court is not necessary for the purpose of serving documents under Regulation 476 of the rules of court. The only requirement is to attach with the document an Arabic translation. For further discussion of this subject, see Drori, Moshe, *Israeli Settlements in Judea and Samaria: Legal Aspects*, published in *Judea and Samaria and Gaza: Views on the Present and Future*, ed. Danial Elazar, American Enterprise Institute for Public Policy Research, Washington D.C., 1982, pp. 68-74.

** The Karp report (published in February 1984) documented the decision of the settlers not to cooperate with the Israeli police in the investigation of crimes.

The Rabbinical Court

Local Arab courts may not look into matters of personal status of Jews. These matters are defined by reference to the Law of Religious Councils, No. 2, of 1938 (which is applicable in the West Bank) to include such matters as marriage, divorce, inheritance and custody.

In 1938, under the British Mandate, nine non-Moslem communities were allowed to have their own courts to hear matters of personal status between members of these communities, but a Rabbinical Court was not among them.

The relevant Military Order[34] empowers the head of the "Civilian Administration" to establish Rabbinical Courts and Rabbinical Appeal Courts.

The Israeli High Court of Justice

It has become appropriate when discussing the West Bank judiciary to refer to the Israeli High Court of Justice because this court, by assuming some of the powers of the Arab High Court of Justice, has become a court to which the residents of the West Bank are increasingly resorting. Having reduced the jurisdiction of the West Bank courts, abolished the Court of Cassation, and reduced the instances when an appeal can be submitted to the High Court of Justice of the West Bank as shown above, Israel has made available its own High Court of Justice to applicants from the West Bank. This has been heralded by Israel as the first occasion in the history of military occupation when citizens of an occupied territory have been allowed a direct appeal to the High Court of the occupying power. It has also been interpreted as a step in the direction of normalization of relations between inhabitants of the West Bank and Israel.

In the foreword to "The Rule of Law in the Areas Administered by Israel", Haim Cohn, a former Justice of the Israeli High Court, explained the basis of the jurisdiction of the Israeli High Court of Justice as follows:[35] "The Court assumed jurisdiction, which in effect is extraterritorial, over the persons of the Military Commanders and their subordinates, the underlying reason being that all organs of the Government of Israel are subject to the jurisdiction of the High Court of Justice in respect of all their acts and omissions, wherever they may have taken place. It is by virtue of this personal — as distinguished from territorial

95

— jurisdiction that the court will order any Military Commander, or any subordinate official in the administered area, to do an act which by law he is obliged to do, or to abstain from doing any act which by law he ought not to do."

When the first case was brought before the Israeli High Court by a petitioner from the West Bank, the then Attorney-General, Meir Shamgar (who is now President of this court), raised no objection to the court's jurisdiction to hear the case. His lead was followed by succeeding Attorneys-General. The possibility of making such an objection still exists, however, despite Justice Cohn's explanation. In a recent case brought before the court regarding treatment of Palestinian prisoners of war at the Ansar Camp in Israeli-occupied Lebanon, the Israeli government argued that the High Court had no jurisdiction over Lebanese soil and that it could not, therefore, hear the case.*

The issue of whether legislative enactments by the military government enjoy the status of primary law, which are unchallengeable, or can be viewed as secondary by-laws and administrative action, which are reviewable, has never been decided by the High court and has only been the subject of *obiter dicta*. In the case of the *Holy Land Christian Society v. Minister of Defence*,[36] one judge, Justice Haim Cohn, was willing to question the legality of a Military Order. In *Suleiman Hilu v. Government of Israel*,[37] Justice Vitkon clearly expressed his opinion that Military Orders are primary legislation beyond the power of the High Court to question. As long as the military governor is the sole unchecked legislator in the West Bank, and his orders are viewed as beyond the scrutiny of the High Court, access to the High Court becomes worthless, since his essential authority remains unchallenged and any reverses suffered by him are quickly remedied by subsequent "legislation".

---

* The reference is to the following cases before the Israeli High Court (all of which were joined together): 593/82, 102/82, 150/82, 690/82 and 271/83. The High Court decided as follows: "a) I.D.F. soldiers were entitled to arrest individuals against whom there were concrete suspicions that such individuals had carried out hostile acts endangering the security of our forces and to hold them in detention in an area occupied by the I.D.F. b) The rules set forth in article 78 of the Fourth Geneva Convention apply to the detainees, and we understand that these were applied in the case of those who are the subject of these petitions. The fact that Israel is not maintaining a military government in the area under consideration does not affect the matter at hand. c) We understand that the respondents are prepared in principle to permit a meeting between a detainee who wishes so and a lawyer, and to allow correspondence with the lawyer for this purpose; of course, in keeping with the security arrangements as required. Therefore, I reject the petitions and cancel the writs that were issued pursuant thereto."

The Palestinians in the occupied territories have in recent years been taking more cases to the Israeli High Court of Justice. The outcome has not been encouraging. The reason for this lies primarily in a series of self-imposed restrictions which the court placed on its proclaimed role which permitted it to avoid dealing with many of the thornier issues raised by the occupation. Amongst these are the following:

(i)   Refusal to apply the Geneva Conventions

The military government maintains and the High Court has agreed[38] that Military Orders are dominant law in the West Bank and that they supercede provisions of the Jordanian law which contradict them. They must be reviewed, if at all, in terms of their compliance with international law.

Yet the High Court has held, in accordance with the view of the Israeli Government, that only customary international law, and not treaty law, is binding on the court. This means that the most advanced and comprehensive statement of international law on the rights of civilians under military occupation, the Fourth Geneva Convention of 1949, is not considered as binding.

Challenges to actions of the military government based on the Geneva Conventions have therefore failed in the High Court.

(ii)   Limited Scrutiny of Claims of "Security Purposes"

The Israeli High Court grants wide latitude to the military government whenever the claim is made that a certain action is taken for "security purposes". In the *Beit El* case, judges accepted the claim that private Arab land confiscated to erect a civilian Jewish settlement was taken for "security purposes".[39] In the *Rafiah* case,[40] Justice Vitkon stated that "security matters, like matters of foreign policy, are not justiciable" and that actions of the military authorities will not be questioned if the Court is satisfied that they were based on security grounds. Also, Justice Landau held that the Court cannot substitute its own military and political opinions for the military opinion of authorities entrusted with maintenance of public order in the "Administered Territories".

The area of review, therefore, becomes very narrow indeed. One case where the courts did hold against the military government was the celebrated *Elon Moreh*[41] case. In that case, which has been discussed, very special circumstances existed. The military government attempted to expropriate proven private Palestinian land for a Jewish civilian settlement in that location. In addition, Gush Emunim settlers insisted in court that their motivation was biblical/political and not security related. The court found that both security and other motives existed and that the other motives were dominant, so they ordered the dismantlement of the settlement.

Narrow as the decision was in the *Elon Moreh* case, it implied a willingness on the part of the High Court, under certain conditions, to examine claims of security purposes. Nonetheless, the principle of judicial reluctance to examine the veracity of claims of "security purposes" continues to be dominant in the Israeli High Court.

(iii) Use of Quasi-Judicial Bodies as Substitutes for Courts

As has been seen, following the *Elon Moreh* decision, the military government began to use a new method to acquire Arab lands without risking review by the High Court. Instead of relying upon unspecified "security needs", the authorities now merely declare areas they wish to expropriate to be "state" lands. Any challenge to this designation has to be made before the military Objections Committee.

(iv) Psychological Barriers

The understandable reluctance of the population to lend credibility and legitimacy to the Israeli occupation by appealing to the court has been based on the feeling that it constituted a high political price to be paid for a poor likelihood of success. This price was made greater by the requirement of the High Court that the Palestinian appealing to it refrain from utilising the press and soliciting favourable public opinion, which Palestinians often believe to be more effective than the High Court in remedying their situation.

(v) The expenses involved in resorting to the High Court

Although the court fees are negligible, according to a recent court ruling the losing party must pay both the costs and the lawyer's fees of the winning party. The remunerations which lawyers charge for appearances before the High Court are very high and beyond the means of most average residents of the West Bank.

(vi) The Inaccessibility of the High Court
to West Bank Lawyers

Although Israeli lawyers have been permitted by a special military order to appear before all West Bank courts, Palestinian lawyers from the West Bank cannot appear before the courts in Israel, including the High Court.

In view of the claim that the High Court in Israel is open to the residents of the West Bank, it might have been expected that special permission would be given for Palestinian lawyers to appear before it, but this is not the case. Petitioners to the court from the West Bank can therefore submit petitions only through Israeli lawyers.

★ ★ ★ ★ ★

Despite all the above limitations, there remain some areas where the High Court can be relied upon to offer substantial relief for West Bank Palestinians:

(a) Obtaining orders to halt pending actions by the military government until there is an opportunity to be heard (e.g. to prevent demolition of a house). Such orders in certain cases had until recently been easy to obtain, but it is rare for a Palestinian to win ultimately.

(b) In areas where the military government fails to follow its own stated procedures before carrying out an action. When Mayors Milhem and Kawasmeh were deported, their wives successfully petitioned the High Court for an order to permit their return until they had an opportunity to appear before an Objections Committee (whose powers were merely advisory and whose proceedings were *in camera*). Once the military government availed them of that procedure, however, they were again deported and the High Court refused to invalidate their deportation order.

(c) In areas where a litigant can prove an irrelevant motive or arbitrary action. Were a Palestinian litigant to prove that action by the military government was based on criteria other than the stated ones, he would be likely to prevail. This area is narrowed, however, by the fact that criteria are rarely announced, by the unwillingness of the Court to investigate the motives of the military government and by the wide latitude it automatically grants to claims of security. Cases like *Elon Moreh*, where the Gush Emunim settlers brazenly revealed the true motives of the settlement and where a former Chief of Staff contradicted in court the professional opinion of the Minister of Defence, are very rare indeed.

99

The Israeli High Court could have played a much more significant role in advancing the rule of law in the West Bank, and may still do so in the future, if it removed some of its self-imposed restrictions. In the meantime, it certainly cannot be claimed that access to it gives West Bankers "automatically ... all those rights enjoyed by Israeli residents ... such as freedom of expression or freedom of the press", or that it imposes on the military government a duty to reflect democratic principles which are "additional to those granted to residents of the region by international law", as was claimed in the Israeli reply to *The West Bank and the Rule of Law.*[42]

References

(1) Benvenisti, Meron, The West Bank Data Base Project: A Survey of Israel's Policies, American Enterprise Institute for Public Policy Research, Washington and London, 1984, p. 61.

(2) Emergency Regulations, 1984, para. 3A.

(3) For a full analysis of these regulations, see article by Timothy Hillier available from Law in the Service of Man, Ramallah.

(4) Benvenisti, Meron, op. cit., p. 40.

(5) Ibid.

(6) Palestinian mayors of several towns in the West Bank, including Ramallah, Bireh, Halhoul, and Hebron, have been deported. The mayors of most West Bank towns, including the mayors of all the above mentioned towns and in addition Nablus, Beit Jalla and Jenin, have been dismissed. These dismissals were carried out under the general power of the Area Commander by virtue of Military Order No. 537 of 17 March 1974. Heads of village councils have also been removed and others appointed in their place. Jordanian law, The Mukhtar Law of 1958, stipulates that the village leader shall be elected by all male residents in the area who are over 18 years of age.

(7) Benvenisti, Meron, op. cit., p. 41.

(8) For a fuller comparison between the Jordanian municipality law and the Regulations for the administration of local councils, see article by the present author in *The Review*, International Commission of Jurists, No. 27 of 1981, Geneva.

(9) Benvenisti, Meron, op. cit., p. 41.

(10) Singer, Joel, *The Establishment of a Civil Administration in the Areas Administered by Israel*, in Israel Yearbook on Human Rights, Vol. 12, 1982, p. 274.

(11) Ibid., p. 275.

(12) See "Civilian Administration in the Occupied West Bank", 1982, by the present author and Kuttab, Jonathan for a fuller analysis of Military Order 947.

(13) Military Order Number 412.

(14) Military Order Number 310.

(15) Military Order Number 528.

(16) Military Order Number 267, later amended by Order Number 362.

(17) Military Order Number 379.

101

(18) Military Order Number 555.

(19) See *West Bank and the Rule of Law,* op. cit., pp. 45-50 for a discussion on the reasons and effects of the lawyers' strike.

(20) Military Order Number 1036 announced some of these increases in the fees. Fees are expressed in the stable Jordanian currency which is not subject to the devaluation of the Israeli currency.

(21) Law in the Service of Man has prepared a survey of all cases heard by the military courts in the West Bank in 1983, including the types of cases heard, the charges and sentences.

(22) Military courts were established by Order Number 3, later replaced by Military Order Number 378 which also specified security charges.

(23) Military Order Number 30.

(24) For example, in *The Rule of Law in the Areas Administered by Israel,* op. cit., p. 30.

(25) Article 43 of Military Order Number 378.

(26) Article 47 of Military Order Number 378.

(27) Military Order Number 1101, amending Military Order Number 271.

(28) Article 2(a) of the Emergency Regulations (Offences Committed in Israeli-Held Areas — Jurisdiction and Legal Assistance) (Extension of Validity) Law, 1967.

(29) For full discussion of this law, see previous section.

(30) Military Order Number 30 — see previous section for a full discussion of these courts.

(31) See Military Orders Numbers 783 (as amended by Military Order 1058) and 892.

(32) Benvenisti, op. cit., p. 44.

(33) For an account of the legal system of the Israeli settlements see article by Raja Shehadeh in *The Review* of the International Commission of Jurists, No. 27, December 1981.

(34) Military Order Number 981 dated 11 April 1982, sections 2 and 9.

(35) *The Rule of Law in the Areas Administered by Israel,* op. cit.

(36) *Holy Land Christian Society v. Minister of Defence,* High Court of Justice 337/71 P.D. 26(1).

(37) *Suleiman Hilu v. Government of Israel,* High Court of Justice 302/72 P.D. 27(2) 169-180.

(38) *Kawasmeh v. Minister of Defence* (1981), 35 P.D. (3) 113.

(39) *Suleiman Ayyoub v. Minister of Defence,* 606/78 P.D. 33(2) 113.

(40) *Hilu v. Government of Israel,* op. cit.

(41) *Dwaikat v. Government of Israel,* 1980, 34 P.D. (1) 1.

(42) *The Rule of Law in the Areas Administered by Israel,* op. cit., p. 39.

102

Part Three:

The Effects of
the Occupier's Law

Chapter Five

The Underlying Policies
and Their Effect on Human Rights

*"Discussion of human rights in Palestine differs markedly from dis-
cussion of human rights in most other locations. With respect to Palestine and its people, human rights deprivations are part of a broader
deprivation of existence as a nation. Individual deprivation cannot be
viewed accurately, therefore, unless it is considered in the context of
the larger deprivation of national existence."*

                — John Quigley*

Introduction

Visitors to the West Bank often comment that they are surprised at
how normal the situation in the occupied territories appears to be. The
army does not seem to have a strong presence, people seem to go about
their business normally, there are many new houses under construction.
It is not at all what they expected to see from following the situation
in their local newspapers or from reports of the human rights situation
produced by Palestinians, Israelis or international investigation teams.

 The observations of these visitors are not incorrect. Except for times
of demonstrations on Palestinian national days or when commemorat-
ing the death of martyred individuals or opposing a new policy of the
occupation, it has been the policy of Israel since the beginning of the
occupation to stay away from the population as far as possible.

---

* In *Palestinian Rights: Denial and Affirmation*, Ed. Ibrahim Abu Lughod, Medina Press,
Wilmette, Illinois, 1982.

Our assessment of the nature of the life of the Palestinians under Israeli rule will not reflect the true and complete picture of the reality unless we take into account the objectives of the policies Israel pursues towards the territory under its control.

It is not my intention here to add another report to the literature on the human rights situation of Palestinians under Israeli occupation. There already exists a large number of such accounts written by groups with different kinds of perspectives and intentions — by Jews concerned about the moral well-being of the Jewish state, and by supporters of the Palestinians concerned with highlighting their plight and increasing support for their struggle.

Inhabitants of the West Bank are not Israeli citizens. They are holders of Jordanian passports and Israel recognises their nationality as Jordanian in the travel documents it issues to them. Yet, Israel does not recognise that the territory is part of Jordan and does not accord inhabitants of the territories the protection guaranteed under international law to protected persons. As such they get neither the privileges of citizens of Israel nor those of Jordan. Their status is comparable to that of alien residents.

But it does not only rest there. The Palestinians in the West Bank are subject to a policy which is deliberately intended to bring about very concrete and definite changes in the occupied territories in order to secure a Jewish majority there so as to enable Israel to annex them.

Those reporting on civil rights often assess the situation of the Palestinians without reference to this policy of the occupation. To do so is to accept the framework laid down by the occupation authorities.

I do not want to derogate from the value and significance of such reports. Yet, I cannot escape the feeling that, however exhaustively such reports may treat the situation, and make known the number of books that are banned and people killed or deprived of their freedom of movement, the overall picture that they leave with the reader is often a distorted one.

When the authorities depose an elected mayor, such an act is considered as a grave violation of the right of the people to elect their own leaders. It is, therefore, a fact worth mentioning in a human rights report. However, by stressing it in isolation from the larger political context, the picture is distorted. It is not as though the correct assessment of the situation of Palestinians in the West Bank can be arrived at by compiling lists of the number of their leaders who were deported or deprived of their elected office or placed under town arrest, etc.; nor from adding to the list of the number of associations that have been banned and the

106

number of books prohibited and the number of school children wounded or killed. If such a compilation could reflect the true situation, then a logical consequence could follow that if only the Israeli authorities ceased harassing the leaders of the population and banning the associations and prohibiting the books, and if the soldiers in the Israeli army could exercise more self-restraint in their treatment of the rest of the population, all would be well. Some have drawn, it is true, the conclusion that such violations are inevitable as long as Israel is occupying a land with close to a million inhabitants who are in opposition to its occupation and that the end of the violations can come only with the end of the occupation. Those who arrive at this conclusion are closer to the truth.

However, it is a fact that from the beginning of the entry of the Israeli army to the West Bank, the government of Israel has called it the liberation of the territories — not their conquest. This description was not mere empty rhetoric. The Israeli policies which then followed, and which are still being followed, are premised on concrete and well-defined attitudes to the area captured and to the people inhabiting it. Only if we take these attitudes fully into account can we begin to make a proper assessment of the human rights situation of the Palestinian inhabitants of the occupied territories and of the true state of the Israeli treatment of the Palestinian population there.

To stress the violations of the civil rights of the inhabitants of the area is to operate within the parameters which Israel has imposed. It is the basic human rights, including the right to self-determination, that should be included in any human rights report. Speaking only about civil rights reflects half the reality.

It has been the practice of Israeli civil rights activists and of the High Court of Justice to steer away from the political issues.

Some may say that such a position, as far as the Court is concerned, is a commendable position. However, the High Court has assumed a very special position in relation to the West Bank. It is purporting to act as a Court of Appeal for the residents there against the actions of the military. By accepting that only the Hague Regulations (which are considered as part of the municipal law of the country) should be applied and not the Geneva Conventions, the Court is allowing itself to be another instrument that lends legal validity to actions by the government which are in essence illegal. In other words, the Court is not acting as an impartial arbitrator.

Similarly, human rights groups in Israel such as the Association for Civil Rights, refused at first to be involved in the protection of the civil

107

rights of Palestinians. They have now changed this attitude but their activities remain limited to civil rights.

The law professors at the Hebrew University who lobbied the Attorney General to make an investigation of settlers' vigilante activities that resulted in the Karp Report*, also acted within the same framework. Their interest was in the settlers' illegal activities — they failed to include with their protest the fact that the settlers' very existence in the West Bank is illegal and the taking of land for settlements is similarly illegal. Their starting point was the acceptance of the existence of the settlements, and they were then concerned about the settlers' activities, once they were there.

When Israeli Jews make pronouncements as to how they would like their country to behave towards the non-Jews amongst them, respecting their full civil rights, I believe that many are being very serious and sincere. Israel is a country with an image amongst other Jews in the diaspora and amongst Western countries of a democracy which has affirmed its commitment to the rule of law and to the protection of the basic rights of its inhabitants.

At the same time, very few Israelis would accept Israel as anything other than a Jewish state. How then could the million and a half Palestinians (which would be the total number of Palestinians in Israel if the occupied areas were annexed) be granted full civil rights and Israel (which has a Jewish population of about 3.4 million) remain a Jewish state?

Those in Israel whose commitment to the continuation of the Jewish democratic state is stronger than that to the larger state of Eretz Israel, do not support the annexation of the territories. Nevertheless, only a small number of this group would allow the Palestinians to exercise their basic human rights to self-determination. What then do they propose? They take a strong position against vigilante settlers' activities which lead to the breaking of windows of Palestine homes or against the destruction of Palestinian homes by way of reprisal, while remaining silent in the face of the acquisition of thousands of dunums of Palestinian land to make Jewish settlement in the West Bank possible.

My intention in this chapter is to discuss the policy towards the Palestinian population in relation to the general policy of annexation and to discuss the human rights situation as being the natural and inevitable consequence of pursuing such a policy. That is to say that the individual violations are not themselves the cause of the evil but only the effect

* Prepared in December 1982 and published in February 1984.

which arises necessarily from a definite and deliberate policy. It is this policy which should be attacked and reversed. Only then can we expect an improvement in the human rights situation of the Palestinians.

Israel uses the security argument to defend the legality of its practices under international law, claiming that they are necessary for the protection of its state and its army. It is true that international law takes full cognizance of the need of the occupier to safeguard the security of its army, and permits restrictions that are indeed necessary for that security. Is Israel's security argument then legally supportable, and which of its practices are legitimate under the international conventions?

Israel's Concept of Security

In the case of *Suleiman Tawfik Ayoub et al v. The Minister of Defence*[1] which was heard before the High Court of Justice in Israel, the appellants challenged the military government's decision to establish the Jewish settlement of Beit El. The government argued in its affidavit submitted to the court that:

"16(a) [the] establishment of the settlement in the area of the Beit El [army] camp not only does not conflict with the military requirement but actually serves it, in that it is a part of the security conception of the Government which bases the security system *inter alia* on Jewish settlements. In accordance with this concept all Israeli settlements in the territories occupied by the I[srael] D[efence] F[orces] constitute part of the I.D.F.'s regional defence system . . . In times of calm these settlements mainly serve the purpose of presence and control of vital areas, maintaining observation, and the like. The importance of these settlements is enhanced in particular in time of war when the regular army forces are shifted, in the main, from their bases for purposes of operational activity and the said settlements constitute the principal component of presence and security control in the areas in which they are located."

I have already discussed, in Chapter One, the case of *Elon Moreh*, which was heard later by the same court, after the above case. In the *Elon Moreh* case a counter argument was presented to the court by Israeli military experts who testified that in their opinion civilian settlements not only do not help security but are in fact a liability in security terms in the case of war.

The official Israeli view (which continues to be held) is that Israeli civilian presence in the occupied territories is necessary for security. Indeed, the concept of security is so far-reaching that it is capable of being taken, in some circumstances, to permit anything that does not conflict with the military requirement.

Widening the scope of the notion of security to this extent makes it irreconcilable with the law of belligerent occupation.

If the presence of civilians of the occupying power in occupied territories is necessary for the security of the occupier then all the actions taken to support this presence will be legitimised, including the acquisition of land and natural resources and the construction of an infrastructure to support that presence, regardless of the extent to which the occupied people are thereby deprived of their legal rights and property.

It follows further that actions taken to suppress the development of the inhabitants of the occupied territories and to encourage them to leave will also be legally excusable as necessary for the security of the occupying power since those inhabitants will necessarily be hostile to the settler policy.

For example, ridiculous as it may seem, the military authorities for a long time refused on security grounds to permit the establishment of a needlework cooperative supported by the Mennonite Central Committee. The YWCA was for three years refused a permit to establish a centre in the West Bank, also on the grounds of security.

We must anticipate that the use of the security justification is only a temporary matter. Several pointers support such a conclusion. In the case brought to the Israeli High Court by the Arab Teachers' Housing Cooperative, in 1982,* against withdrawal by the planning authority of building licences which had been granted to the teachers to build their houses, the court accepted the reasons given by the authority for withdrawing the licences — namely that the position of the houses conflicts with the road plan, which is part of a West Bank road scheme drawn up by the Israeli Planning Department operating in the West Bank (see *supra*). In accepting this reason, the Court said that the length of the occupation renders actions by the occupier which otherwise would be considered contrary to international law, acceptable. The court considered the two criteria that any such action should be for the benefit of the local population or for the security of the forces. The road scheme

---

* Jamiat Askan al-Malmoun, al-Taounia al-Mahdoda al Msawlia, Co-operative Society v. Commanding Officer of the IDF and the Higher Planning Commission, SCJ No. 393/82.

in question is designed to link the settlements to Israel and to construct roads which avoid the Arab population centres. Nevertheless, the argument made before the Court that the road scheme is not really benefitting the local Palestinian population was not accepted. The Israeli High Court had in an earlier case (*The Electricity Company for the District of Jerusalem Ltd. v. Minister of Defence et. al.* (1972) P.D. 27(1) 124, 138 F) recognised Israeli settlers as part of the population of the West Bank.

As long as the Court considers Jewish settlers to be part of the local population all the purport of the restrictions imposed by the above criteria of international law designed to protect the civilian population under occupation will be distorted. It is to be expected therefore that in its future decisions the Court will be putting less stress on security justifications and more on the benefits to be derived from the actions of the military by the 'local' population. When this happens, the circle will have been completed. Legal provisions which have been used to safeguard the interests of occupied people will be used by the occupier to defend policies that are being practised to benefit primarily the citizens of the occupier. It is not difficult to appreciate that then the very purpose of the international conventions will thereby be defeated.

Such a situation already exists as far as planning laws are concerned. I have already discussed (in Chapter Two) the damage which these plans will cause to the Palestinian inhabitants and how they are designed to benefit the 30,000 Jewish settlers in the area. The preamble to the Order which empowers the Military Officer to assume full control over planning reads, "Whereas I consider it necessary for the orderly management of development and construction operations in the area, and for securing proper planning and licensing procedures, I order . . . ".

Meron Benvenisti, who has studied the new plans put forward by the military, observed that: "From the perspective of 30,000 Israel settlers, proper planning and licensing procedures seems to have been carried out smoothly. From the perspective of 750,000 West Bank Palestinians, the preamble reads like a macabre joke."*

---

* Benvenisti, Meron "West Bank Data Base Project: A Survey of Israel's Policies", American Enterprise Institute for Public Policy Research, Washington and London, 1984, p. 28.

The Consequences of The General Policy
on The Palestinian Population

The security justification, whether or not it can be supported in fact or in law, is an excuse put forward after the fact to add legitimacy to the general policy of replacing the Palestinian population by a Jewish one.

In the following pages I will describe some of the main consequences of this policy to the lives of the Palestinian inhabitants of the occupied territories.

The right to self-determination

The policy Israel is pursuing in the West Bank deprives the population of their basic human right to determine their own future through disrupting the demographic unity of the land (the manner in which this is being done was described in Chapter One of this study). Planting Jewish settlers in the area makes the emergence of a Palestinian state very difficult.

The same objective is pursued through depriving the Palestinians of their right to participate in political activities. In this way, they are being prohibited from developing politically and participating in any political process. Here again, security is cited as the excuse. Security is enlarged to become a concept of political control.

The Israeli propaganda machine has sought to portray (both within Israel and abroad) the Palestinians inside and outside the West Bank as supporters of terrorism and as the bitter enemies of Israel, who will never accept Israel's existence. For obvious reasons, the campaign was at its height before the invasion of Lebanon.

This blanket description, or rather caricature, leads to the harassment of all Palestinians because, being Palestinian, they are considered a security threat to Israel. The reasoning that underlies the policy is that to be a Palestinian is to be subversive; to be subversive is to endanger security.

In the Israeli thinking there is a relationship between independent Palestinian political activity and "security" offences. An Israeli diplomat in the United States accused an American philanthropic church organisation running charitable work in the West Bank of supporting the Palestine Liberation Organisation. When the representative wanted to know why this was so, the diplomat answered: "You are helping Palestinians in the West Bank. The Palestinians support the PLO. Therefore, you are helping the PLO."

112

This is not the place to argue about the nature and policies of the PLO. The organisation is on record as accepting a Palestinian state side by side with Israel, but no distinction is made by Israel between extremist and moderate Palestinians. Israel does not accept any Palestinians with a nationalist stance whether or not they accept Israel's existence.

General Chaim Herzog (now Israel's president) revealed in 1974 that in the early years of the occupation, the Labour government refused to permit any independent political expression on the part of the Palestinian population, even rejecting the request of pro-Jordanian "notables" to form an anti-PLO grouping (cf. Noam Chomsky's book, *The Fateful Triangle*, p. 54).

Given the consistency of the Israeli position of refusing to recognise the national existence of the Palestinians, whose "problem" is considered to be only a refugee problem to be solved in the context of negotiations with the Arab states, the refusal to allow Palestinians independent political activity is not surprising. The only Palestinian presence in the West Bank acceptable to Israel is that of a docile minority acquiescing in permanent Israeli domination. Consistent with this is Israel's policy of discouraging Palestinian economic development. A cement factory project in Hebron, for example, has been denied a permit for several years. The Hebrew papers reported in October 1984 that this was because Israeli cement factories were not selling enough cement.*

The alien resident status

Professor Yuval Ne'eman, Secretary of the Tehiya party and former Minister of Science, said in an interview given to the *Jerusalem Post*:**

"All these territories must be annexed to Israel: the Golan, Judea and Samaria and Gaza. As to the Arab population here, it does exist — between 400,000 and 450,000 are refugees whom the Egyptians and the Jordanians consciously and consistently perpetuated in that status. Their humanitarian problem will not be resolved in a hypothetical Palestinian state, because they are not natives of those areas.

---

* For other examples, see article by Susan Hattis Rolef in the *Jerusalem Post* Oct. 1, 1984, "Partners in a Dialogue", where the writer argues that the military authorities have "simply not allowed any genuine economic development (in the West Bank) to take place."
** International edition, 14 to 20 October, 1979.

They must be resettled as part of a real peace settlement in Kuwait, Saudi Arabia and the other Arab oil countries which have the wherewithal to resettle them. As to the remaining Arabs, they should be given three choices:

1. Those completely opposed to living in a Jewish state could choose the option taken by the Algerian Jews, who left Algeria when it became independent, although their forebears settled in the area long before the Arabs;

2. Those wanting to remain in their native towns and villages but not to participate in Israel's national life could remain as resident aliens, a status not unknown in Western democracies;

3. Those who, like Israel's Druze minority, want to remain and become fully integrated in Israel, would be given every opportunity to do so."

Israel has made the choice for the Palestinians (without consulting them). It has in effect given them the status of alien residents.

At present all Palestinians in the West Bank are holders of Israeli identification cards issued after the census of the population which was carried out in September 1967. They also all hold Jordanian passports but these are of no practical use in the West Bank. The Israeli identification cards contain information about the holder, including his religion. It may be stamped (according to the ninth amendment of Order 297) "with any stamp or any symbol or indication . . . for reasons of the security of the area". To be found without an identity card is considered to be an offence under the security orders. The card is needed to carry out any activity which involves the authorities. The card is not, however, the property of its holder and may be confiscated by any soldier without reason or receipt. This being the significance of the identity card, it is often used as an instrument of oppression and harassment in an arbitrary and extra-judicial manner. It is common practice to take away the cards of a group of Palestinians and order them to report daily to the military government. No reasons are given and no interrogation takes place and no charges are pressed.

Without their identity cards, the Palestinians will be breaking the law if they are found anywhere outside their homes. This means that they have to obey the orders to report to headquarters. This procedure can go on for many days. And in this way a person can be punished without proffering any legal excuse or having to go through any court. There are many examples of the use of the identification card in extra-judicial punishment. The cards of ex-prisoners are stamped rendering it very difficult for them to obtain licences to travel, work, drive, etc.

When leaving the West Bank, the identity card is taken at the point of exit. A travel document is issued by the Israeli Ministry of Interior in which the nationality is stated as Jordanian. On this travel document is stamped a return visa. If a Palestinian does not return within the time limit prescribed in his permit, his card is not returned to him and he loses his right of residency in the West Bank.

The present legal status of the Palestinians in the occupied territory is similar to, but not as privileged as, the status of an alien resident in the United States. In the U.S. the alien resident becomes eligible for full American citizenship after five years. A Palestinian in the West Bank, however, under the present conditions, never becomes eligible for a citizenship which would ensure his right to stay in the West Bank. The Palestinian in the West Bank, although living in his own country, is treated as a permanent alien resident.

The Classification of Palestinian Society
By The Military

In a meeting of the Civilian Administration[2] held on 29 October 1982, the Acting Head of the Civilian Administration at the time classified leaders of the Palestinian population in the West Bank in the following groups:

(a) In the first group he placed what he called the radical heads of the municipalities who to him represent the rejection front and are the leading members of the "National Guidance Committee";

(b) Members of the second group he called "the Jordanian block" which did include supporters of Jordan, but which, as he believes, has become more supportive of the Palestine Liberation Organisation since Jordan ceased to assume responsibility for the Palestinians after the Rabat conference which named the PLO as the leader of the Palestinians. In this group he included a number of mayors, heads of Chambers of Commerce and what he called moderate realistic figures who have close ties to Jordan.

115

The members of this group, he claimed, did not take any steps without first getting Jordan's consent;

(c) The members of the third group, he said, are those with whom the Civilian Administration has begun to nurture relations. The members of this group are totally dependent on the military administration and include the heads of the village leagues, moderate mayors and mayors who have been appointed by the Administration. This group is independent of any external influence;

(d) The 12,000 employees of the military government constitute the fourth group.

The Head of the Civilian Administration recommended the following policies towards members of each group:

(i) The struggle against the nationalists in the first group is a continuous pursuit, he said. Pressure against its members may not be stopped even after they are deposed from their posts. It is the duty of the military governor of each district in the West Bank to make recommendations concerning the manner of dealing with them and to submit reports to the Area Commander indicating those to be controlled;

(ii) A continuous attempt should be made to neutralise the members of the pro-Jordanian group by making them dependent on the Administration;

(iii) Continued assistance should be afforded to members of the village leagues in every possible manner. The Commanding Officers are instructed to make visits to the appointed municipal councils and the village leagues and to submit reports concerning the outcome of their visits;

(iv) Those who are employees of the military government should be turned into "the army of the Civilian Administration". And, as with the village leagues, members of this group must be "assisted towards political ends" in order that they may be used politically in the future.

The Head of the Civilian Administration explained how support of this group is to be given and what end it should serve. Punitive action should be taken against the bad elements to remove them from the system, whereas complete support should be extended to the positive active elements. This should include the granting of permits, raising of salaries, re-assessment of privileges, and the granting of special identification cards to the senior employees of the military government. It must be remembered, however, he said, that this support is not for its own sake, but rather for the fulfilment of a political end and for the future political manipulation of this class. Commanding officers must submit suggestions as to who should be dismissed by giving them pensions or submitting them to a disciplinary court. Commanders of subdistricts should submit weekly reports concerning the manner in which the negative elements in the first and second groups have been handled. They should also send lists of these to the police under the heading: "Names for administrative handling".

Although this classification was discussed in 1982, it continues to apply today and to serve as a guideline. To help the reader appreciate the extent of the powers of control available to the military officers which make them able to render life easier or unbearable for a Palestinian in the West Bank, some of the powers of control available to the military commanders will be described.

Powers of Control Exercised by The Military

General powers of control

Every aspect of the life of a Palestinian under occupation is controlled through military regulations.

In addition to being physically restricted from a large area of the land in the West Bank (no less than 40% of the total area) which has been acquired for Jewish settlement and which the Palestinian is prohibited from entering, there are specific restrictions on the freedom of movement of Palestinians.[3] No Palestinian may leave the West Bank without obtaining permission to do so from the authorities. This includes staying overnight within the pre-1967 borders of Israel. The military governor in the area within which the Palestinian resides is empowered to issue such a permit. Such permission is generally denied to Palestinians who have served a term of imprisonment for what are termed "security offences". It is also denied indiscriminately and without reason being given to others.* This can mean that those who have children or other members of their family outside the area can be prevented from seeing them because a permit is also needed for them to come to the West Bank. The occupied territory then becomes, for people denied these permits, a large prison, an isolation ward.**

Driving licences and licences for vehicles are also given only after the application has been endorsed by the military authorities. For several months during 1983-84, all the residents at the Dheisheh refugee camp were denied these permits. This also meant that those who depended on driving for their livelihood could not renew their driving licences.[4]

Many professionals, such as lawyers, pharmacists, surveyors, cannot obtain the licences they need to practice their profession without the approval of the military authorities.[5]

Eligibility for election to the executive board of a trade union is also subject to military approval[6] and so is the employment by West Bank businesses of non-West Bank residents.[7] Even a garage owner must register the particulars of every vehicle he services.[8]

Control is also exercised over certain businesses of Palestinians. It is necessary to obtain permission to open a bank[9] (no such permission has been granted since 1967), or to start an insurance[10] or publishing company.[11]

Restrictions can also frustrate other businesses for which a specific permission from the military is not required. No transaction in real property can proceed without permission.[12] An application to have a

---

* There are many examples of the imposition of this restriction. Muhammad Masad, an academic assistant in the Cultural Studies Department of BirZeit University, was refused permission to travel in order to complete his studies in the U.S.A. The refusal extended from April 1983 until March 1984. Abdel Karim Samara, who was studying in Toulouse, France, for a diploma during the academic year 1981-82 and then was intending to start a thesis, returned to the West Bank to visit his family and to collect some documents for his diploma in June 1982. He was then prevented by the authorities from returning to France. Awni Awad Ayed Diabes, an assistant researcher at the Arab Scientific Institute for Research in El Bireh, studied in Belgium, and his wife is Belgian. In past years he has travelled abroad several times, but since returning with his wife in February 1983 he has been prevented from leaving the country for Amman on two occasions without any explanation being given.

** Samieha Khalil, for example, who heads the Women's Family Rejuvenation Society in Bireh, and who is a widow, has been prevented from leaving the area to see her children — all of whom are outside. For more than two years permission to leave was refused her and permission for her children to come to the West Bank to visit her was likewise refused. In both cases, the military authorities gave no reasons for their refusal of the permission. In August 1984, one of her children was finally allowed to visit her. Permission for the other children to visit has still not been granted.

118

telephone installed or even transferred from one place to another cannot be processed without military approval. Similarly, signing a lease with a term of over three years requires permission. Imports and exports (whether for agricultural products or any other goods) cannot take place without military approval.[13] The registration of companies and trademarks is also under the control of a military officer and so is the establishment of cooperatives and charitable societies.

The power to grant or refuse permits is, therefore, a very powerful instrument in the hands of the military officers. A person who is deprived of permits will have a very difficult time. This is why, when the military classify the population into different categories, life is made difficult for members of that category which is out of favour. Permits are used to implement a carrot-and-stick policy.

Control over development

A historical review of the Military Orders dealing with control of development in the West Bank shows how the Military Orders reflect changes in the policy of Israel towards the West Bank.

Prior to January 1982, the Military Orders concerning the commercial life of the West Bank seem to have been intended as a means of exerting general control over the business sector of the population. For example, an Order of August 1967[14] prohibited any non-resident from starting any business in the West Bank or from being employed in the West Bank by any project (whether commercial or not) without obtaining a special permit from the military authorities.[15] Towards the same end, the officer in the Israeli Army in charge of the Judiciary was appointed as the Registrar of Companies and Trademarks.[16] The registration of companies in the West Bank is, therefore, left to his discretion. The authority to hear appeals against his decisions has been removed from the local courts and transferred to the military Objections Committee.[17]

Before 1982 no serious control was exercised over the flow to the West Bank of funds to finance projects carried out by entrepreneurs, cooperatives or charitable organisations. However, since the beginning of 1982, a whole series of controls of this kind has been imposed by Military Orders, of which some examples will be given here. The first of these is Military Order Number 952,[18] dated 20 January 1982, concerning control of currency. Immediately after the occupation, all banks which were in operation in the area were closed. The only banks now operating are Israeli banks. There are also many money changers, and it is against the operations of the money changers that the Order is primarily intended. The Order prohibits any resident of the West Bank from buying foreign currency from a licensed money changer except for one of the reasons specified in the Order. These are limited to the importation of goods and services and the transferring of money (not to exceed $3,000 annually) to a dependent relative residing outside the area. The same amount is the maximum permitted to be carried by persons travelling outside the area and no more than $500 of the total is to be in cash.

The Order also requires every resident of the area who has a bank account outside the area to inform the authorities of this fact and of the amount deposited. Similarly, Article 3(c) of the Order imposes a requirement on the owners of immovable property located outside the area to inform the authorities about it by presenting a full report on the details of their ownership. Order 1118 (as amended) dated 3 July imposes a tax on the importation of services.

An Order of 9 June 1982 prohibits the receipt or entry of money into the area by any resident of the area except by permit.[19] The Order defines bringing money into the area to include any money received or brought in, whether it was received or brought in by the resident himself or through another directly or indirectly and whether or not for the provision of a service or the granting of consideration. It also prohibits bringing money to the area from "the enemy" except with a permit.

"Resident of the area" is defined as a holder of an identity card issued by virtue of Military Order Number 297. The definition of resident also includes any organisation established according to the law in force in the area or which is organised or administered in the area.[20] The "area" is defined as including the State of Israel and any other area falling under the control of the Israeli Defence Forces. The "enemy" is defined as any force which is in a state of war with the State of Israel, or which declares this about itself, whether or not a state of war has been declared or whether or not military activities are waged, and anyone supporting any hostile organisation as defined in an Order[21] concerning restriction on training or contact with a hostile organisation outside the area, whether directly or indirectly. "Hostile organisation" is defined in the same Order as follows:

"any person or group of persons which aims at endangering the security of the public or the Israel Defence Army or which endangers public order in Israel or in the area which the Israel Defence Forces control".

Another Order[22] declares the establishment of a fund to be called "The Fund for the Development of Judea and Samaria". This fund, according to the internal regulations published on 9 June 1982, shall be administered by a board of directors whose decisions must be endorsed by the Head of the Civilian Administration. The Order on the importation of money prohibits the receipt of money in the area from "the enemy" unless the money is intended to be transferred to this fund. The same Order empowers the Head of the Civilian Administration, or whomever he may appoint, to grant permits for bringing money into the area as he sees fit by written permission, which may be general or specific and may be for a single specified person or a specified group of persons. The prohibition also extends to visitors who are not resident in the occupied areas, but who may wish to bring money in during their visits to the West Bank. The receipt of a permit under this Order does not exonerate the recipient of the permit from obtaining the permits required under the Order on currency control. Violation of this Order subjects the violator to large fines or to imprisonment for up to five years or both.

The internal regulations of the Fund for the Development of Judea and Samaria state that its board of directors shall decide the way in which the money may be held and the manner in which it shall be used. Applications for obtaining money from the Fund may be submitted by a local authority or by a juridical body. (The Jewish settlements in the West Bank are established as local authorities. Arab population centres are governed by either municipal or village councils.) Applications must be submitted through the governor in the district where the local council or juridical body is located. The board of directors of the Fund may accept or refuse such applications. They may, also, grant money or grants on their own initiative for the execution of projects for the development of the area (Articles 10 and 11 of the Internal Regulations).

An Order of 11 July 1982[23] prohibits the acceptance by a public institution of any loan, contribution, gift or annuity whether in the form of money or in other property except by permit from the "person responsible". The term "acceptance" is defined to include "acceptance by the organisation itself or through another whether directly or indirectly for or without consideration". The "person responsible" (who is appointed for the purpose of this Order by the Head of the Civilian Administration, established in November 1981) is prohibited from issuing a permit if the money is from the "enemy" unless the property to be received is in the form of currency. In that case, the permit will only be granted for the purpose of depositing the currency in the ownership of the "Fund for the Development of Judea and Samaria", established by virtue of Order Number 974.

All moneys received by a public institution must be deposited, as soon as received, in a bank which the person responsible authorises in the area.

Thirty days after the issuance of Order 998, every public institution had to submit to the person responsible statements of all its bank accounts in the area for his approval, and 60 days after its issuance it had to submit statements of all its bank accounts outside the area and deposit any balance in a bank account in the area. No money could be withdrawn except after obtaining a permit from the person responsible.

A public institution, immediately after obtaining the approval of the person responsible for its bank account, must deposit in it all its moneys that are not deposited in a bank account or that are deposited in a bank account which has not been approved by the person responsible. Statements of account, showing the amount deposited and endorsed by the manager of the branch of the bank where the money is deposited, must be presented to the person responsible.

The punishment for offenders violating this Order is imprisonment for up to two years and/or payment of a fine.

Since the last quarter of 1982, residents of the West Bank have been required to fill out forms for income tax purposes providing full information about all their possessions inside and outside the West Bank, whether movable or immovable. These forms are not issued in conformity with the Jordanian Income Tax Law of 1964,[24] which continues to be in force in the West Bank as amended by Military Orders. They seem to be intended to serve the twin purpose of better enabling the authorities to control the flow of funds from outside by assessing the increases in the person's possessions, and of enabling the income tax authorities to exercise stricter control.

Whereas an Order issued on 22 June 1967 declared that all tax laws shall remain unchanged, changes have in fact been made to the tax laws and their effect is to require the West Bank residents to pay increased taxes. The following are the Orders which have made changes in the amounts of tax to be paid: Military Orders 509, 533, 543, 586, 612, 636, 655, 725, 754, 770, 782, 791, 816, 835, 873, 900, 924, 943, 958, 976, and 978.

The Jordanian Income Tax Law has also been amended by the

replacement of Chapter 14, concerning the means of collecting the tax, by another chapter which now requires the payment of advances.[26]

The tax officers in the West Bank towns are now Israelis replacing the Arab employees who held these posts until recently. Assessments were formerly subject to two stages of appeal in the local courts. However, the tribunal which is now competent to hear tax appeals is the military Objections Committee.* Since this tribunal does not make decisions, but only recommendations which may be accepted or rejected by the Area Commander, a proper right of appeal to an independent court or tribunal has been denied to West Bank residents.

The three groups responsible for the day-to-day violations of the basic rights of Palestinians in the West Bank are the military, the village leagues and mayors appointed by Israel, and the Jewish settlers. Many of the activities of the settlers mentioned in the third section have been documented in the Karp report, published by the Attorney-General of Israel in February 1984. Unfortunately, no action has yet been taken to apply the recommendations of the report to curb similar future violations.

The following discussion of human rights violations is divided accordingly into three sections. In all cases, the ultimate aim is to make the daily lives of Palestinians in the occupied territories intolerable to encourage them to emigrate. As will be evident, absent from the discussion is reference to the more extreme sectors in Israeli society who are overtly racist, and have been described as such within Israel, such as the Kach movement of Rabbi Meir Kahane (now a member of the Israeli Knesset) who advocates the outright forceful expulsion of all Palestinians (including those who hold Israeli citizenship) from Israel and the occupied territories. Every country has its lunatic fringe. Britain has the National Front and the United States the Klu Klux Klan. To quote their views as though they were representative would be misleading and dishonest.

---

* (See Part I, *supra*).

Chapter Six

Violations of Palestinian
Human Rights in the West Bank

Violations by The Military Authorities of the Right
To Security of the Person And The Right to Life

In the West Bank, the army is the source of all new legislation,[27] some of which has been described. It is also the authority which implements these laws. It also controls the local courts which arbitrate in cases of legal disputes and appoints the judges to these courts. The army has established its own system of justice to deal with offences against a large number of the laws which constitute the occupier's law now in force in the West Bank.

As previously described, although the area is not annexed to Israel, Israeli law has through various means been extended to areas under the direct control of Israeli settlements which constitute, according to some estimates,[28] as much as 40% of the total area of the West Bank. The majority of the population living in the rest of the West Bank are subject to the occupier's law and its occupation army. Their subjugation to the provisions of this law is total.

In a case before an Israeli military regional court, file no. 325/82, in which the General Chief of Staff of the Israeli army, Rafael Eitan, was summoned to testify, the directives and guidelines which the highest authority in the army gave to the units in the occupied territories were given in evidence. The trial is worth discussing at length here.

Hebron brutality cases[29]

The trial, which took place during the winter of 1983, was one of the rare instances where members of the Israeli army have been brought

124

to account for their actions in the West Bank. The background to the case is itself of interest. It was brought only as a result of the efforts of three members of the Israeli organisation, Peace Now,[30] who had been on reserve duty in the West Bank. Their action was motivated by their belief that the assaults and brutality that they had witnessed against the civilian population by members of the Israeli Forces constituted a danger to the character of the Israeli army itself. After completing their reserve duty, the three met with the OC Central Command, Major General Uri Orr, to tell him of the events they had witnessed. Feeling that this was not sufficient, the three men then convened a press conference which took place on 10 May 1982. Here, they made public their allegations of assault and brutality committed by Israeli soldiers during the period March to April 1982 when the 'civilian administration' dismissed the Palestinian mayors of Nablus, Ramallah, and El Bireh, and Israeli troops "killed 10 Palestinians and wounded 90 others during the worst riots in the region in years" (*Jerusalem Post* of 15 October 1982). As a result, the army began an investigation of the claims and found them to be "partly justified". On 14 October 1982, an army spokesman announced that seven soldiers would be courtmartialled on charges of aggravated assault, illegal use of weapons, improper behaviour and breach of discipline.[31]

On 11 November, one of the seven, a sergeant, was found guilty of beating teenage prisoners in Hebron and was sentenced to six months in prison and six months suspended sentence.[32] On 7 November 1982, seven soldiers, including a major and three sergeants, went on trial at Jaffa Military Court. The trial lasted (periodically, on and off) until February 1983 and evidence was heard from a number of important figures, including the OC Central Command, Major-General Uri Orr, and the Chief of Staff himself, Rafael Eitan.

The Court reached its verdict on 17 February 1983. Three of the defendants were acquitted, among them the Deputy Military Governor of Hebron, Major David Mofaz, on the grounds of insufficient proof of the charges alleged. The other four were found guilty and were sentenced to prison terms of between two and six months. In their judgment, the judges stressed that the soldiers had been under great pressure: "The lives and well-being of IDF soldiers cannot be treated lightly. The local population must know that they assume risks when they generate tension in the area. One cannot demand that IDF soldiers wear kid gloves when they are being stoned."[33] The transcript of the trial has remained an official secret and the only details available about the

125

evidence submitted at the trial were in the daily Israeli press reports.

Some of the charges related to the detention of pupils from Hebron's Islamic High School at the Military Governor's headquarters. A sergeant who had already been sentenced gave evidence and reportedly told the court: "We pushed them, slapped them and kicked them. The major just stood by and watched. Everyone hit them as hard as he could. Afterwards, I left the shed where this was happening because I couldn't stand beating up people who couldn't fight back." Two names were missing from the list of the accused: Colonel Ya'acov Hartabi, Military Commander of the West Bank, and the Commander of Hebron, Lieutenant-Colonel Shalom Lugassi, who, it was alleged, issued orders for the beatings. On page 12 of their verdict, the judges wrote: "to carry out Hartabi's orders — to shoot at solar water heaters, to break watches, to assemble passers-by or people outside their homes in groups of six or eight in order to beat them up — could in no way be considered as a legal order." Lieutenant Mathias, one of the witnesses, told how local inhabitants were rounded up and made to learn to sing the 'Hatikva' (the Israeli National Anthem) and to shout insults. Captain Artsi told the court: "One day, after stones had been thrown in the village of Sa'ir, it was decided to round up all the local inhabitants. Anyone we saw we put on a bus and we drove them north until we ran out of petrol. They were then made to get out and make their own way home on foot. It was Lugassi who gave this order."[34] Lieutenant Akiva Berlowitz recalled an incident which took place in the School of Tarik Ben Ziad:

"I was present during this incident. It was morning, tyres had been burnt and stones thrown. We arrived in the area under the command of Lugassi and entered the school classrooms. The local inhabitants had been made to come out. I don't remember what happened to them outside. In the classroom those who behaved were O.K. Those who were not good were beaten and taken outside. There was an argument with the headmaster and Lugassi beat him."

The line of defence followed by the defence lawyer, namely that "the root of the evil was the directives from above", proved successful in this case. It was confirmed by the backing which the military establishment gave to its people even when excesses were uncovered. The defence lawyer submitted to the court a written summary of an interview that Major General Uri Orr held with the accused after the charge sheet against him had been presented. Orr wrote: "I explained to the officer that he would get my support during the trial and afterwards. In addition, he would remain in his position in the command." The defence lawyer's contentions were also supported by the testimony given that "The directives I issue are in written form. Agitators are to be dealt with firmly and to be detained . . . sanctions are imposed in the territories, collective punishment . . . I issued an order that parents of rioters are to be punished. There is an order in the territories that if the children are not punishable, the parents are to be punished. To detain them and release them, detain and release. As long as it is legal, it's fine. . . . I issued a directive for punishing *mukhtars* (village elders) in the territories . . . The Civil Administration should make use of sanctions in places where there are problems. For example, prevention of benefits that are within the military government's power. Also clarification talks, this for purposes of punishment."

The defence attorney presented various documents to the court indicating that the Chief of Staff's orders were indeed issued in writing as he testified. A cable sent out in April 1982, constituting "the Chief of Staff's summary of the discussion held on the 26th," states in paragraph 4: "We must persist in the punishment of parents". On 2 May 1982, the Chief of Staff put out a cable which contained the following message:

"A detention camp must be set up urgently at Beit-Bad.[35] The camp is to serve for detention when use needs to be made of the legal measures allowing detention for interrogation (without trial) for a period of time dictated by the law, their release for a day or two and their re-arrest.

"It must be made quite clear to the *mukhtars* that they bear personal responsibility for what happens in their area of residence, and that they will also be detained when problems arise in their area of jurisdiction . . . the civil administration should refrain from summoning persons for warning talks (we humiliate ourselves) and instead of talks, should carry out arrests. The residents of the Jewish settlements must travel with arms, and when they are attacked open fire. We must see to it that this subject is made known to the Arab inhabitants."

In a military government meeting held in 1980, the Chief of Staff's response to a remark made by a staff officer, that achievements had been made in the welfare of the inhabitants of the occupied areas, was that he was not interested in achievements but in emigration.

To the Knesset Foreign Affairs and Defence Committee, the Chief of Staff said that if Israel established 100 settlements between Jerusalem and Nablus, the Arabs would no longer be able to throw stones at Israeli traffic but "would only be able to scurry about like drugged cockroaches in a bottle".[36]

Such are the beliefs and attitudes held by those in the highest positions of power over the occupied territories. As Professor Gordon Allport of Harvard University demonstrated in his study, "The Nature of Prejudice", there is a progression from "verbal aggression to violence, from rumour to riot, from gossip to genocide".

The examples given below of violations of basic rights prove that this progression is evident in the occupied territories.

Loss of life by shooting

In an affidavit,[37] Nur El Deen Abdel Kader Khalil Jaradat, aged 18, from the village of Salir, near Hebron, describes how Abdel Raheem Jaradat (18 years) lost his life by shooting:

On Thursday, 29 April 1982 at 7.15 in the morning, I walked to school as usual with Abdel Raheem Jaradat who is in the graduating class. As soon as we arrived at the school, Abdel Raheem went to his class which was doing extra hours to make up for time lost due to closure of the school. I and the other students remained outside in the schoolyard. We then heard the sound of shots in the nearby town of Halhoul. A little later a car passed by on its way to Hebron. The driver was blowing the horn indicating that something unusual had happened. We stopped the car and asked the driver what the matter was. He told us that he had with him a wounded student from Halhoul High School. The driver also told us about the death of a student, Jamal Musa El Shaladeh, aged 17, from bullet wounds after being shot at by Israeli soldiers in the demonstration which had taken place at the Halhoul School.

"After hearing this, all the students (including those from the graduating class) got together in the yard. We were joined by the people from the village and we all went to the house of the murdered student, Jamel Musa El Shaladeh.

"At 12 noon, we saw a bus full of soldiers and Israeli army patrols entering the village and firing shots in the air and at the group which had gathered near the house of the murdered student. With some other students, Abdel Raheem and I tried to walk to the centre of

128

the village. But when we found the soldiers shooting in all directions we went towards the mountain to take shelter. Abdel Raheem, however, insisted on getting to the centre to find out if there were any wounded persons as a result of the shooting, and he would not be persuaded otherwise. So we had to leave him and go. When he was about 150 metres from us we saw three soldiers climbing the mountain on which we were. Abdel Raheem could not see them. We called to him, but he did not answer. In the meanwhile, the soldiers continued firing. We called louder but in vain. Then we saw Abdel Raheem fall to the ground. We tried to get to him to give him first aid, but the three soldiers had reached the place where he fell. We walked back a short distance, then saw a group of women coming screaming to the place where his body fell, trying to save him, but the soldiers prevented them from reaching him and Abdel Raheem remained on the ground. The soldiers prevented anyone from helping him."

In November, a paratroop officer was found guilty of causing the death of Abdel Raheem Abdel Kader Jaradat by negligence. He was given a four-month suspended sentence.[38]

There have been many reports of loss of life by shooting. In December 1982, another soldier was convicted of illegal use of arms which resulted in the death of one Palestinian and the wounding of two others. Mati Golan commented on the court sentence in an article in the Israel daily, Ha'aretz, saying:

"The court sentenced the sergeant to three months in prison and even this was only a suspended sentence ... The practical lesson is that one can shoot at and kill people in Judea and Samaria, i.e., West Bank, in breach of the law, without being punished in any real sense."

During the twelve months that followed the establishment of the "Civilian Administration," the number of confirmed cases of loss of life by shooting was fifteen. Of these, ten were committed by soldiers in the Israeli army who shot at unarmed civilians. The bullet wounds in all cases were in the abdomen, chest or head. Four others were shot by settlers and one by members of the village leagues. Of the fifteen who lost their lives, eight were labourers, five were students, one was a housewife and one was unemployed.[39]

In November 1983 an 11-year-old girl was killed by settlers. On 28 January 1984 a Palestinian was shot by a soldier in Nablus and another in Jenin on 1 January 1984. In April 1984, a student from Najah

129

University was found dead. On 22 and 23 November 1984, two people were killed by soldiers in Birzeit and Ramallah. The soldiers delayed the ambulance carrying the wounded, amongst whom was Sharaf Tibi from Birzeit who died of his wounds before arriving at the hospital.

With the exception of the Israeli backed and funded village leagues, whose leaders are issued with guns, the West Bank's Palestinians are forbidden to possess weapons. Among the growing number of Jewish settlers, however, all adults including women have the right to carry "personal weapons," so long as they have had minimal weapon training. But guns sometimes fall into the hands of extremist settlers who have no licences. A 19-year-old American citizen, Yisrael Fuchs, who lived in a settlement near Hebron, was convicted in the summer of 1983 for shooting at an Arab car with a gun for which he had no permit. Fuchs is a member of the Kach movement which advocates expulsion of all the Palestinians from the West Bank.

In an article published in the Israeli daily, *Ha'aretz*, on 5 April 1982, Amnon Rubinstein pointed out the difficulties which the police face in investigating cases of shooting by settlers, when they attempt to do so. The settlers, he said, refuse to be questioned by the police. "The police doesn't dare question or arrest Jewish suspects, fearing a violent confrontation with the settlers." Another difficulty is that the settlers have workshops for manufacturing arms, and they can make changes in the weapons to disprove any ballistic tests. Mr. Rubinstein gives the example of Ilan Tor, who after being cleared by the police of suspicion of killing an Arab, "admitted that he had 'dealt' with his weapon before submitting it to the police for tests". Mr. Rubinstein poses the question of whether there is an attempt at encouraging private revenge and punishment campaigns.[40] The civil courts in Israel have in certain instances dealt leniently with Israelis accused of previous crimes against Palestinians. The Tel Aviv District Court released Ephraim Segal of Elon Moreh settlement on bail; he is charged with being an accessory in the murder of 11-year-old Aisha Al-Bahsh of Nablus (see *Jerusalem Post* 20 July 1984).

Between 18 March 1982 and 6 May 1982, there were 365 reported cases of wounding.[41] Of these, 251 were caused by bullets and the rest from beatings. In March 1984, seven labourers were wounded by settlers while travelling on a bus on the road between Birzeit and Ramallah on their way to work. Also during March 1984, one Palestinian was shot by soldiers, and in July 1984 five residents of the Dheisheh refugee camp were wounded when a soldier opened fire at short range

130

without provocation.

The following description of the blinding in one eye of Muhamad Hassan Abu Amra in Gaza is taken from a report made of the incident by the League of Human and Citizens' Rights, of Tel Aviv.

In the afternoon of 1 May 1984, Muhamad Hassan Abu Amra of Gaza was plastering a structure which he had built without a building permit. A military jeep arrived and a red-haired military officer approached Muhamad and ordered him to remove the structure immediately. Muhamad agreed to do so. The officer took Muhamad's identity card and told him that he would not get it back until the structure was destroyed. Then the officer ordered Muhamad to accompany him to the building where the licencing authority was housed, in the El Rimal quarter. This is how Muhamad describes the events that followed:

"As I entered his office, the red-haired officer slapped me in the face. He beat me without any reason, without any provocation from me, simply abuse in bad faith. He wanted to degrade me; and in fact I was, and told him: 'Since you beat me, I will not tear down the structure now, do with me as you please!' The red-haired officer left the room and in his stead another officer entered, heavy-set and dark skinned. The fat officer grabbed me by the shoulder and forced me into the adjoining room and there he punched me straight into my left eye. Because of the punch, blood and other fluids started pouring out of my eye. The fat officer left the room. I lay on the floor, my eye bleeding, suffering from the pain. At around four in the afternoon, a military vehicle took me to the government eye hospital, El Nasser. After being examined, I was immediately operated on and my left eye was removed. It is true that a number of years ago, I underwent surgery of the left eye in the English hospital* of Jerusalem. I then had a white spot on the eye and it was removed. After the operation, which was successful, I was able to see well from that eye."

The following details are taken from an affidavit given to Law In The Service of Man by a victim of an incident where civilians were shot at without any apparent provocation:

On 3 July 1984, residents of the Dheisheh Camp were on their way to a picnic on the occasion of the Ramadan Feast when their bus was

---

* The St. John Orthopedic Hospital.

stopped at a checkpoint near Rachel's tomb in Bethlehem. The soldiers came up to the bus, searched it, and checked the identity cards of the travellers. Then, one of the soldiers asked 15 young men to get out of the bus and he searched them very carefully. After this, he asked them to get back onto the bus. The bus was not allowed to continue towards its destination. After a long delay, during which time the bus was sent back and forth to the military headquarters in Bethlehem, an officer, who was referred to as Haim, arrived in a Ford civilian car. He got onto the bus and ordered 13 of the male passengers to get out. This order was accompanied by threats and beatings. The 13 men were ordered to stand by the bus in front of a nearby wall. Some were told to keep their hands up, others to sit down. Then the officer started to beat some of the men, which caused the women and children in the bus to cry and shout. Then Haim got onto the bus and said that there were more passengers on it than the law allows. One passenger answered that the number of passengers did not exceed 60 persons which is the legal amount allowed. At this point, Haim dragged this passenger down to the area where the 13 were standing and sitting, pulling him by his hair.

In the words of the affiant this is what happened next:

".... After an hour of waiting, I was exhausted from the heat and from holding up my hands and I tried to ask permission from the soldier to let me have some water because I was beginning to feel dizzy. I suffer from a disease which causes me to have dizziness from time to time. But the soldier refused my request. One of my friends who is aware of my disease, asked for water on my behalf when he saw that I had fallen on the ground from the dizziness. But again the soldier refused and this time he shot into the air. When the other passengers in the bus heard the shooting they began to cry out in fear, thinking that one of us was hit. Haim at this point ordered me to go back to where the others were standing but I could not. He began to threaten me with death if I spoke and then suddenly he shot at me but I didn't feel anything. Then he shot again and I fell to the ground and saw that blood was coming from my legs. At this point, the other passengers got out of the bus and were crying. I heard the soldiers shooting and when someone tried to pick me up to take me to hospital, the soldiers shot at them and wounded one of them ..."

The wounded were finally taken to hospital but were not allowed to remain until treatment was over. The same soldiers who carried out the shooting came to the hospital and took one of the wounded to Al-Fara'a prison, despite the objections raised by the doctor treating him. Law In The Service Of Man wrote to the authorities objecting to the practice — which is common — of removing wounded people from hospital and transferring them to prisons where medical facilities that are needed to complete the treatment commenced are not available, it also requested that the soldiers who opened fire without lawful excuse be tried. It was learned that one of the Palestinians who were wounded was charged, although the soldier who did the shooting was not.

Harassment and illegal punishment without trial

Curfews

"There is nothing better than a curfew", said one settler from Shilo to the Israeli daily, *Ha'aretz,* reporter, Amnon Abramovitz, "We then have a private road".

Immediately after occupation by the Israeli army, the West Bank was placed under a general curfew[42] which was lifted gradually as the army had the opportunity to assume complete control over the population. Thereafter, curfews were not so common. Since the beginning of 1983, however, the use of curfew as a collective punishment has been on the increase.

The village of Thahrieh in the Hebron area has a population of approximately 20,000. During the first few months of 1983, the village spent half the time under curfew restrictions. The following statement was made under oath by Atallah Alawi, a 40-year-old teacher from this village. It chronicles some of the events of the curfews imposed between January and April 1983.

"The town of Thahrieh has been under siege more than once through the imposition of curfew by the occupation authorities. On 29 January 1983, curfew was imposed because some young men threw stones and the authorities claimed that as a result of this an Israeli girl was killed.[43] Curfew continued for 20 days, during which time all the residents were prevented from leaving their homes and people from outside the town were prevented from entering the town.

"During the curfew, the town lived in anxiety. This was because when curfew was imposed, no end to it was declared. That is why throughout the 20 days people were anxious, especially in view of the shortage of food and medicine. About 5,000 workers, living in

133

the town, work outside. During the curfew they were unable to go to work and were therefore prevented from earning any income for their families.

"I work as a teacher in a school outside the town. As with the others, I also suffered this form of collective punishment. My students, most of whom are from outside the town, were deprived of my services so the punishment affected not only the townspeople of Thahrieh, but also those outside.

"The harassments which people in the town of Thahrieh encountered during the curfew were many. For example, on 12 February, the curfew was still in force. I had to go outside the town to send the grades of the High School Government Exam (the Tawjihi) but I needed a permit from the authorities. In fact, I did obtain a permit, and as I was walking in one of the streets with my permit a number of Israeli soldiers came and arrested me. They took me to Al-Fara'a prison along with eight other persons from Thahrieh. I also learned of the existence of others from Thahrieh in the prison. I spent four days in the prison without interrogation. Then I was released. At the end of my term five young men from the town accused of throwing the stones which resulted in the death of the Israeli girl were brought in. The houses of their parents were sealed.

"On 2 March the town was again placed under curfew which remained in force until 12 April — approximately 40 days. During this period, the authorities put two military posts at the entrances to the town forbidding anyone from entering or leaving the town except by permit from the village league. The authorities also welded shut about one hundred stores as well as three flour mills which are the only flour mills in town. After curfew was lifted, the authorities permitted the re-opening of the stores and the mills but only after their owners gave an undertaking that they will investigate and submit the names of those who threw stones.

"Curfew was also accompanied by a general atmosphere of terror due to shooting in the air and restricting us by prohibiting us from moving from one house to another or opening windows or standing on balconies or rooftops. We were also not allowed to obtain essential provisions except during the one hour which we were allowed in some days to move around to get food and medicine. During this period all of the transactions pertaining to the town were suspended and all permits were withdrawn. On 10 April curfew was lifted for three hours. I heard this announcement over the loudspeakers of the mosque near my house. It was also announced that all residents must attend an important meeting at the town mosque. In that meeting some of the members of the village council who are associated with the village leagues suggested to the residents the necessity to organise troops of guards to keep the peace and look out for the young men who throw stones. But this suggestion was refused by the residents. The head of the village council submitted a list of people who are out of favour. Amongst these were myself and four others, namely Dr. Mahmoud Saadeh, Jamil Yunis Harb, Jihad Kamel Ettal and Muhriz Ali Ettal. Indeed, at eleven that evening on 10 April, the five of us were arrested and transferred to the military government H.Q. in Hebron where we were held in a shack without food, blankets or interrogation all night and all during the day of 11 April. I was only taken for interrogation at four in the afternoon along with Dr. Saadeh. We were accused of throwing stones. Then I was taken along with two other young men, Jamil Yunis Harb and Jihad Kamel Ettal to Al-Fara'a prison. Dr. Saadeh and Muhriz Ettal were kept in Hebron. I was kept at Al-Fara'a for five days during which I was not interrogated or asked any questions. Then I was released along with Jamil and Jihad.

"There is a section of Al-Fara'a called the Stable which is in fact an old stable which the British and Jordanian armies used for their horses. In that section I was placed along with four others in a horse-pen. In the past the stable housed 25 horses; it now has 114 human beings and the number sometimes reaches 140."

In the city of Nablus which is the commercial centre of the West Bank, where all the activity happens in the old city, curfew was imposed on the old city on the following dates in February and March of 1982:

In February — 3, 8, 14, 15, 26, 27 and 28
In March — 1, 2, 3, 5, 6, 7, 8, 9, 10, 14, 17 and 21[44]

During the same period curfews were imposed on other places in the West Bank, amongst them were the villages of Yatta and the town of Halhoul, both of them in the vicinity of Hebron. Curfews were also imposed on the following refugee camps: Jalazoun, Ballata, Amari, Dheisheh and Kalandia. During the imposition of the curfews many days passed when permission was not given for foodstuffs or medical supplies to be brought into the camps. This resulted in shortages. Also, the services which the United Nations Relief and Works Agency provides and on which many families in the camp depend were not allowed to continue. Breaches of the curfew resulted in the arrests of many young men living in the camps, on whom large fines were imposed.

In most cases the curfew was lifted only after the army had taken control of houses in strategic positions and established permanent posts at the entrances of the towns or camps. It has also been observed since the lifting of curfews that the army has increased its rounds inside the towns and camps and its harassment of the inhabitants there. The following is a description by Adnan Abu Jibne, a 28-year-old resident of Kalandia refugee camp, of life under curfew,* given in a statement under oath:

> "On Friday, 11 March, 1983, at about six in the morning I heard through the loudspeakers of the camp mosque that "By order of the military government of the Ramallah area, curfew is imposed until further notice. Whoever violates the curfew will be subjected to the severest punishment". When I heard this announcement I was preparing to go to my work at the Makased Hospital in Jerusalem. I also had an appointment with my fiancée to make some tests at the hospital. I stood by watching the condition of the camp after hearing the announcement and saw soldiers going to all the lanes in the camp. Some were taking positions on the roofs of the higher houses to enable them to watch clearly the condition of the camp. Other groups were taking positions in four main directions of the camp; each had a walkie-talkie, weapon, club and tear-gas canisters. I must explain here that curfew in the camp means that the residents may not leave their houses, that is, one may not open a door or a window. The situation at the camp makes it difficult to observe these orders because the ordinary family in the camp lives in separate rooms which are not connected so that the kitchen and the toilet may be at some distance from the rest of the rooms of the dwelling. This being the case, moving from one part of the house to the other rendered the resident in breach of the curfew. This being the case, each family has its own incidents with the soldiers. Although these incidents are different, they are all essentially the same. I wish to relate here the

---

* This curfew lasted for 24 days. According to a report in the *Jerusalem Post* 1 April 1983: "Military sources confirmed that during this period three adults in the camp died of 'purely natural causes,' while local Arab sources claim that at least two infants also died because of inadequate medical care."

136

incidents which took place between the members of my family with the soldiers on this Friday. I had been sitting in my house with my father, young brothers and fiancée when we were surprised to see two soldiers enter our house in an aggressive way. This was about three in the afternoon of Friday. When they entered, they asked us for our identity cards and we gave them to the soldiers. When I asked them for the reason for breaking into our house, the soldier who had the looks of a Moroccan answered that a member of the camp had thrown a stone at them. I said that none of us threw a stone and no one has entered our house except him. But the soldier disregarded this and left us, taking with him my identity card and that of my father and threatening that 'We will see you in court'.

"After half an hour we were surprised by the entry into our house of a large number of soldiers, about nine, accompanied by the two soldiers who had broken into our house earlier on. As they entered I heard one of them say in Hebrew, 'Who is the one you spoke about?' Immediately someone said, pointing a finger at my fiancée, 'Why does she spit on the soldier?' The commander of the unit ordered that her identity card also be taken. But my fiancée refused to give it before she was heard. After the commander heard her story in detail, and how the two soldiers had previously entered our house, the soldiers denied having done so. When the officer asked the soldiers whether they were sure that my father and I were running away from the soldiers in the camp lanes they answered that they were. Then the officer ordered that our cards be returned, and we understood that all this was an attempt by the two soldiers to arouse us only. This is one of hundreds of similar stories about treatment the inhabitants of the camp are subjected to.

"On the second day, Saturday the 12th, which is a day of rest for the labourers when they buy provisions for their household, some labourers tried to go to the stores to buy bread, kerosene and milk, but the soldiers prevented them and ordered them to stay indoors. Anyone leaving the house had his identity card confiscated regardless of the motive for which he was leaving his house. The confiscation of the cards was also accompanied by attacks by the soldiers on the people by assaulting them, cursing at them and ridiculing them. This continued to be the case all day Saturday.

"On Sunday the 13th, at about eight-thirty in the morning I was supposed to leave the house to go to Makased Hospital to carry out the tests for my fiancée who was in the house with us. Despite the curfew, I decided that since my house is situated in the land of west Ram, curfew does not extend to us. So I left my house with my fiancée to go to the hospital. I met the soldier who had earlier broken into our house and who had accused my fiancée of spitting at him. He did not stand in my way and left me until I reached the main street and got on the bus. But as soon as I sat in the bus, a soldier's patrol pursued the bus and stopped it and one officer and two soldiers ascended the bus and came directly towards me and my fiancée.

"They ordered us to leave the bus and ordered me to ride with them in the jeep, leaving my fiancée behind in the street. I was taken to the police station in the camp where I was ordered to stand with my face to the wall. Many other residents of the camp were also there, amongst them the owner of a store who told me how he was accused of opening his store. He had done so, he said, in order to provide milk for a woman whose child was fed milk from the camp infirmary, which was closed because of the curfew along with the other clinics and the kitchen, which provided two meals for the very poor members of the camp.

"I then turned to look to my left and saw a man of 40, called Abdel Nabi, who was also accused of breaking curfew when he had gone in search of grain for his sheep on which he depends for his source of income, and which latter were about to die. I also heard more and more incidents, all of which brought me to the conclusion that the residents of the camp did not break curfew because they wanted to but because the soldiers do not respond to their pressing needs. For example, the soldiers took the identity card of Abu El Abed Shihab who is 65 years old, because he was apprehended in the street while on his way to his shop to bring medicine for his asthma from which he suffers.

"I remained standing opposite the wall with the soldiers around me until 10.30 in the morning, during which time I was listening to the stories of the camp residents. After this I was transported to the police station in Ramallah, to the interrogation section. I was surprised to find there large numbers of the residents of the Jalazoun, Amari and Kalandia refugee camps. I found there also a court summons for me. The charge against me was that I broke the curfew and was seen with my 65-year-old father outside the house. The interrogator asked that I dictate to him my statement and said that he would write it in Hebrew. After an argument, the interrogator agreed

138

to allow me to write my statement in my own hand, in Arabic. I then waited for approximately three hours to be taken to jail as I had been informed that I would be detained until the court hearing. Then, after three hours I was allowed to leave on bail pending the court case.

"While I was at the police station, I saw three children of the residents of Kalandia camp, aged between eight to eleven years old, who were accused of throwing stones at soldiers. I had heard one soldier asking another in Hebrew, why and how he brought these children. The soldier who brought them answered, 'I was bored and tired and so I brought them with me.' There were also two other young men of between 13 to 14 years of age, also from Amari camp, who were brought from inside their homes. There were also two other men from Ramallah, aged between 30 to 35 years old who were accused of throwing stones at a bus when they were going, at seven in the morning, to their work, and there were scores of other cases.

"In the station I saw with my own eyes scores of young men being carried in army jeeps to Al-Fara'a prison near Nablus to be detained until the trial. I stayed in the station until four o'clock on Sunday. Then I was allowed to go home.

"On Monday and Tuesday, 14 and 15 March, curfew was officially lifted and this was announced on the loudspeakers. However, passage was not allowed through the main entrance of the camp, and private cars were also not allowed to park by that entrance. In fact, practically speaking, curfew was not lifted since large numbers of soldiers continued to roam in the camp lanes and the schools continued to be closed. There are two schools in the camp, primary and secondary, for boys and for girls with two shifts per day. Also all the United Nations Relief and Works Agency services centres inside the camp were closed.

"During these two days when curfew was lifted, the arrest of all those whose identity cards were confiscated during the previous days began. The arrests took place during the late hours of the night from ten at night. Those arrested were placed at the entrance to the camp and ordered to remain seated on the ground until the morning hours during which period they were subjected to beatings, insults and humiliations. Then in the morning they were transferred to the Barracks at the Ramallah jail.

"On Wednesday, 19 March, I went to the court with my lawyer and found more than 60 people waiting for trial. The ages ranged from 20 to 70. Those younger than 20 were being sent to Al-Fara'a prison. All during that day I remained waiting at the court from 8:30 in the morning until 4:30 in the evening. During this period my lawyer went to the prosecutor to ask when the time was fixed for my trial. I asked my lawyer to ask him generally about the other inhabitants of the camp. The prosecutor told him that he was not aware of those waiting outside and that they had no cases in the court files. This was despite the fact that those standing outside had been summoned by official notices which stated that their trials were today. The trials were adjourned until Wednesday, 26 March.

"A group of the people went to the police officer in Ramallah to inform him that they had had no trial. So the officer said that they could return to the camp to wait there for new summonses. So they returned to the prison to inform the prosecutor of this. But the prosecutor refused to let them go and ordered them to continue to wait. Everyone waited until four in the afternoon, when the prosecutor came and told the inhabitants that they must confess to the charges made against them so that the trial could proceed quickly. And so in court all the people were led to the courtroom where the judge spoke addressing everyone and saying that there was no necessity to deny and it would be better to admit the charges made against them in order to facilitate the trial. He also said that these charges were not serious. And he began to call the people three at once and he began to read the charges and then pass judgment. The sentence was that they must pay a fine of three thousand shekels (approximately $75) per person or spend 15 days in jail.

"When the accused was asked about the charge made against him, the Judge would listen to his brief defence, but he did not take into consideration the truth or lack of it in what the accused said. The only thing that was taken into consideration was that the accused broke the curfew, without considering the cause which made him do so. In two hours the Judge was able to pass sentence on each and every one of the 40 or so accused. While I was in court that day, I heard and saw many incidents. I heard, for example, how some aged people were accused of breaking curfew as they were going to the mosque to pray and of others who were taken out of their homes for no apparent reason and of those who were stopped in Ramallah and Bireh and accused of breaking curfew, even though they had been outside the camp when curfew was imposed. Others had broken curfew to bring milk to the children or medicine or grain for the sheep.

140

"That day ended after we had all been sentenced to pay the fines within three days of the date of the judgment or to spend 15 days in jail, and we had to choose between these two."

Arrest, search and detention

Both under the military orders and in practice, the Palestinians in the West Bank do not enjoy the right to freedom from arbitrary arrest. By virtue of Articles 78 and 81 of Military Order 378, a soldier in the Israeli army has the power to search premises and arrest upon suspicion without a warrant. It is estimated that 200,000 security prisoners and detainees (20% of the population) have passed through Israeli prisons.

These powers are frequently and arbitrarily used with the result that a Palestinian in the West Bank is likely to be stopped by soldiers anywhere and at any time, have his house entered and searched, and be arrested without any need for the soldiers to show reasonable cause or to present a warrant.

The following description was given by Jihad Fahme Saleem, a 20-year-old painter from Nablus, in a statement made under oath. The events described took place in February 1982.

"At around six in the evening I was returning home from work. The situation in the town was normal. My companions and I were met by an army jeep on patrol duty. We were called and our identification cards were taken from us. The commander of the group did a body search of me. I was asked to raise one trouser leg and then the other leg. I didn't understand and raised the same leg. He asked me to stand on the side as he searched my companions. Then he asked them to leave. I was taken in the jeep and then I was ordered to carry barbed wire and broken glass in my bare hands. Then after about a quarter of an hour I was again put in the jeep and taken to Wadi Toufah near the municipal courtyard where there is a hill. I was made to crawl on my stomach up and down the hill, army style. I was made to crawl on the threat of being shot if I refused. After going up and down the hill, the soldier asked me what I was doing in the street. I told him that I had gone to fetch food for my family. So he said, 'I will tell you what you must eat. Go ahead and eat grass.' I protested that I am not an animal and will not eat grass. I said that it could be poisonous and may harm a human being. So he said, 'Yes, a human being. What do *you* care?' He pushed my head with force to the ground and I began eating grass and chewing it. He opened my

141

mouth to make sure that I was swallowing what I had in my mouth.

"This continued for a quarter of an hour. Then he asked me if I was full, and he began kicking me with great force and telling me, 'You will all not submit unless we treat you with force'. I said, 'But I did nothing to deserve this'. But he laughed and said, 'I am sorry; please, if you like, punish me,' and he tried to force his weapon on me. I refused, but he made me carry it. And he said, 'By God, show me how clever you can be. Take revenge on me'. Here I cried and pleaded that I do not know how to use guns and that I only wanted him to leave me alone and to let me return to my house. Then we got up to the street, and he said that he would drive the jeep and that I must run behind it or else he would not return my identification card. So I ran for about a hundred meters. Then he stopped and gave me my card and said, 'Now, you know very well how I look. So if you ever see me, get off the street and tell your friends to do the same.' "

The above is not an isolated case. There are other known incidents of brutality and dehumanising treatment by soldiers. Night calls are also common. Abdul Hakim Kana'ain, a 24-year-old student from Birzeit University, described in a statement under oath the events of the night of 11 January 1983. He said that he heard laughter outside his house. He opened the door and soldiers came into his house where he was studying with a friend. A thorough search of the house was carried out and, when nothing incriminating was found, the soldiers grabbed copies of magazines published in Jerusalem. A report was made which he was asked to sign but he refused. He was hit by the soldiers and threatened with death. Then he and his friend were taken in the jeep to the centre of the town to the Post Office where a group of about 15 soldiers were present. There they were transferred to a big car in which were many soldiers and where they were beaten severely until they got to Ramallah. There they were taken to the Ramallah prison.

The weather was cold and his body was aching from the beating he had received from clubs, boots and fists. After their names were taken, they were put in the army barracks used for detention. It was cold there and smelly water seeped through holes in the walls. The student and his friend were given two blankets but no mattresses, food or drink. "I shivered all night long. In the morning the soldier who had arrested us the night before returned. He beat us and cursed us. This was repeated again until Friday when at 11 in the morning we were released. I still do not know the reason for my arrest."

As a result of the detention of large numbers of people, sometimes by rounding up and arresting groups of 20 or more people, and the renewal of the period of arrest beyond the 18 days allowed by Military Order 378, the places of detention become full to their utmost capacity.

To avoid this problem, what have become known as "quick trials" (which have been mentioned in Part II of this study) are carried out. These are distinguished from the normal military trials by the speed with which the whole legal process is completed. They usually occur following mass arrests at demonstrations. Those arrested are brought before a makeshift court, sometimes at night, before there has been any chance to contact defence witnesses or lawyers. Often, it is even before the parents of the accused know that they have been arrested. The trials are often over within ten minutes. Sometimes the accused are told that they will get a light sentence if they enter a guilty plea. During the year 1982/83, hundreds — usually between the ages of 13 and 21 — were dealt with in this way. Those found guilty usually have to pay very heavy fines, often amounting to several thousand dollars, accompanied sometimes by a prison sentence.[45]

A case was submitted to the Israeli High Court to test the position which the High Court would take in similar cases. The following is an account of the case which appeared in *Ma'ariv Weekly Magazine* on 8 April 1983.*

"Three 13-year-old girls are on trial for throwing stones at a mechanised patrol of the security forces.

"Under the Israeli Law of Youth, a minor cannot conduct his own defence, and it is the court's duty to appoint a defence lawyer for a minor — a demand which, incidentally, has its parallel in Jordanian law. But we are speaking about a military trial being conducted under edicts of a military government.

"So, three girls are confronting a military prosecutor, a witness for the prosecution and His Honour Judge (in the reserves) Hanoch Keinan.

"The prosecution witness, who happens to be a settler from Neve Horon, tells the court that while he was on patrol stones were thrown that were observed to have originated in a group of girls who ran into the patrol. He got out of the vehicle, made a flanking

---

* As often happens in cases which find their way to the High Court, the respondent offers a compromise to the petitioner in order to prevent the case being decided by the High Court, for fear that a precedent will be set. In this case, the petition was also withdrawn before the court could hear it and decide on the legal point in question.

movement, located the three throwers, pulled them out of the group, and here they are before your honour.

"Testimony that even the greenest defence lawyers could refute, if there was a defence lawyer. An interpreter is at the defendants' disposal, but they (the 13-year-olds) don't avail themselves of his services in order to launch a scathing cross-examination. Thus, the prosecution wraps up this stage of the proceedings. My witnesses, says the prosecutor.

"The girls take the witness stand. 'It wasn't me,' says the first. 'It wasn't me,' says the second. 'It wasn't me,' says the third.

"The Israeli Law of Youth says that in the absence of a defence lawyer, the judge is to assist in the interrogation of the witnesses. And his Honour Judge Keinan does in fact launch into action.

" 'Over to you, Hanoch.'

" 'I don't believe you,' he tells the girls upon completion of the questioning.

"The military prosecutor, yawning out of boredom and having lost interest in the proceedings since he thought, apparently, that there was no case to be made here, comes to life when he hears the judge's comment. Recovering, he launches a withering interrogation.

" 'We were coming home from school,' the girls say in reply to his questions, 'when suddenly this man came up to us and said we had thrown stones.'

" 'I don't believe the defendants,' the judge writes in his judgment. Bringing us to the stage of arguments regarding punishment.

"The prosecutor, fully recovered, his adrenalin pumping along at a great old rate: 'Your Honour, we have here a terrible phenomenon. The plague of the land. Stones.'

"His Honour: 'Girls, what do you have to say?'

"The girls: 'We have nothing to say.'

"So, his Honour moves on to writing the judgment, in which he gives free rein to his secret judicial longings. In a learned style that characterises the justices of the Supreme Court, he vents a judgment of elegant eloquence: not for me the ideology of stone-throwers, for whom there can be but one verdict, etc. etc.

"One girl is sentenced to a fine of 700,000 Israel pounds. The other two being sisters, they get a reduction: a million pounds between the two of them. If the fine is not paid within seven days of the judgment, their fathers will be jailed for six months!

"You have to know that there is no appeal against such a judgment.

144

It can be annulled or softened by appeal to the High Court of Justice under circumstances or pardon or — though I'm not sure of this — if the father volunteers for some village league or other.

"It later turns out that the father of the girl who has been fined 700,000 pounds is totally destitute and chronically ill, working two days a week as a baker. Not exactly your type who can direct his broker to sell off some stock so he can meet a draconian fine and fulfill a judgment that crushes the destitute and grinds down the poor.

"In the appeal to the High Court of Justice (194/83) it was argued that:

"(a)   This is not justice ('mishpat') but injustice ('mishpah'). (A play on words taken from Isaiah 5:7).

"(b)   The judge may fine the father but not send him to jail.

"(c)   The judge had a duty, which he did not fulfill, to summon the father and hear him, and not send him to prison *in absentia*.

"The High Court (Justice Moshe Baisky) acceded to the attorney's request and issued an interim order postponing implementation of the sentence."

When the person sentenced is a juvenile and is unable to pay the fine imposed by the court, the parents are made to pay and are liable to imprisonment if they fail to do so.[46] Payment is usually demanded immediately. Every day of delay in the payment of the fine renders the person sentenced liable for payment of an increase or imprisonment for him or his parents.[47] Order 1083 now makes it mandatory for the courts to give the parents who are to be punished for the actions of their children the chance to respond before sentence is passed upon them.

Another method of punishment without trial used frequently is confiscation of identification cards. Since, as has already been mentioned above, it is an offence to be found outside one's house without the identification card, withdrawal of this card enables the authorities to impose any condition on its holder. Sometimes they are made to wait all day and all night in the courtyard of the military headquarters. At other times they are made to report daily to the headquarters.

In the village of Arrabeh in the last week of November 1982, all the male inhabitants between the ages of 16 and 60 were rounded up and told to report to the military headquarters. The reason for the demand was that graffiti had been written on the walls in the town. The men

145

had to wait at the headquarters from eight in the morning until midnight. A thousand men were made to report in this manner for six days in succession.

When the identification cards of students enrolled in foreign universities who return to the West Bank for a vacation are confiscated, the students are unable to leave the area to pursue their education abroad. Sometimes upon presenting themselves at border posts with valid exit permits they are still refused permission to leave the area on the instructions of the security forces.

The practice that has been followed since the beginning of the occupation is that on leaving the West Bank holders of identity cards must leave them at the place of departure. On leaving, they must obtain exit visas. If the duration of the stay abroad is prolonged, the exit visa must be renewed. Failure to do so can result in the loss of residence rights in the West Bank. Often renewal is made extremely difficult and has been refused. The list of cases where Palestinians have lost their right to reside permanently and work in the West Bank is a very long one.[48]

Town arrest

The practice of using administrative detention as a means of restricting the freedom of the detainee without trial has been generally stopped. But it has been replaced by the imposition of restriction orders which are generally valid for six months and usually restrict the movement of the person concerned to the area of his town of residence, and make him subject to other conditions such as the necessity to report to the police station once or twice every day. At the end of 1982, 57 people had been placed under this "town arrest" in the West Bank (including Jerusalem). They included engineers, farmers, students, labourers, lawyers, teachers, pharmacists, journalists, accountants, newspaper editors, priests and physicians.[49] In August 1984, 50 people were under town arrest.

In its 1984 Annual Report, Amnesty International expressed concern about the increasing use of such restriction orders, stating its belief that "many people were restricted for the non-violent expression of their political opinions" and opposing "the imposition of such measures in all cases since those restricted were not charged or tried and had no effective right to refute the evidence against them." Amnesty International also published in October 1984 a separate report on town arrests and restriction orders in the occupied territories.

146

Al-Fara'a prison[50]

The conditions at Al-Fara'a prison*

Information on the conditions at Al-Fara'a prison has been obtained by Law in the Service of Man from interviews with former prisoners, prisoners' relatives and lawyers. Most of the approximately 250 prisoners at Al-Fara'a are young people, many of them between the ages of 15 and 18. Arrested students from West Bank universities, including Birzeit, are frequently sent to Al-Fara'a.

Established in April 1982 (when tension in the West Bank was at its highest) as a detention centre for people suspected of endangering "security" in the West Bank, and against whom in most cases no specific charge could be made, Al-Fara'a prison is distinguished from the other West Bank prisons (Jenin, Tulkarem, Nablus, Ramallah, Hebron)**, in various ways:

Difficult physical conditions

The derelict buildings of a previous British (and later Jordanian) army camp were quickly opened as a prison, which makes living conditions there particularly uncomfortable. This is especially true for the "stables", i.e., former horse stables dating from the time of the British. In addition, during periods of widespread arrests, tents are erected outside the buildings to contain the overflow of prisoners. Up to 50 prisoners may be confined in each tent, which measures 3 meters by 6 meters, and which is kept closed for large periods of the day. Infections are frequent because of the dirt in the tents and the general lack of hygiene.

Isolation

During the period of their detention at Al-Fara'a — normally up to 18 days, as allowed by Military Order 378, but sometimes that period is extended — most prisoners are completely cut off from the outside world and have no contact with a lawyer. They do not even have the protection of visits by delegates of the International Committee of the Red Cross for the first 14 days.

---

* Law in the Service of Man published a report on the conditions at this prison, in the winter and summer of 1984.

** where prisoners also complain about overcrowding, inadequate food and medical care, physical maltreatment, etc.

Strict regime

Unlike other prisons, Al-Fara'a is guarded and controlled by the army. Additional rules of behaviour have been introduced at Al-Fara'a, resulting in a stricter regime, for instance:

a) Prisoners must stand up when soldiers enter their rooms or tents; in the presence of soldiers they must always keep their arms behind their backs.

b) Prisoners have to put their hand up before speaking to a soldier.

c) No talking between prisoners is allowed in the presence of soldiers, except with prior permission.

d) At mealtimes prisoners must remain standing until given permission to sit down.

e) Prisoners sometimes have their heads forcibly shaved upon entry to Al-Fara'a.

Punishment inflicted for any infringement of the rules of behaviour consists, in particular, in putting the prisoner in an isolation cell or depriving him of food.

Maltreatment

Until January 1984, Al-Fara'a had been used solely as a detention centre, while interrogation and investigations were carried out elsewhere. Since January 1984, it has been used as an interrogation centre, and there have been many allegations from prisoners about maltreatment, used as a means of obtaining information (or sometimes as a punishment). For instance:

a) Prisoners are forced to stay for long periods (often several days) with their hands tied behind their backs and hoods over their heads.

b) Hooded prisoners are sometimes forced to stand outside in the courtyard without clothes, and may be hit by the soldiers in passing.

c) Prisoners are sometimes kept in very small cells, the floor of which can be covered with water to a depth of about 10 cm. Ten isolation cells have recently been constructed. Those cells measure 60 cm by 170 cm and are often used by more than one prisoner during the period of interrogation (i.e., usually for several days). The cells have just one small window (measuring about 30 cm by 20 cm) and no toilet Sometimes, but not always, prisoners are provided with a bucket.

d) Several reports collected mention the practice of putting a stick or a pen between each finger of the prisoner's hand, and squeezing hard.

e) Prisoners are forced to take very hot showers followed by very cold ones in rapid succession.

f) Prisoners are obliged to stand for long periods continually moving their heads from left to right, or with their arms outstretched.

Particularly pathetic is the interview of a 15-year-old boy who was arrested at 1.30 a.m. on 22 January 1984:

"When I got to Al-Fara'a prison, my personal possessions were taken, and I went to the doctor's room for a check — I didn't have any illness — and was taken from there to the 'stable'. There, I was handcuffed with one hand over my shoulder and the other behind my back, and they put a bag over my head. Then they took me into the toilets. They forced me to sit down in the water there inside the toilets, and I stayed there for two days. During this time I was subjected to ugly interrogation: they beat me with an electric cable and ordered me to turn round and round for a long time, so that I got giddy and nauseous. They made me stand cross-like in the middle of the interrogation room for an hour and a half, after which I simply was not aware of what was happening to me, as I was in a heavy faint because of the interrogation. When I came to, I found a nurse beside me calling me by my name, and he gave me some tablets.

"Half an hour later I was returned to interrogation. They used extremely bad methods of interrogation. They kicked me with their army boots on my shins and used insults and bad language, saying, for example, that they would bring my sister and do what they liked with her. This went on for a long time. I told them I was innocent, but they didn't believe me and kept on torturing me for 12 days on end. During this period many charges were made against me, but I confessed only to one, which was throwing stones at a car with an Israeli number. After 12 days, they put me in the rooms and I stayed there for two months. During those two months, I was taken to court four times. The fifth time, I was sentenced. The judge was satisfied with my term of detention (two months) and sentenced me to two months suspended for three years. I was released at 7.30 p.m. on 22 March 1984."

Al-Fara'a since January 1984

Since January 1984 there has been a change in the methods used, although not in the goals, at Al-Fara'a. In the autumn of 1983, the former "stable" was converted into a number of interrogation offices and cells. The detainees are no longer detained without charge in the prison, but are interrogated on a number of counts, usually participating in demonstrations of stone-throwing, and are subjected to brutal physical and mental punishment during interrogation, aimed at procuring a confession. Frequently, the detainee refuses to confess on a false charge and is later released without trial; at other times, he does confess, primarily to avoid further maltreatment, and is usually subsequently convicted and sentenced generally on the basis of this confession. Many former detainees have stated under oath that they falsely confessed to acts they had not committed in order to stop the punishment.

This, and the substantial evidence of both physical brutality and severely degrading treatment, indicate that despite the introduction of interrogation at Al-Fara'a, the aims of the prison remain the same: to degrade the prisoner and his integrity as a human being and to intimidate both him and the society to which he will return, and not to fulfill the normal purpose of a prison — to punish those who are actually guilty.

Amnesty International have reported in their study entitled *Torture in the Eighties,* published in 1984, on pages 233 and 234 that:

"Amnesty International has continued to receive reports of ill-treatment during the period under review in the form of testimonies from former detainees held in the Occupied Territories, statements from lawyers and eyewitness accounts. The frequency and consistency of these reports indicate that some Palestinians from the Occupied Territories arrested for security reasons and interrogated by the Shin Beth, intelligence services, in a number of different detention centres have been hooded, handcuffed and forced to stand without moving for many hours at a time for several days, and have been exposed while naked to cold showers or cold air ventilators for long periods of time. Detainees have also been deprived of food, sleep and toilet and medical facilities and have been subjected to abuse, insults and threats against themselves and the female members of their families.

"Amnesty International has also received a number of detailed reports of individual prisoners being beaten, sometimes severely, during interrogation in the Occupied Territories. One such case is that of Nassim Abd Al Jalil Audi Ahmad Daoud from Yabroud, who was

150

arrested on 30 January 1982 and interrogated in a detention centre about his activities as a member of Al Fatah organisation. He alleged that, while hooded, handcuffed and sometimes stripped naked, he was, over a period of two weeks, beaten all over the body, including the genitals, with clubs and fists. His head was also repeatedly hit and banged against the wall, causing injury and necessitating medical treatment.

"There have been many reports of Palestinians in the Occupied Territories being ill-treated as a form of harassment and intimidation by the Israeli Defence Forces (IDF), either immediately upon arrest or in places of short-term detention. These allegations referred to military premises in Hebron and Ramallah and Al-Fara'a detention centre near Nablus."

Access to detainees — the agreement with the
International Committee of the Red Cross

Since 1967, when the occupation of the West Bank began, the International Committee of the Red Cross has taken the position that the provisions of the Fourth Geneva Convention are applicable. In its Annual Report of 1968, the International Committee of the Red Cross reported that:

"In spite of International Committee of the Red Cross efforts, the Israeli Government stated that it wished to leave the question of the application of the IVth Convention in Israeli-occupied territory 'open for the moment', preferring to act on a pragmatic basis and to grant delegates practical facilities."

The question continues to be open to this moment. The Israeli government claims that although it does not accept that the convention applies in law, it is in fact abiding by its humanitarian standards. After negotiations over several years, an arrangement was made in 1978 which continues to be the basis of the relationship between the International Committee of the Red Cross (ICRC) and Israel.[51] According to it, the delegates of the International Committee of the Red Cross may visit detainees within 14 days from their arrest. They will be notified of the arrest 12 days after it takes place. The military authorities are abiding by their undertaking and it seems to be the case that with very few exceptions, notification of all arrests of prisoners who remain in detention over 12 days are reported to the ICRC.* However, sometimes the authorities

---

* It was reported, however, that in July and August of 1984 this was not the case.

detain prisoners for 11 days, release them for a day and then re-arrest them for a similar period and so on. Such detainees are not reported.

According to the terms of the agreement, the ICRC delegate may speak to the detainee on the 14th day of detention only about his personal situation and the state of his health. The delegate may not recommend that the detainee appoint a lawyer.[52] According to Article 11 of Military Order Number 29, the right of an accused to see a lawyer is subject to the discretion of the prison authorities. There are cases known to the author of this study when the military court judge recommended that because of the particulars of the case, the accused appoint a lawyer. However, the accused is often unable to do so since very often the only contact he is able to make with the outside is with the ICRC delegate who cannot be of much assistance because, under the terms of the agreement referred to above, a delegate is prohibited from transmitting any information whatsoever to an outside body or to the family of the detainee other than the date of arrest, the place and date of visit and the detainee's state of health. In at least two cases known to the author, when a detainee complained of harsh treatment to an ICRC delegate, he was subsequently severely punished by prison officers for so doing.*

In its annual reports the ICRC mentions the number of arrests they have been informed of and the number of visits their delegates have carried out. When considering the effectiveness of the ICRC's role in the West Bank, the argument put forth is that it is better for a detainee to be visited after 14 days than not to be visited at all. It is also a service for the families of the accused to be informed of the arrest (when the arrest is reported to the ICRC), rather than to remain completely in the dark. However, the total isolation of prisoners from any outside contact for 14 days (and in some cases for much longer) is a long enough period. In the opinion of many ex-prisoners, the visits of the ICRC were of little, if any, significance or practical help.

Violation of The Right to Property

In Part I of this study the methods used to acquire land from Palestinians have been described, as well as the regional planning schemes which restrict the use of lands not yet acquired. It will be recalled that,

---

* Law in the Service of Man wrote to the ICRC, bringing these cases to its attention, and it is known that the ICRC is taking this matter very seriously.

152

according to the estimate of the West Bank Data Base project,[53] up to 40% of the total area of land in the Occupied West Bank (excluding Jerusalem) has already been acquired by Israelis.

The discussion here will be confined to restrictions on the right to water and to the demolition of houses as an extra-judicial punishment.

Water rights

An Order of August 1967[54] vests in the person appointed by the Commander as "the person responsible" all the powers by virtue of:

"Any law, order, decree, or regulation dealing with water, its transportation, extraction, export, consumption, sale, distribution, inspection of its use, purification, allotment of shares, the establishment of water projects, measurement, prevention of contamination, carrying out of studies and measurements in anything that deals with water matters, drilling wells, hearing of objections and all proceedings dealing with this, fixing of sites for water works, giving of licences required by any of the above laws, etc., fixing and collecting fees, taxes and any payments for any of the above and any other matter which has not been mentioned specifically above which deals in any way whatsoever with water subjects."

The Jordanian Law on the Supervision of Water, No. 31 of 1953 provides for the necessity of obtaining the approval of the Manager of the Department of Irrigation and Water for any irrigation scheme. This is a civil department which grants permission unless convinced that the irrigation scheme will cause damage to any land or any other scheme or road. Military Order Number 158[55] provides that installations for drawing subterranean water may be set up only in accordance with the provisions of the Order. Article 4(A) of the Order states that "it shall not be permissible for any person to set up or to assemble or to possess or to operate a water installation unless he has obtained a licence from the Area Commander."

Owners of such water installations are then exempted from the necessity under Jordanian law of obtaining a permit for the irrigation scheme. Those who, prior to 19 November 1967, owned such installations have to submit applications to the Area Commander for new licences. The Commander may refuse to grant the licence without showing any cause. The Order also gives him the power to cancel any licence or amend it or make it conditional or change any of its conditions as he wishes. Finally, to make the power of granting licences for irrigation projects completely discretionary and under the absolute control of the military authorities, the requirement that any matter relating to the law must be published by posting it in the village in question and by sending a notice to the inhabitants of the village, is done away with. The Area Commander can now 'publish' the matter merely by posting it in his office.

The importance of the amendments made by this Order can be appreciated when the case of the "Auja" spring is recalled. It was by virtue of this Order that the Jewish settlers in that area were able to obtain a licence to dig a well near the Arab spring, causing it to dry up in 1979 and the plants of the nearby farmers to wither. If the previous law had been applicable, such a licence would have been denied because of the damage that would be caused by the irrigation scheme to adjacent schemes and lands.

Throughout the 16 years of occupation no more than five permits were given to Palestinian residents to dig wells.* Water is provided very adequately to Jewish settlements in the West Bank. This is a clear example of a law introduced neither for the security of the Israeli forces, nor for the benefit of the local population, but in order to further the interests of Israel, in this case its settlement policy which is in itself a violation of international law.

House demolition

The practice of destroying Arab houses as a means of reprisal has been used since the beginning of the occupation. In recent years it has even occurred following an accusation that a stone was thrown by a member of a particular family. In its 1968 annual report, the International Committee of the Red Cross (ICRC) wrote that "the International Committee delegates in Israel repeatedly petitioned the Israeli civilian and military authorities to cease these practices which are contrary to articles 33 and 53 of the IVth Geneva Convention and to ask for the reconstruction of the damaged houses or for financial compensation to be paid.

"According to Article 33, 'No protected person may be punished for an offence he or she has not personally committed. Collective penalties and likewise all measures of intimidation or of terrorism are prohibited.' "

The director of Department of Principles and Law at the ICRC, Mr. Jacques Moreillon, has interpreted Article 53 as follows: "Article 53 of the Fourth Geneva Convention of 12 August 1949 states as follows:

---

* Higher figures for the number of permits issued have been given by some Israeli sources, but permits also have to be obtained for improvement or renewal of an existing well, and these permits may have been included in the total.

" 'Any destruction by the Occupying Power of real or personal property belonging individually or collectively to private persons, or to the State, or to other public authorities, or to social or cooperative organizations, is prohibited, except where such destruction is rendered absolutely necessary by military operations.'

"In the opinion of the ICRC, the expression 'military operations' must be construed to mean the movements, manoeuvres and other action taken by the armed forces *with a view to fighting.* Destruction of property as mentioned in Article 53 cannot be justified under the terms of that article unless such destruction is absolutely necessary — i.e. materially indispensable — for the armed forces to engage in action, such as making way for them.

"This exception to the prohibition cannot justify destruction as a punishment or deterrent, since to preclude this type of destruction is an essential aim of the article.

"The authors of the Commentary on the Fourth Convention were in full agreement with the ICRC on this, as confirmed by Mr. Jean Pictet, under whose direction the Commentary was published."*

According to figures held by the ICRC, a total of 56 houses have been destroyed by the Israeli forces since 1976. In addition, 19 homes were sealed from 1976 up to April 1983.[56]

George Michael Comsieh is a 50-year old labourer residing in Beit Sahur. His son was accused of throwing stones at an army patrol and was arrested. The following night his house was demolished. Mr. Comsieh's account of the demolition, given under oath, is as follows:

"On 14 November 1982, at 2.00 a.m., a number of Israeli soldiers rushed into our house and began to search. They did not find anything. They then said that they wanted my son Waleed who is a 16-year-old school student. They took him with them to the police station in Jerusalem [known as] the Russian compound. The following night, we were surprised to see a large number of Israeli soldiers enter the house with an army officer. The officer told me to listen and began reading an order which stated that they wanted to demolish our house because our son, Waleed, had been accused of throwing stones at an Israeli patrol. We were given 30 minutes to evacuate our house. We were surprised and could not do much in half an hour as most of the family were still asleep. The soldiers began throwing some of the

---

* From a letter by Mr. Moreillon dated 25 November 1981.

furniture out of the house causing a lot of it to break. The rest of the furniture remained in the house. The soldiers placed explosives and blew up the house. So, in a few minutes, my house, which was 14 metres by 14 metres with two floors, and on each floor there were four nice rooms, a sitting room, a verandah, a bathroom and a kitchen, had been destroyed. This quick action did not give us the opportunity to ask for an injunction at the High Court of Justice. I believe this action is against any human law. This house does not belong to my son but is my property, and now the whole family is in need of a home to live in."

Following this demolition, the Bethlehem municipality refused to participate in the Christmas celebrations. This refusal was withdrawn when the Military Governor issued permission to rebuild and promised to release Mr. Comsieh's son. Building permission was granted, but the son was not released and was ultimately tried and convicted of throwing petrol bombs and sentenced to three-and-a-half years in prison. Following the demolition, the family lived in a tent. The publicity this caused led the Military Governor to object to their living in a tent. Some weeks later, an armed group set fire to the tent and the family moved in with neighbours.

Violations of Freedom of Thought, Expression and Education

Freedom of thought and expression

There is strict limitation in the West Bank over freedom of thought and expression. Although some Israeli and American writers have recently brought these restrictions to the attention of the international public, they have, in fact, existed since the beginning of the occupation. The following are the Military Orders which introduced these restrictions:

— Military Order No. 50[57] prohibits either the bringing to the area of any 'newspaper' or its 'publication' without a permit from the officer appointed by the Area Commander for the purposes of this Order.

The definition of 'newspaper' includes all publications containing news or information or narrative or comments, or discussions or analysis of news, or any other matter which is of interest to the public written in any language whether published in Israel or anywhere else, for sale, for

156

consideration or gratuitously at specified or unspecified periods. 'Publication,' as defined in the Order, includes all forms of dissemination, handing over, or distribution.

On 6 August 1980, Order 50 was amended to include a paragraph which stated that in order to remove any doubt "any publication which has not been entered in the list of prohibited publications. . . shall not be considered a publication permitted to be brought into or published in the [West Bank] unless a permit has been issued for it." The 'person responsible' is prohibited from giving a permit for any publication on the prohibited list.

Although the Order seems, from its title, to be dealing with newspapers, in fact it includes all publications of whatever nature. The prohibition does not apply only to publications brought in for commercial or public use. Even if an individual brings in a single copy for his own library without obtaining a permit he is in violation of the Order and is liable to imprisonment for up to five years and a fine of 150 Jordanian dinars (equal to $400) or both.

— Military Order No. 101[58], article 6, prohibits residents of the West Bank from printing and publishing "any publication, advertisement, proclamation, picture or any other document" which contains any article with "a political significance" except after obtaining a licence from the Military Commander. 'Printing' is defined in the Order to include "carving on stone, typing on a typewriter, copying, photographing, or any other manner of representation or of communicating expressions, numbers, symbols, pictures, maps, paintings, decorations or any other similar material." Amendment No. 3* to the Order widened its scope by prohibiting publication or possession of all other forms of audio-visual material including cassettes and videos.

— Article 88 of the Defence (Emergency) Regulations of 1945[59] provides as follows:

  "1) The censor may by Order prohibit the importation or exportation or the printing or publishing of any publication (which prohibition shall be deemed to extend to any copy or portion of such publication or of any issue or number thereof), the importation, exportation, printing or publishing of which, in his opinion, would be or be likely to be or become, prejudicial for the defence of Palestine or to the public safety or to public order.

---

* By Order Number 1079.

"2) Any person who contravenes any order under this regulation and the proprietor and editor of the publication, in relation to which the contravention occurs, and any person (unless in the opinion of the court he ought fairly to be excused) who has in his possession or his control or in premises of which he is the occupier, any publication prohibited under this regulation or who posts, delivers or receives any such publication, shall be guilty of an offence against these regulations."

A list[60] of books that have been prohibited under this Order and regulation (mainly Arabic titles but including some English titles) is published at various times. The lists that have been published so far cover more than a thousand titles, including:

Christopher MARLOWE	*The Jew of Malta*
Phillip GILLON	*A Zionist Asks for a Palestinian State*
George ANTONIUS	*The Arab Awakening*
Yigal ALLON	*The Origins and Organisation of the Israeli Army*
Ghassan KANAFANI	*The Small Lamp* (a children's book)
Nizar KABANI	*The Complete Poetic Works of Nizar Kabani*
Arnold TOYNBEE	*Palestine Crime and Defence*
Livia ROKOCH	*Israel's Sacred Terrorism* — A Study Based on Moshe Sharett's Diaries

UN Resolutions concerning Palestine and the Arab-Israeli Conflict, 1980

(These titles have been translated from the list of prohibited books provided, in Arabic, by the Israeli authorities.)

— Military Order Number 107[61] prohibits anyone in the area from using the text books appearing in the Appendix attached to the Order. Violation of the Order renders the offender liable to imprisonment of one year and/or a fine. The Appendix includes about 60 school books, including grammar, history (a book on the history of the Crusades is amongst them), geography, philosophy, civic studies and Arabic literature. In the Report of the Commissioner-General of the United Nations Relief and Works Agency for Palestine Refugees in the Near East, 1 July 1980, it was reported that of 83 textbooks approved by Unesco, the Israeli occupying authorities refused import permits for 13.

The effect of these orders is to prohibit absolutely the right of any resident of the West Bank to acquire any printed matter from abroad (including Israel) before he gets a permit from the military authorities. The prohibition does not only apply to books, photographs, posters and any printed matter: Military Order 101 has been interpreted as applying to paintings.

In April, 1980, for example, Bethlehem University students were prohibited from wearing white T-shirts which had streaks of green, black and red because these constitute the colours of the new Palestinian flag. The University was warned against allowing students to wear such shirts.

Najah University was closed on 1 August 1984 on the grounds that illegal literature was found at the University. In May 1984, an artist from Gaza, Fathi Ismail Ghabin, was sentenced to a one-year term of imprisonment, half of which he actually had to serve, and the other representing a fine of 37,000 shekels, because of a painting which he had produced. He was charged with distributing inciting material.*

Posters of paintings by Palestinian artists from the West Bank were confiscated at the Allenby Bridge. During the negotiations with the military legal advisor which followed, in which this author was involved, it was explained that the criteria which the military authorities use for banning posters are as follows:

— posters including any one of the following elements are forbidden:

  — the four colours of the Palestinian flag near each other,
  — calligraphy including the word 'Palestine',
  — depiction of guns, grenades or rifles, etc.

The posters were not returned.

Gallery 79, an art gallery in Ramallah, was closed on 21 September 1980, and paintings on exhibition were confiscated and to date have not been returned. They included one depicting a man with cheek in hand entitled "permit denied".

Applications, for example, by the universities in the West Bank for permits to bring in periodicals needed by the students for their studies were refused. One refusal of such an application by Birzeit University was made on 19 November 1979. The titles for which the permit was requested are available at the Hebrew University library in Jerusalem,

---

* See article by Amnon Raz in the Jerusalem magazine *Hadashot* (published in Hebrew), on 16 May 1984.

but Birzeit University may not even photocopy the parts required by the students and bring them into the West Bank.

Press censorship of newspapers published in Jerusalem for distribution in the West Bank is very stringent. According to Israeli law, only matters which are related to army security may be censored, but in practice all the material in the newspapers published by Arabs in Jerusalem is subject to censorship. It is estimated by those working at these newspapers that around 30% of all their editorials, for example, are refused publication by the censor.[62]

In 1983, the three Arabic daily newspapers in Jerusalem were prohibited from publishing and then publication was allowed after new three-month permits were issued. These were made subject to a condition that the authorities have the right to confiscate any issue and prohibit its circulation notwithstanding the fact that they had previously approved all its contents.

This does, in fact, frequently occur. The taxi in which the newspapers are transported is stopped and the newspapers are confiscated. Attempts to avoid this 'afterthought censorship' have resulted in strong warnings to agents and distributors. In addition, two daily-newspaper editors were placed under town arrest for a period of approximately two years and were prevented from going to work.

Newspapers face difficulties in obtaining telephones, telexes and international news agency services.

A large number of individuals in the West Bank have been charged and sentenced for possessing prohibited books. Some examples are given below. It must be noted that in view of the wide scope of the prohibition on books, it is almost always possible to find at the house of any literate person in the West Bank books or pictures which would fall under the definition of prohibited books under one or other of the Orders mentioned above. This being the case, the army can always justify its entry and search of a house and the arrest of its residents on the grounds that they were looking for prohibited books. The existence of any such 'prohibited books' then becomes the basis for a court case for which many have been sentenced to prison terms and fines.*

It is worth noting that the official spokesman of the military government ment denied the existence of the list of banned books made by virtue

---

* Amnesty International in its 1984 Annual Report, expresses concern "that the possession of 'illegal literature' is frequently used as a pretext to arrest and detain individuals, particularly students, most of whom are then released without charge or trial" (p. 344).

of Order 101 as described above. He apparently tried to confuse those Israeli and foreign journalists who were concerned about this practice by referring to a list published in 1976 and later cancelled. The journalists, however, pursued the matter and ascertained the facts and denounced the practice which has continued just as widely as before.[63]

The following are examples of some cases involving censorship:

— On 15 April 1983, the Arab College of Nursing in El Bireh was closed for two weeks by the military authorities after it was claimed that prohibited books were found on display at a book fair held at the College;

— on 11 December 1981 about 65 people were arrested for watching a film at a club in the Kalandia Refugee Camp. They were kept out in the cold all night and some were imprisoned for a week;

— Hamdi Farraj, a journalist from Bethlehem, had his whole library of 500 books confiscated. Twelve books were brought in evidence at his subsequent trial where he was sentenced to 17 days imprisonment, a fine and a suspended sentence. When his lawyer demanded the return of the other 488 books, he was informed that they had accidentally been burned;

— in November 1984 threats were made that the literacy programme run by local charitable organisations, which serves 4,000 people throughout the West Bank, should be stopped on the basis that the book used was prohibited.

Freedom of education

The restrictions placed by the authorities affect all educational institutions whether government, private or under the supervision of the United Nations Relief and Works Agency (UNRWA), including schools, universities and vocational training centres.

Some of the restrictions on textbooks and reference books generally were described in the previous section. In this section some of the main effects of the violation of the freedom of education will be discussed.

The closure of educational institutions

It is a common grievance of all those responsible for the administration of educational insitutions that their closure makes it very difficult to plan the academic year and complete the required curricula.

Closures are due to various reasons.

Closure of schools and universities by the military authorities, usually as a form of punishment for student demonstrations, accounts for the greatest loss of school days. Birzeit University, for example, was closed for the following days during the period 26 March 1979 to June 1984:

Dates of Closure of Birzeit University
by the Military Authorities

From 26 March 1979	to 1 April 1979	(4 days)
From 3 May 1979	to 2 July 1979	(2 months)
From 14 November 1980	to 22 November 1980	(1 week)
From 4 November 1981	to 4 January 1982	(2 months)
From 16 February 1982	to 16 April 1982	(2 months)
From 8 July 1982	to 8 October 1982	(3 months)
From 2 February 1984	to 2 May 1984	(3 months) (old campus)
From 2 April 1984	to 2 May 1984	(1 month) (new campus)

In May 1982, the Israeli military occupation forces began a new practice of unofficially closing the University of An-Najah by erecting roadblocks at all entrances leading to the campus, thus effectively preventing students and faculty members from reaching the campus. Consequently, during the whole of 1982, the University was closed for a total of 22 days.

The comprehensive list below shows that 1983 saw a continuation, and, in fact, a massive escalation of these practices.

— Closed by roadblocks: 11 January 1983 to 26 January 1983; 18 February 1983, 10 April 1983, 17 April 1983.

— Closed by Military Order: 6 June 1983 to 4 September 1983.

— Closed by roadblocks: 13, 17, 19, 21, 23, 26, 29, 30 November 1983; and 3, 12, 13, 14, 18, 20, 26 and 27 December 1983.

The University was also ordered closed during the period 1 August 1984 to 1 December 1984 (four months) on the grounds that illegal literature and posters and some knives and chains were found on the premises. The literature and posters were in fact brought for a Palestinian cultural exhibit which had already been displayed elsewhere. Palestinian paintings were confiscated by soldiers.

Sometimes the educational institutions are closed through the

162

extension of official vacations. In April 1983, the Officer in Charge of Education, who is not directly responsible for the administration of private schools, ordered these schools to extend their spring vacation. At other times, schools such as Yatta School, near Hebron, are forcibly closed by settlers. Strikes by the students or faculty members in protest against policies of the military authorities also account for some of the loss of school days.

To compensate for lost time, some universities and schools have attempted to hold classes in other halls or in private homes. The authorities reacted very strongly against this imprisoning students, putting up roadblocks and threatening those who were taking part in these make-up classes.

Following the closure of Birzeit University in the summer of 1982, the University arranged classes for the students in Jerusalem. In a statement given under oath to Law in the Service of Man, Suha, a student of Birzeit University (who has requested that her real name not be used) described how on Thursday, 15 July 1982, after the closure of the University she went with other students to attend make-up classes in Jerusalem. On being recognised as students by the soldiers, she and other students were driven by bus to the police station in the Russian compound in Jerusalem. She heard the soldiers curse the students and say: "You are not students, you are shit". Each of the students was asked: "Why did you come to Jerusalem?" — to which they answered that they came to make up for the classes they were losing. The soldiers would say: "We know all you Birzeit students, you are rascals, but we will teach you".

They were then all taken to a yard and kept there until midday, after which they were taken to Ramallah where a water truck was emptied onto the students. At 8 p.m. the soldiers told them to go home and forget the idea of making up classes. They were given back their identity cards but not before they had been marked and were told to return the next day to the military governor in their respective towns. Suha describes the mark put on their identity cards as "a blue shape on the front page of each identity card near the personal photograph".

Recent closures of Bethlehem University include a three-week period from 10 March 1983 and a two-week period from 3 November 1983.

Harassment of students

Students in the West Bank are probably subjected more than any other group to constant acts of harassment by the authorities.

Harassment takes place as the students are on their way to their schools or universities when they are sometimes stopped, searched and either arrested or their identification cards are confiscated. The soldiers seem to act on the premise that all students are guilty until they can prove their innocence.

Harassment also takes the form of breaking into student hostels and private homes and carrying out searches and beating and humiliating the students as well as their families.

The Birzeit University public relations officer reported that on 10, 11, and 12 May 1982, for example, the Zaituna, Al Hambra and Rabah student hostels of the University were attacked by soldiers. The soldiers carried out searches, damaged furniture, locks, telephone lines, and broke glass. They confiscated books and student identification cards and declared that these visits and searches were merely to serve as a warning.

The following description was made in a press release issued by Birzeit University on 24 March 1983 of the events which took place the previous night:

"Army jeeps arrived at the back entrance of Birzeit University about 7.15 p.m. Soldiers entered cafés near the gate where students were eating dinner and watching television. They rounded up about 50 students and made them go to various parts of the village and paint over slogans. They were then made to stand with their faces to the wall and hands held high. They were to remain in that position until well after midnight.

"More soldiers arrived on the scene about an hour later and began to enter student homes in the area. Six students were arrested: Abdul Halim Abu Askar, Nawad Daoud Ibrahim, Naim Mahmoud Jarrar, Subhi Abdel Khadr Jabbar, Shawkat Mohammed Jabbar and Ra'id Salah. Books were confiscated from a number of houses.

"Meanwhile, about 100 students were trapped in the University library, afraid to emerge, while other students fled to the hills to escape the soldiers' harassment. When University officials arrived on the scene about 11 p.m., the army refused to answer their inquiries about the source of the problem or to make any provision for the trapped students or for students still forced to stand against the wall."

According to the University, these actions were unprovoked.

On 23 February 1984 at 2 a.m., soldiers raided the Salam Asfour Hostel, housing about 60 Birzeit students and broke down two doors as they forced their way into the room of Mohsin Abu Ramadan. As Mohsin Abu Ramadan was not in his room, other students were wakened and beaten. The soldiers stayed for more than an hour and when they left they took with them all of Mohsin's personal possessions, including books, clothes and even his carpets from the floor. Earlier in the same evening, soldiers had raided the house of Ali Nimr Bardawi in Birzeit. He was not at home either, and the soldiers ransacked his house and took a collection of his paintings with them.

The families of students are often harassed also, as is illustrated by the following two cases which have been reported by the Public Relations Office of Birzeit University:

Iyman Lebadi

On 29 March 1984, soldiers went to the family home of Iyman Lebadi. Iyman was not at home. The soldiers left verbal instructions that he should report to Tulkarem Military Headquarters, but no official summons was issued. The soldiers returned on 31 March in the middle of the night and detained Iyman's father; he was released the next morning. On 3 April, soldiers again raided the family home at night. This time they detained Iyman's brother and threatened to hold him until Iyman gave himself up. The brother was released after two nights in detention.

On 14 April an army patrol under the command of an officer calling himself Captain Uri went to the family home. The officer threatened Iyman's father with dismissal from his job as a teacher in a government school unless Iyman presented himself at Tulkarem Military Headquarters the next morning. The next day Iyman's father went to Birzeit to discuss the problem with his son, and Iyman decided to give himself up.

Iyman was arrested on 15 April and held for two weeks in Al-Fara'a prison. On 29 April he was released without having been charged.

Sha'wan Al Jabaarin

During April 1984 soldiers went several times to the family home of Sha'wan Al Jabaarin in the Hebron district. On 24 April an army patrol came at night and detained Sha'wan's brother, Nadiim. The soldiers promised that Nadiim would be released as soon as Sha'wan reported to Hebron Military Headquarters.

On 30 April Sha'wan went to the Hebron headquarters. He was

interrogated and released on the same day, without any charge. His brother, nevertheless, remained in detention until 10 May.

Other forms of harassment include prevention of travel abroad to continue education or to work, confiscation of identity cards, imposition of restriction orders and repeated calls for interviews with the military government with the aim of disrupting the students' lives.

The following is a typical case of confiscation of identity cards of students:

On 10 October 1983, three Birzeit students, Amin Abu Ghazal, Saab Fariq Alawi and Bashar Thahar, had their identity cards confiscated when soldiers raided their home in Abu Qash. No reason was given for the raid and no charges resulted from it.

On 11 October, the students waited the whole day at the Ramallah Military Headquarters, but to no avail. They returned on 12 October with a Birzeit staff member and were told by a guard that their IDs were in Nablus. The students' attorney then contacted Nablus and was told the IDs were not there. He then addressed himself to the office of the Legal Adviser to the West Bank military government and was told the IDs were in Nablus; the Legal Adviser issued a paper for the students, telling the Nablus authorities to return the IDs.

On 27 November, the students went to Nablus and were turned away. They tried again the next day and were told the IDs were in Ramallah (contrary to what the Legal Adviser had said). They tried again after the Legal Adviser had made an appointment for them with the responsible officer in Nablus, but he told them only that they must get their IDs back "from the soldiers who took them".

Eventually, the students went to the Nablus Identity Card Office to apply for new identity cards. They again met with some obstruction, but finally received their new IDs on 16 March 1984.

An example of bureaucratic obstruction to travelling abroad follows:

Muhammad Masad, an academic assistant in the Cultural Studies Department of Birzeit University, was selected to study for an M.A. degree in the U.S.A. at the expense of the University. He received notification of his acceptance at the University of Wisconsin at the end of April 1983. Soon afterwards he applied for a "laissez-passer" from the Tulkarem Identity Card Office to enable him to travel, but he was turned away. Masad reapplied on several occasions but to no avail.

His U.S. entry visa was issued on 21 October 1983 (already two months later than the scheduled start of his study programme). He tried again to obtain the "laissez-passer", but was refused again and

166

again. Letters from the Birzeit University and copies of the letter of acceptance from Wisconsin had no effect on the authorities.

Masad then turned to a lawyer, Muhammad Na'amneh, for assistance. The lawyer wrote to the Assistant Legal Adviser to the military governor in Beit El on 16 January 1984. On 28 January, she replied, saying that Masad would not face any problems in obtaining his "laissez-passer". Masad therefore returned to the Tulkarem Identity Card Office but was still confronted with bureaucratic obstruction. On several occasions he was again turned away and told to come back the next day. It took more than 40 days after the receipt of the Assistant Legal Officer's reply for the "laissez-passer" to be issued.

Masad was finally able to travel to the U.S. in March 1984, having thus missed the major part of the academic year 1983-84.

Students serving prison sentences in Israeli prisons are allowed to continue their education. This was previously the case for students from the West Bank universities. However, at the end of 1983, when the Birzeit University applied to continue this education programme for its students serving sentences in Israeli prisons, the prison authority refused to allow the education programme to continue and referred the matter to the Civilian Administration.

Arrest of students before their matriculation examinations

In June 1983, just before the government matriculation examinations (Tawjihi), about 40 students were arrested by the Israeli military and detained for sufficient time for them to miss their exams. The students were held for four or five days and then released. During their period of detention they were not told the reason for their arrest, they were not questioned and they were all released without being charged. The effect of their arrest was that the students missed the examinations and had to wait another year before they could sit them again. One of the students was told by his arresting officer that this was the purpose of the arrest.[64] The same process was again repreated the next year, but the number of arrested students was smaller.

Discouragement of development of the educational institutions

Many of the schools and universities complain of lack of educational facilities. In the case of government schools, the development of the schools is very inadequate. In the case of privately run institutions,

167

permits for important necessary facilities such as laboratory equipment, are often withheld or delayed.

In addition to the prohibition on importing books for the newly constructed library of Bethlehem University, the Civilian Administrator refused to grant permission for building a gymnasium to serve the University. Birzeit and Najah Universities face similar restrictions due to delays or refusal to grant permits to build essential premises to meet the expanding needs of these universities.

For example, Birzeit has not been granted a licence to build a Fine Arts Faculty within the zone designated for that purpose since 1975 and approved as a University Planning Zone. The licence was applied for in November 1983 and was still not granted at the time or writing (October 1984). The licence to enlarge the University Zone to accommodate other buildings and facilities needed by the University and applied for in February 1984 had also not been granted at the time of writing. The bias of the Israeli Planning Department in the West Bank was evident from the fact that a local resident was allowed to continue building in the area within the University's proposed enlarged campus, despite the existence of many legal objections against the licence which the University brought to the attention of the Planning Authority. The Authority also failed to remove a fence built without licence inside the approved University zone, despite pleas to the Planning Authority to do so. The University has petitioned the Israeli High Court of Justice, claiming bias by the Planning Authority against the University. As of September 1984, the Court had not arrived at a decision in this case.

Contrary to the 1950 Agreement and Protocol on the Importation of Educational, Scientific and Cultural Materials, Birzeit University is required to pay full customs duties and taxes on all educational equipment purchased for the University.

Most foreign teachers of West Bank universities stay in the West Bank by means of tourist visas that have to be renewed every three months, for which purpose they normally have to leave the country at the end of each three-month period, and then return. Work permits are rarely granted.

Attempts by the authorities to create a gulf
between the universities and the rest of society

One of the aims of university education in the West Bank is to increase the students' understanding of their own society and to prepare

168

them to serve it as best they can. With the aim of maintaining contact between campus and society, some universities require a number of hours of voluntary service by the students for public projects. During the olive-picking season, many students, therefore, volunteer their services because there is a shortage of manual labour. In October 1982, the students from Birzeit University who went to the town of Salfit to assist the villagers in their olive-picking were arrested by the soldiers, beaten and insulted and prevented from carrying on with their voluntary work. No charges were brought against them, but the message was clear.

Sami, whose real name is not used, describes the harassment faced by the students when they went olive-picking:

"On the evening of Saturday, 3 October 1982, I went along with 120 other students from Birzeit University to the town of Salfit for the purpose of picking olives. This contribution to the villages by the university students has become an annual tradition, which the Committee for Voluntary Work at Birzeit University sponsors. The completion of a number of hours voluntary service is also now a requirement at the university for graduation.

"On Sunday, 4 October 1982, having spent the evening with the villagers, we took off early in the morning to begin our work picking olives. We spent the day doing this, and at five in the afternoon we returned to the houses of our hosts, the villagers we were helping. At six that same evening, the volunteers and a large number of the hosts were gathered at the Salfit municipality building. Our hosts entertained us to a party which ended at 7.30 p.m. when everyone went home. Meanwhile, three Israeli army vehicles, in which there were approximately 12 soldiers, began roaming around the town.

"On Monday, 5 October, at eight in the morning, we carried on our work in the fields, picking olives. Our work that day ended at five in the afternoon. During that period I saw a policeman on a motorcycle driving around and watching us. He took the identity card of one volunteer, and I do not know whether he confiscated it or returned it to its owner. This same policeman also asked a number of the volunteers for their identity cards.

"At seven in the evening on the same day, we went down to the village intending to buy some food and some cigarettes. A border police jeep followed me and a group of students with whom I was walking, and they asked for our identity cards. There were six of us, five from Birzeit and one of our hosts. After they had collected our identity cards, they asked us to go to the Salfit police station at ten that night. At ten o'clock, I went with three other students to the police station. The other two (of the five students) were girls and they did not come with us. When we arrived at the police station, the border police asked about the two girls and where they were staying. We told them that we did not know exactly where they were staying. All we knew was that they had worked with us picking olives. They then took me and the three other students who were with me in a police jeep and began driving around the town looking for the two girls.

"At a certain place in the middle of the town, they stopped the jeep and asked us to tell them where the girls were staying. But we honestly did not know where they were staying. After that they took me out of the jeep and began beating me with clubs and the butts of their guns and kicking me with their boots. There were five soldiers beating me. As a result of their beating, I fell to the ground. One of them kicked me in the face with his boots and another in the stomach. My left eye became swollen as a result of this. I screamed but they increased their kicks, ordering me to shut up and cursing me. They then carried me to another place and again they said that I must direct them to the place where the two girls were staying. They threatened to take me to the settlement, Ariel, so that the settlers there would hit me. I was silent and they continued their beating, provocation and curses.

"When it was getting to midnight, they carried me to another place, and there they gave me four identity cards and asked me to go to the police station. When I arrived there, I gave the identity cards to the policeman responsible and I found the three other students there. The policeman told me that he had orders from the Commander of the border police unit that we were to stand in the courtyard of the police station without speaking to each other, and we were not allowed anything to drink or to have anything to protect us from the cold. We were kept standing in the courtyard until six in the morning in the biting cold.

"At six, a policeman came to the police station. He telephoned the headquarters in Tulkarem and reported that he had four students who had been brought in by the border police and asked what he should do with us. He was told to give us our identity cards and release us.

170

"Upon my return home, after being released, I felt severe pain in my left eye which was completely closed. I could not see anything with it. I was taken to the Salfit clinic for treatment. My eye still hurts."*

Military Order Number 854[65]

This Order, which was promulgated on 6 July 1980, imposed perhaps the strictest restriction on academic freedom in the West Bank. The Order amends the Jordanian law on Education and Culture of 1964 which applies to elementary and high schools and to vocational training centres but not to universities. Order 854 brought the universities of the West Bank within the ambit of the law, thereby imposing on them restrictions normally placed only on elementary and high schools.

The Order empowers the military authorities to exercise complete control over whomever may be accepted by the university as a student, teacher or principal. It requires all students who do not hold identity cards issued by the Area Commander of the West Bank to obtain a permit from the Area Commander before they can enroll as students. It also gives the authorities powers over licencing teachers, both foreign and local.

Using its newly acquired powers under the order, the military authorities, in the fall of 1982, required of all "non-resident" teachers at West Bank and Gaza universities (that is to say, all persons not holding military-issued identity cards, even if they had actually been born in the occupied territories), that they sign a statement, along with their work-permit applications, whereby they would deny any support, "direct or indirect", to the PLO or any other "terrorist" organisation. The implications of this "loyalty oath", if signed, were far-reaching: they could include the duty to report on students' and colleagues' conversations inside and outside the classroom, as well as on the presence of literature or cultural exhibits which could be deemed to be in support of a "terrorist" organisation.

---

* Discouragement of voluntarism and community self help by the military authority is prevalent and is evident from the restrictions which the social welfare department places on charitable organisations to the extent that the authorities make it clear that serving the community is almost subversive activity. A good illustration of this is the harassment of a woman like Samiha Khalil, head of the Society for the Rehabilitation of the Family (supra), who is punished for her excellent service to the community by being prohibited from travelling to visit her children, all but one of whom are not allowed to visit her in the West Bank.

The promulgation of the order and its application in the form of the "loyalty oath" for non-residents led to strong protest by the student population of the West Bank. Having refused to sign the statement, at least 25 lecturers from An-Najah National University in Nablus and 19 from Birzeit University were barred from teaching or summarily deported.

The following affidavit is taken from a British national, Mark Cheverton, who was working in the biology department at Bethlehem University. Following his refusal to sign the aforementioned "loyalty oath", which he considered to be a highly political document, he was ordered to leave the country by the military authorities. He describes the events that led up to his being told to leave and gives his reasons for refusing to sign the statement.

"I arrived at Bethlehem University two months ago (2 September 1982) to teach biology as a laboratory instructor. I applied for a work permit to do so, and, as is normal practice, commenced work immediately, preparing for the new academic year by writing a manual for laboratory biochemistry. In applying for a work permit, I signed a statement agreeing to abide by the laws of the region.

"Term was scheduled to begin on 20 September, but when I arrived in the morning a road block prevented me and other teachers and students from entering the university. The soldiers told me to go to the military government in Bethlehem to sign a statement. When I went, I found that the statement was highly political and I declined to sign it because of this. I went to seek advice from my consulate, university and fellow teachers.

"The military government continued to prevent the university from opening until a fortnight later (4 October). Then Col. Bahar, 'Civil Governor of Bethlehem', summoned the teachers who had recently applied for work permits to see him on 7 October. We were given a pep talk during which we were advised not to involve ourselves in the politics of another country. However, contrary to this order, he asked us to sign this political statement.

"One week ago (28 October) I was summoned again by Col. Bahar, this time on my own, and asked to sign this political statement in order to receive my work permit. I again declined to involve myself in this political issue. The governor instructed me that I must leave today (5 November) if I did not sign.

172

"Today I am being deported for my refusal to make a political statement.

"There are already ample provisions on the statute books for security measures, and I had moreover signed a statement that I agree to abide by these laws when I applied for a work permit. Thus, the only possible purpose of this statement is political. The statement is clearly political in its nature and intent, as it refers explicitly to only one organisation and to no others.

"I will be leaving the country this afternoon, forced to leave against my will. I want to help people through education, but this is being denied. In conscience, I cannot sign this statement and the only alternative is deportation."*

In November 1983, The World University Service and The International Commission of Jurists sent a mission to investigate academic freedom in the occupied territories. The following are some of their conclusions:

(i)   The pattern of Israel's treatment of the West Bank universities over the past five years has been "one of harassment going beyond what might be reasonably justified on the grounds of public order or security";

(ii) There is a "clear and urgent need to reconsider the wide range of administrative measures and practices affecting the universities", in particular those restricting the import of foreign funds and planning refusals;

(iii) Military Order 854 should be rescinded, as "the extraordinary powers over academic life for which it provides naturally led to a storm of protest", and it represents "a potential threat" to academic life which "creates distrust and prevents sensible co-existence"; and

(iv) There should be greater recognition of the role the universities can play in the economic, intellectual, cultural and political development of the area, and greater contact between Palestinian and Israeli universities.

---

* A compromise formula for the statement was eventually agreed upon and signed by some of the remaining teachers in early 1984, but work permits have still not been issued.

The Village Leagues

This group, referred to earlier, which the Head of the Civilian Administration placed in the third category according to his classification of West Bank political society, was established in 1978. The support given to its members and to the political and military ends which the administration hoped it would fulfill, began after the signing of the Camp David Accord. Israel was trying to save face by implementing its version of the 'autonomy' plan and needed the presence of a local group through which it could claim popular acquiescence to its plan.

The village leagues are established by virtue of an Order[66] which amends the Jordanian Law on the administration of villages[67] by adding to Article 32 of the Law the following two sub-sections:

"(a) The Area Commander is empowered to permit the establishment of societies for the purpose of increasing cooperation and ties between village councils in the area concerning the matters dealt with in this law provided that he is convinced that the matter is necessary for the purpose of implementing the objectives of this law and provided that this does not affect public order and security in the area.

"(b) The society established as in (a) above shall have a juridical personality and the manner of its constitution, administration, operation, dissolution and inspection shall be determined by issuing regulations."

The first such 'league' to be established was in the Hebron area. The memorandum of association of the Hebron village league provides as follows:[68]

The objectives of the Hebron village league as stated in its "Basic Regulations" are the following:

(a) to settle all disputes and differences between the inhabitants of the district;

(b) to encourage the organisation of cooperatives to help farmers improve their economic conditions;

(c) to encourage the organisation of charitable societies for the service of the needy and the rehabilitation of the disabled;

174

(d)   the development of agricultural techniques and their modernisation.

(e)   planning and executing development and industrialisation of agriculture and carrying out all activities which lead to the increase of income of the individual and the group;

(f)   the establishment of public companies for the service of the inhabitants of the district;

(g)   carrying out any activities of a social or financial nature within the limits of the laws in force.

In practice, the leagues go beyond the objectives laid out in their articles. Their centres of operation are not in the villages they were ostensibly formed to serve, but in the main cities. The heads of the leagues are appointed, and it is not clear what constitutes membership or what the terms of affiliation exactly are. Many of the members of these leagues are armed with sub-machine guns provided by the Israeli army and are trained by the army in the use of these weapons. In some areas, the village league members patrol the area with arms and in their own jeeps.[69] Most of them are recruited from the lowest ranks of society and from amongst society's outcasts. Evidence from affidavits collected by Law in the Service of Man indicates that the leagues go to greater excesses than even the members of the Israeli army. The delegation of power to carry guns and to assume some of the powers of the Israeli army is transferred by virtue of Order 180.[70] It is done in the following somewhat obtuse manner:

"No person may carry arms or ammunition . . . without permission issued by the Area Commander, or whoever stands in his stead. No person may carry arms or ammunition . . . in a manner which contravenes the conditions of that permission."

Article 5 of Military Order 947[71] empowers the Head of the Civilian Administration to delegate some of the powers vested in him by virtue of this order. In many cases, such as for permits to travel, the endorsement of the Head of the village league in the city or village where the applicant for the permit lives must be obtained. Other powers are also exercised by the village league in an attempt to increase the league's influence.

The policy of nurturing and supporting the village leagues has been pursued now for several years. If it was, indeed, the policy of the military authorities to promote the village leagues as a political force to

175

which the authorities could point as an indication of public support for their political activities, the village leagues have not been successful. If, however (as I believe is the more likely and attainable aim), the leagues were meant to be developed into an army militia which would support the central Israeli policy of encouraging the emigration of the Palestinians from the West Bank by dividing and thereby weakening the population, and by making life intolerable (which will save the Israeli army from having to do some of the "dirty work" which the army may in time become less willing to do), then the leagues have been more successful.

The use by the military authorities of their appointed village leagues as agents to implement the policy of harassment of the population in the occupied territories is on the increase.

In an article by the Israeli writer and journalist, Amos Elon, published in the Israeli newspaper, *Ha'aretz*, on 19 March 1982, the office and character of Bishara Kumsiyeh, the Head of the Bethlehem village league, is described:

"The entrance to the office of Bishara Kumsiyeh, head of the villagers' association in the Bethlehem region, is blocked by a Border Police command car and half a dozen unshaved young men, sloppily dressed, armed with sub-machine guns. Soldiers in proper uniforms are also seated in the command car. But who are these seeming guerrillas in Kafiyas over old wind coats or in sweaters with holes? They are Bedouins from the Taamreh and Abdiyeh tribes who serve as the new security forces of the villagers' associations in the Bethlehem, Ramallah and Hebron regions. Here in Bethlehem they are paid 5,000 IS a month. They have licences issued by the Israeli Military Authorities permitting them to carry arms (an Uzi sub-machine gun) and 50 bullets.

"Who is your commander? The son of Bishara Kumsiyeh. Are they a militia? This is considered a negative name, they say. Why? Because it reminds one of Major Hadad in South Lebanon. So what are they? Security forces. How many of them? 30 at the moment. Have they been trained? Yes. Where? In an Israeli army camp near Kfar Etzion. Transportation means? Jeeps.

"Everyone who comes to the house is carefully questioned. Where, who, why, when. The young interrogator keeps his finger on the trigger. Apart from the Uzi, he is also armed with a knife and a pistol, stuck in his belt. He hesitates. One of the men is sent inside

176

and returns with the approval.

"Inside, further armed men, further control. This is how visitors reach the office of Bishara Kumsiyeh, owner of this small private army, financed by the Israeli government. He is a rich local business-man who leads the villagers' association, and thus is one of the great hopes of the Israeli authorities. The hopes for anti-PLO leaders in the West Bank are focused on men such as Bishara Kumsiyeh in Bethle-hem, Mustafa Dudin in Hebron, and their like.

"The offices are large and comfortable. This used to be the Bethle-hem Post Office and telephone exchange. Many rooms filled with desks and empty chairs. Armed young men lean on the walls. There is no one here except for them. There are nets over the windows against bombs.

"Bishara Kumsiyeh himself waits in the backroom. He is a heavy man with a fleshy face. His large hands on the table; the only item on the table is a calendar issued by a known Tel Aviv arms distribution company. On the wall a poster advertising a similar company. Bishara Kumsiyeh offers his guests tea made with Israeli tea bags. His eyes remain frozen in their sockets when he raises his voice to say that he is angry. No, he is not frightened by the declarations of the Jordanian PM threatening the villagers' associations. The associations are no more than a means for developing the villages. They express the will of the people, more than the politicians who pretend to speak for the people. The Jordanian PM is a Nazi! Nazi! If he goes on like this, the Jordan bridge will have to be closed. That far? Yes. Is he afraid? Definitely not. The associations are stronger than ever He says that thousands are armed. How many are paid? He doesn t remember the number. It is only PLO and Jordanian agents who threaten the associations, but they shall know how to protect them-selves. They have all the means to do so, sums up Bishara Kumsiyeh.

"Leaving his room one passes an old guardsman seated by a small table, surrounded by armed men. When he sees the people leaving Kumsiyeh's room, the old man jumps up shouting: "At your service, master. Damn the Jordanian Kingdom. Damn King Hussein!". In his belt a large knife and a pistol. Several of the men present in the room repeat the sentence after him. For a short moment this strange scene reminds me of pictures from Lebanon, the 1948 war or the events of 1936-1939, until I see the differences.

"Are Arab armed militias being organised in the West Bank with the approval of the army and with its organisational and financial encouragement? The word 'militia' is probably exaggerated, at least at this stage. On the other hand, the term 'security units' no longer fits, especially in these days of escalated conflict in the West Bank, not only with the PLO but with Jordan as well. The truth lies somewhere in between. Against the PLO camp and the Jordanian Camp that had always claimed to represent the interests of the Palestinian inhabitants in the occupied territories, the Military Authorities have tried to develop in recent months a third force, the villagers' associations. 'Security units' or 'militia' are an integral part of this third force. No one knows how strong they are. The leaders of the associations talk of thousands, and we heard about hundreds who had been trained by the Israeli army. Is the truth once again somewhere in between?

"Just as the associations are not only a means to transfer public funds to those that Israel favours, but also a means for political manipulation using the managing authorities they are given, so the many young armed men around them are not only bodyguards, as they claim. We hear that these young armed men are used with the knowledge of the authorities for policing tasks and for political harassment.

"People who drove through Ramallah at night in the past month report that they were stopped and questioned by armed patrols of the village association. Others reported about mixed patrols of Israeli soldiers and association men. On another occasion such an armed patrol broke into the house of a known PLO supporter, beat him, confiscated books and documents and took the man to the police station. If these reports are true, Israel shall not be the first occupation force to try to control using a native militia."

The village leagues have caused great suffering and terrorised the population.

In the following affidavit, the deponent tells of how she was interrupted while at work in her field by the arrival of armed members of the village league. She describes the events that followed their arrival, which involved beatings and shootings, leaving one person with gunshot wounds and one dead. The action of the army that followed the shootings is also recounted:

"On Saturday, 9 June 1982, at about 8.00 o'clock in the morning, I left home with my daughter, who is 30 years old, and married to one of the residents of our village. We went to our field, which lies about 225 metres from my house and no more than 25 metres from the home of (X). Upon arriving at the field, we began working, but were interrupted a quarter of an hour later when we were attacked by three strangers whom I had never met before. They wore civilian clothing, spoke Arabic and carried weapons whose make I don't know. They stepped down from a white jeep and proceeded to shoot in the air, while four other men remained in the jeep which was parked near the house of X, which is about 250 metres from the main street in the village.

"Consequently, and because of the shooting, my daughter and I began screaming and calling for help, but one of the armed men grabbed my daughter's hair and began dragging her along the ground. Another of the armed men did the same to me. They were joined by a fourth armed man from the jeep and they proceeded to beat us with sticks. Our pleas for mercy were to no avail — 'In God's name! For God's sake! May God protect us!' But the armed men continued to beat us. Then they dragged us to where the jeep was standing, next to the house of X.

"Suddenly, I noticed my sons D and A and their cousins H and S attacking the armed men, who were still beating us with sticks and the butts of their rifles, with stones. The armed men shot at my sons and their cousins, particularly H, who was shot on the inside of his right foot, and I saw him limping hurriedly into the house of X. My son D followed him, but the presence of the armed men initially prevented D from following his cousin H inside.

"They started shooting at him and were joined by the three men who had remained in the jeep. Meanwhile, my daughter and I tried to protect D by hiding him behind us and I tried to cover him with my body and hands. This caused one of the armed men to strike me on the hand with a stick, which broke my left hand, an injury from which I am still suffering.

"Then two of the armed men carried me into the car which stood about 10 metres from the house. I saw my daughter and heard her yelling at one of the children inside the house, ordering him to open the door and enable D to enter the house after H. The child did open the door. D entered and closed the door behind him. When that happened, the armed men grabbed my daughter and dragged her and put her with me in the car. They then started to break the doors and windows of the house in which H and D were, as well as shooting, but they were unable to get into the house. This forced them to

179

go up to the roof. Two of them went up there and broke down the door to the stairwell.

"When these two succeeded in entering the house, they opened the door for the other armed men. I saw D leaving the house hurriedly and escaping to the back of the house, from the left side. I was alarmed when one of the armed men followed him, shooting at him, and they both disappeared from my view. Then I heard shouting and I did not know the reason, but the armed man who was standing next to the car asked the person he had called Mohammad whether the person hit was 'one of us or one of them' ('us' being the armed men, and 'them' being the villagers). Mohammad informed him that it was one of 'them'. I sensed then the armed man being overcome with a palpable sense of fear. He started muttering beside the car and calling the rest of the armed men to flee. He ordered us to leave the jeep quickly, and all seven got in and drove off in the direction of the road leading to . . ., which is 7 kilometres from the village. They also took with them H who had been hit in the foot and A who is a sick young man.

"I rushed to the back of the house where the shouting had come from and found my son D lying on the ground with his arms outstretched and blood seeping from his mouth. I was shocked at this sight and began sucking his blood, thinking he was injured in the mouth, but when I placed my hand under his head to pull him towards me, my fingers sank into the back of his bloodied head. D continued to snort feebly and I stayed with him until my son A came with his cousin S. Together we carried D to the main street which was about 250 metres away and awaited a car to take D to the hospital.

"Half an hour later a Peugeot car owned by a blacksmith from . . ., who happened to be working in our village that day, came by. He stopped his car and helped us to carry D and sped away with my son A, 22 years old, and his cousins F, 21 years old, and S, 24 years old, and one of the villagers. As soon as we arrived at the hospital in . . ., the nurses took D directly to the first-aid and operations room and I waited outside, but they allowed his brother to go in with him.

"Shortly afterwards, A returned to me. I asked him about D's condition, and he told me that one of the doctors had ordered his transfer to the Hadassa Hospital in Jerusalem because of the seriousness of his condition. He was transferred by a Jordanian Red Crescent ambulance to the Hadassa Hospital. He was accompanied by his cousins F and S, while my son and I waited for them in . . ., since the nurses prevented me from travelling with D in the ambulance.

"About an hour and a half later the ambulance returned and they told me that D needed blood. A and five other young men, two from our village and three from . . . went by taxi to the Hadassa Hospital to donate blood. When my son returned to the village at about 3.00 p.m., he told me that D had died before he and the other blood donors had arrived.

"At about 3.30, ten military vehicles, packed with soldiers and an Arab police car arrived at the village. They ordered a crowd of about 400 men, women and children, who had gathered to await the arrival of the body of the martyr, to move towards the centre of the village and to gather there without making any disturbance. Otherwise, they would take necessary measures to maintain the peace. These orders were spoken by policeman J. The crowd obeyed. The military vehicles and police cars continued to patrol the streets, while about ten soldiers surrounded the crowd.

"At about 8.00 p.m., eight soldiers and three Arab policemen, including policeman J, came with a list of 15 young men. J read out the names and found ten of them, including my son A, and ordered them to go into two vehicles (one a police car, the other an army vehicle). As my son later told me, they led them to the headquarters of the military governor in . . ., where they spent the night outside in the cold. The next day they were taken to Al-Fara'a prison in Nablus, where they stayed for twelve days.

"At about 10.00 p.m., the soldiers ordered those gathered to go home and informed them that they would be notified as soon as the body arrived. The villagers responded to the orders of the soldiers, but my relatives and I continued to demand the body of my son. It was finally returned on Wednesday, 23 June 1982, at about 3.00 p.m., when about twelve military vehicles and a police van came to the village with the body. As soon as they arrived, they imposed a curfew on the village and started shooting in the air. They requested three of the relatives of the martyr to attend the funeral ceremony. They permitted my brothers and me to see him before the burial. The villagers insisted on being present at the burial ceremony and were permitted to do so by the soldiers provided they kept quiet."

In 1983-84, following the adverse publicity which the leagues got in the media, the presence of the leagues in the cities has become less evident. But contrary to the belief of many, the leagues continued to operate and increase their power in the villages.

It is clear by now that Israel is not offering the Palestinians any measure of political independence. The assumption, therefore, that the leagues are being prepared to assume any political power is groundless. However, it is consistent with Israeli policy to attempt to influence life in West Bank Palestinian society whereby types of organisation such as the village leagues become the dominant power in the society. It also appears to be Israel's policy to have Palestinian society return to the traditional tribal law — the *Qanoun Ashaari* — and have the tribal courts replace the regular courts.

When a murder occurred in Tulkarem in the spring of 1984, the members of the village league in the area got together and formed a tribal court and drew up conditions which they attempted, with the acquiescence of the military government, to impose on both the family of the accused and on the regular court that was looking into the matter. They ruled that the family of the accused should be exiled from the area and that the court could not release the accused on bail.

The regular courts have not yet been replaced by tribal courts, which latter have not been in operation as the sole arbitrators of disputes for more than a hundred years. But with the deterioration that is taking place in the local courts (and which the authorities encourage) the Tulkarem case may have been a test by the authorities of a new policy to give the leagues judicial powers in addition to their vigilante activities.

Mayors and Local Committees

The appointed mayors in several towns have a record of behaving harshly and arbitrarily towards the residents of their towns. The worst case is that of Jenin.[72]

On 6 July 1982, the mayor and local council of Jenin became the fifth municipal council to be dismissed by the Israeli authorities. The council was replaced by a three-man committee headed by a local businessman, Shehab Sanouri.

The Committee took over all the powers and responsibilities of the elected council, which include the provision of water and electricity. It became clear that the committee was treating the duty to provide these basic amenities as a favour to be granted or withheld on an

182

arbitrary basis.

The following are some cases of the cutting off of the electricity and water supplies to residents of the town of Jenin by the municipal council appointed by the military authorities.[73]

1. On 6 October 1982, water and electricity supplies were cut off from the office of Engineer Wafa Mira'. They were reconnected on 23 November 1982.

2. From 9 October to 15 October 1982, water and electricity supplies were cut off to café owner Mahmoud Muhamad Balsheh on the grounds that he "was not providing the public with services", having failed to provide coffee to the municipal workers.

3. Water and electricity supplies were cut for a period of one month beginning on 7 October 1982 to the house of Muhamad Hasouneh, where seven people live, on the grounds that he had tampered with the water meter. An employee of the Authority denied that there had been any interference with the meter.

4. Water and electricity supplies were cut off to the bakery of Mousah Issa Abu Ajaj for five days without reason.

5. The pharmacy of Naser El Nafa'a was without water and electricity for 45 days, and his house, where seven people live, was also without water and electricity for two days at the beginning of October 1982.

6. Water and electricity supplies were cut off for three days to the Eastern quarter of the town of Jenin, where approximately 3,000 people reside, after graffiti against the municipal council was found on the walls.

7. Water supply was cut off to the house of Adli Khalil Abdulah Asreiri on 6 November 1982. He made a complaint against the municipal council, which retaliated by cutting off the electricity as well on 15 December 1982.

8. Water supply was cut off to the house of Bassam Sulieman Mustafa Arkawi on 6 November 1982 and it was reconnected the next day. The electricity was cut on 13 December and was reconnected four days later after he made a new contract with the council and was forced to pay a contribution to them.

9. Electricity and water supplies were cut off to the house of Abdel Karim Mahmound Yusuf Abu Na'ah on 14 December 1982 because he acted as a surety for Bassam Arkawi. When he withdrew, his

water and electricity were reconnected. Bassam had to find some-one from the town of Nablus to act as his surety.

10. As a result of a fight between the children of four residents of Jenin with the children of the appointed mayor of Jenin, Shihab Sanouri, water and electricity supplies were cut from the houses of their parents for periods of seven to twelve days.

Violations by Jewish Settlers

The means by which the land has been taken to establish Jewish settlements in the occupied territories has been described in this study; the legal system that has been set up to enable the enforcement of different sets of laws for Jews and Palestinians has also been described. This section deals with the consequences of the present policy on the human rights situation of the Palestinians in the West Bank.

The Case of Kiryat Arba, a Jewish settlement near Hebron

"Things are happening at Kiryat Arba", wrote Michael Meron in Ha'aretz on 29 October 1982, referring to the negligence of the security forces in dealing with offences committed by the settlers of Kiryat Arba against the Palestinian population.

"People are detained by the security forces very secretly and are released surprisingly fast, bailing themselves out. One of the paragraphs in their 'freedom agreement' is not to talk to journalists. One of the charges: planting bombs. Amongst those detainees is Moshe Rosenthal who is in charge of security at Kiryat Arba."

Tzvi Katzover, the brother of a Kiryat Arba councillor told Mr. Meron that "after an incident they get organised spontaneously and go out to the streets. On several occasions they broke windows in houses and cars belonging to Arabs. If they happen to meet an Arab on the street at the same time, they would also beat him up . . .". The writer continues:

"Tzvi Katzover wants to maintain good relations with his Arab neigh-bours. But knowing them well, he knows that they only understand the language of force. The Arabs don't understand democracy, he says. They understand a different language. With them you must use collective punishments in order to deter."

184

The conclusion which journalist Amnon Rubinstein reaches in an article entitled "Outside the Rule of Law" (published in *Ha'aretz* on 5 April 1982) is that: "Two classes of residents have been created in the territories: Arabs who are subject to the military government, and Jews who come under the aegis of Israeli law".

Kiryat Arba is the oldest of the Jewish settlements in the West Bank, having been established in 1972. It is also the most inhabited and the closest to Hebron, an Arab city with 60,000 inhabitants, in the West Bank. The relations between the Jewish settlers of Kiryat Arba and the neighbouring Palestinians can be taken as representative of the relations between the two communities generally throughout the West Bank. For this reason, most of the examples described here about the human rights violations suffered by the Palestinian West Bank population at the hands of Jewish settlers will be drawn from the Hebron area. It must be stressed, however, that it is not only the settlers in this settlement who commit violations of human rights. Similar incidents have also occurred involving other Jewish settlements in the West Bank.*

A recent public opinion poll conducted in Israel and published by the *Jerusalem Post* on 13 January 1984, showed that 18.7 percent of the Israeli public supports terrorist activities by extremist Jewish groups against the Palestinian civilian population in the Israeli occupied territories. Amongst supporters of the then ruling Likud coalition, the percentage reached 26.2. For further discussion of official and public support for Jewish terrorists, see Introduction.

Violations of the right to life

Most settlers above the age of 18 years are either regular or reserve members of the Israeli army. In either capacity they often serve in the West Bank along with the other soldiers in the Israeli army. Their readiness to use their arms to shoot at civilians, documented in the report of the Assistant Attorney-General, Yehudit Karp, exceeds that of the other soldiers. When shooting takes place by soldiers, it is not possible, however, to discover whether the injury or death was caused by a settler soldier or a non-settler. Violations committed by the army have been discussed in a previous section. The examples given here are only

---

* Both the Karp report and the report of the International Center for Peace in the Middle East mention many more examples of settler vigilante activities which have not been investigated by the authorities.

185

of incidents perpetrated by settlers wearing civilian clothes.

The Ja'abari family was sitting at home one night watching television. Their house is close to Kiryat Arba. Outside, the Jewish Feast of Purim was being celebrated by the settlers. The Feast of Purim, as described in the Book of Esther, chapter 9, commemorates the day when "the king's command and edict were about to be executed on the very day when the enemies of the Jews hoped to get the mastery over them, but which had been changed to a day when the Jews should get the mastery over their foes". The events that took place that evening were described by Fatima Ja'abari, the mother of the victim, in a statement under oath. She said:

> "We were sitting at home watching television when suddenly we heard the sound of shots inside the house. Bullets penetrated the walls, windows and doors, and the shrapnel went all over the room where the members of my family (whose number is 14) were sitting. But the bullets did not hit anyone except my daughter, Alia, aged five, sitting absorbed in the TV programme. I saw that she was wounded on her leg and she fell on the floor, losing consciousness. I went from one room to another to try and find out who did it. I saw eight armed people walking on the street and chanting in a loud voice in both English and Hebrew. I made my children interpret what was being said. It was "Leave this land, this is the land of Israel. We shall slaughter you."

An article by Dani Rubinstein in the Israel daily, *Davar*, on 9 April 1982 carried a report of another shooting near Hebron:

> "Two Israeli contractors came upon a stone roadblock at the village of Beni Naim, east of Kiryat Arba. They were hit by stones and turned back to Kiryat Arba. There they found some settlers, including Avi Nir, and left again for Beni Naim. Once again, they came up to the stones. Avi Nir opened fire and is suspected of killing a boy from the village, who was taken to the Hebron Hospital where he died. The police spokesman said that the matter would be investigated and that a man from Kiryat Arba was wanted for questioning."

Avi Nir was allowed to spend a week at work as usual before finally being persuaded to make a statement to the Bethlehem police. No one has ever been charged as a result of the fatal shooting.

The reluctance to investigate the matter on the part of the police was shown in another incident, referred to in the same article, which occurred some weeks previously. Settlers from the settlement of Shilo had met stone throwers on the main road and opened fire on them. An Arab boy from the village of Sinjel was killed and a settler from Shilo, Nathan Natanson, was detained as the suspected murderer. After two days the police changed the charge from murder to manslaughter and he was discharged on bail.

Miriam Yusuf Khalil, from the town of Sinjil, mother of a 17-year-old student, Muhamad Abdullah Yusuf, who was murdered by the settlers, said that on Monday, 15 March 1982 her son left home to go to school in Sinjil. When the other students returned and he didn't, she learned that there was a demonstration that day in Sinjil and that Mohamed Salim Saif, a student from Abween, had been arrested and Ayman Khalil Khasib, a student from Aroura, was kidnapped.* The next day the mother went to the police station to inquire about her son. There she met an officer called Dabbas who told her that her son was amongst those who were arrested.

Two days later she went again to the police station and took with her some winter clothing for her son. The police officer took the clothing which they promised to give her son. Two days later, on 20 March, shepherds from the town found the corpse of her son on a nearby hill, 150 metres away from the main Nablus-Ramallah Road. The police, the army and a doctor examined the body, which was then buried. But by then news of the murder had reached the newspapers and it was reported in many of the Israeli dailies. A large number of soldiers came back, imposed curfews on the town and forced some residents to dig out the body which was taken for an autopsy and returned four days later at 1.30 in the morning. Relatives of the deceased were forced at gunpoint to re-bury the body.

There were reports also of killings by settlers in other parts of the West Bank.

On 26 October 1982, Hisham Lutfi Abu Muslam, aged 14, from the refugee camp Ballata, near Nablus, was murdered by settlers while he was leaving school where a demonstration was taking place. Maysoon Kannam, aged 12, from the village of Aroub near Hebron, was killed by settlers as she was going to the store during curfew to fetch some food for the family.

---

* There are many known instances of kidnapping by settlers when the person kidnapped was taken into the settlement and intimidated. This is another example of the settlers taking the law into their own hands.

Terrorising the population and destroying property

Sa'deah Al Bakri, a widow who lives close to Kiryat Arba, has suffered from repeated terrorist actions against her by Jewish settlers who are pressuring her to abandon her house so that the land upon which it stands can be acquired to enlarge the settlement. Her suffering became known in Israel, and members of the Peace Now movement offered their assistance against such acts of hooliganism. To many Palestinians and Israelis, Sa'deah Al Bakri is the symbol of steadfastness in the face of the expansionist designs of the Jewish settlers. Below is an account[74] given in a statement made under oath in October 1982 of what this woman has suffered over the years:

"It was our misfortune and that of other people in our area, that the settlement of Kiryat Arba was established on our land. Fourteen dunums of our land were expropriated when Kiryat Arba was first established (east of Hebron). Things didn't stop there, we started being harassed more than others because our house, which was there before the 1967 occupation, was situated about ten metres from the barbed wire fence which surrounded the settlement. The settlers tried hard to tempt my husband to sell them the rest of our land (about three dunums) which was next to the settlement.

"When my husband absolutely refused, the harassment and terrorism started. In 1972, a hand grenade was thrown at our house at about 1.00 a.m., destroying part of our house frontage. My husband was arrested by the military and held for eight months without trial or charge. In 1980, while two of my sons, Nasir, 15, and Eid, 13, were on their way home from a nearby shop, they were chased by some settlers. I was startled by my sons' cries of terror, and when I came to the door the settlers turned and went back to their settlement.

"In 1981, the settlers attacked our land, which we had refused to sell, and brought bulldozers and started working on it. When my seven children and I tried to stop them, they beat us and cursed us but we managed to stop them temporarily and they finally left. But I fear they will return and try to take the land again.

"In February 1982, at 2.00 a.m., two bombs were thrown at our house. Luckily, one hit part of the house that we don't use as it hasn't been furnished yet. The other bomb caused damage to another room. The door was completely destroyed together with some car equipment that my husband used, as he was a driver prior to his death. The next day a military investigation team came, and we showed them the damage and told them what had happened, but all they did was gather up the pieces of shrapnel of the bombs that were on the ground and chase away the reporters who were at our house at the time. On 24 February, 1982, at about 3.00 a.m., another bomb was thrown at our house by the settlers. It hit the wall of the room we were in and damaged it.

"Other harassment has been the fighting of the settlers' children with my children; the breaking of our windows in 1981; and the constant stealing of fruit and vegetables from our land. At this point, we don't know whom to turn to, as our future is in jeopardy, especially since my husband's death in 1977, as he was the one who dealt with these problems. A life like ours with all the harassment and ill-treatment we receive from the settlers is devoid of human rights. Wouldn't it be better to be dead rather than to live under those circumstances?"

Attacks on property

The examples given in this and the following sections are drawn from complaints[75] by residents of the Hebron municipal areas, submitted either to the municipal council (before the dismissal of the council in July 1983) or to the military governor of Hebron with copies to the council. A record of these complaints is kept at the municipality in Hebron.

Many complaints have been submitted about attacks by settlers on vineyards and fruit orchards.

Nimer Muhamad Mousa Gaith, Muhamad Mahmoud Taha, Fahed Ahmad Yacoub Jaber and the widow Hanieh Salim, each complained of attacks on their land with bulldozers by settlers from Kiryat Arba, uprooting of vineyards and fruit trees. One complaint, dated 4 April 1981, described the removal of the soil from the complainant's field to the settlement.

Complaints of settlers throwing bombs near dwellings causing the windows to be shattered, breaking into empty houses and occupying them, and entering inhabited dwellings armed with clubs and daggers and demanding to look around, claiming that they are the owners of the house, have been submitted by Kaid Shaid Danna, Mahmoud Hamous and Hussam Khatib. Adel Nasser Ed Din complained to the Area Commander of the West Bank that settlers entered his house and attempted to put their furniture in it. He evicted them and put on locks, but they broke the locks, removed the doors and carried them to the settlement.

Before his deportation in 1981, Mayor Fahed Kawasmeh complained to the Minister of Defence of settlers entering the house of Abdel Aziz Dawoud Nayroukh, breaking his furniture and attacking his wife. Other complaints describe settlers placing barbed wire on the property of the residents of Hebron.

On 6 February 1983, the Kiryat Arba local council uprooted four high tension electricity pylons belonging to the Hebron municipality, cutting electricity to 25 Arab families in the Boyeira Quarter. The pylons were repaired and electricity reconnected, but on 8 February the settlers again attacked the pylons, causing further damage.

Disposing of sewage over Arab property

Several complaints have been made from 1976 to 1978 concerning the sewage disposal system of the Jewish settlement, Kiryat Arba. The residents of the Wad El Husayn Quarter, near the settlement from the southwest, submitted a petition to the military governor of Hebron on 31 October 1976 in which they complained that the main sewerage pipe of the settlement, which passes through their quarter, had burst and that the sewage was seeping into their drinking water wells and their orchards, causing fruit trees to die, and dangerous insects to gather around their houses. They complained to the local council of Kiryat Arba in 1975 but were told that this was the problem of the Hebron municipality. They complained to the Hebron municipality who promised to raise the matter with the military government. The health department, to which they complained on 4 August 1976, did come and inspect and were appalled at the health conditions the quarter was suffering, and they also promised to get in touch with the military authorities. When nothing was done, the residents sent a complaint, this time to the military governor.

Other complaints to the military governor on the problem of the sewage from the settlement were made on 9 April 1978 by Issa Salieman Errazim, who complained that the sewage gathering around his house was causing a bad smell, attracting flies and mosquitoes, making it impossible for him to sleep and endangering the health of his children.

190

The residents and owners of the lands situated in the part of Hebron called El Zeif also had similar complaints.

Threats and attacks on the person

Over the years there have been many complaints made of the settlers roaming around the houses of Arab residents living near the settlement, exploding bombs, shooting or calling out threats at the residents to entice them to leave. Similar complaints have been made by Arab residents living near the Birkat Avraham Yeshiva in the Old City in Jerusalem where the students refused to repair a severe sewage leak into the families' rooms. See report in *Al-Fajr* English weekly, 3 August 1984.

Haj Abdel Rahim Muran complained to the Mayor of Hebron on 5 September 1976 that at about 11.00 in the evening on 4 September 1976 settlers from Kiryat Arba attacked his house, assaulted his family and went out to the vineyards and uprooted them.

A petition signed by 5 people addressed to the military governor of Hebron and to the mayor, describes attacks by settlers on the houses of the complainants. The settlers threw stones at their houses, shot at the complainants and caused a lot of damage and fright. The windows of the houses were shattered and the settlers assaulted the women. The residents informed the police and the army but neither seemed concerned. One officer told the complainants that "the police know who is responsible and they will call them when they feel like it".

Other complaints describe attacks made against the guard of the Ibrahimi mosque in Hebron on 30 April 1976. The guard had intervened on behalf of a child of about five years of age whom a settler was attacking. But the settler screamed at the guard and drew his gun at him threatening to shoot him. The guard called the police who let him go. Kayed Said Da'ana complained on 21 February 1982 that the settlers were circling his house at night and looking into the house through the windows. He describes that he was awakened when he heard them trying to break into the house. Then he heard an explosion which shattered the door.

Walid Bahjat Taher Es Sharief complained on 14 March 1983 of finding a box by the door of his house. He informed the police who discovered that in the box was bread, meat and a bomb. The police exploded the bomb.

The Mayor of Hebron complained on 1 March 1983 that a bomb exploded outside Al Qazazin mosque in Hebron on Friday, 25 February at midday, shortly before about 3,000 worshippers left the mosque. He writes that "two local inhabitants were injured when the device went off under a pile of stones next to the mosque . . . and two cars parked in the same area were seriously damaged." In the same complaint, the Mayor refers to an earlier incident which took place on 29 October 1982, in the soccer field in Hebron where a bomb went off 30 minutes before the beginning of the match, injuring two people. A large number of spectators were expected to attend the soccer game.

The Jewish settlement inside Arab Hebron

In the spring of 1968, a group of supposed "Swiss tourists" under the leadership of Rabbi Moshe Levinger, booked into Hebron's Park Hotel. This was the beginning of the Jewish settlement inside Arab Hebron. The succession of events was narrated in an editorial in the *Jerusalem Post* on 12 July 1983.

"The settlers were granted permission in 1970 to establish Kiryat Arba as a wholly Jewish suburb north of Hebron. At the time, that was a signal achievement for the settlers. But while they seemed to have their hands busy expanding Kiryat Arba, the settlers did not abandon their real purpose: of a Jewish return to the heart of Hebron and perhaps more, no matter what the cost.

"The first overt step towards realisation of that dream was the unauthorised occupation of Hebron's Haddassah Building by a group of Kiryat Arba women and children in the spring of 1979. Prime Minister Begin, to his credit, criticised the invasion. 'In this country,' he told the cabinet, 'there will be no squatting and no seizing of houses in Hebron, and there will be none in Tel Aviv either. When people just march in and take over houses, they have to be expelled.'

"But expelled they were not, and in fact their numbers increased. When a year later, Arab terrorists killed Yeshiva school student, Jehoshua Sloma, in Hebron, the illicit occupancy was legalised. When a little later six Hebron Jews were murdered by terrorists, the cabinet agreed that a 'proper Zionist response' would be to revive the Jewish community in the town, and Hebron's Mayor Fahd Kawasma was dismissed."

That was how Kiryat Arba and what the journalist David Richardson has described (in an article entitled "Hebron Test") as "the three tiny islands of Jewish revivalism in the heart of the city" came to exist.

In Richardson's words, this settlement is "the source and training ground for the most uncompromising Israeli drive to reclaim all of Judea and Samaria" (i.e. the West Bank).

'And the moment is now'

In a grazing area off the main road to the Arab village of Dahriya, south of Hebron, about 500 Jews, most of them young and religious, assembled on 22 February 1983 to mourn the death of Esther Ohana, who died of her wounds after the stoning of the car in which she was travelling three weeks before.

Eighteen thousand residents of Dahriya, who had been on a 23-hour curfew for 19 days, were locked up in their houses. Those close to the grazing area where the ceremony was being held could hear what was going on. Few could understand what was being said, because Hebrew is not a language which the Palestinians in the West Bank understand.

"He who does not mete out death to murderers, to all those who throw stones", Rabbi Moshe Levinger said to the assembly, "is himself responsible for the murder of Esther Ohana. *God is the Lord of Vengeance.* A normal situation calls for love, singing and friendship – but there comes a moment for vengeance . . . and the moment is now." (Reported in the *Jerusalem Post* on 23 February 1983).

The following days provided several occasions for vengeance, but as it turned out the full opportunity for that came only four months later. Meanwhile, many clashes occurred, some of which were reported and are mentioned here. All the reports are from the *Jerusalem Post.*

On 1 March 1983, the *Post* reported that:

"Clashes between Jewish settlers in the Hebron area and their Arab neighbours continued for the second day yesterday. A resident of the village of Yatta complained that his car came under fire as he passed the Kach settlement of El Nakam (God's vengeance) outside Hebron, and passengers on a bus from Kiryat Arba alighted and stoned passing Arab traffic after their bus was hit by a stone as it passed the Dheisheh refugee camp."

Quoting a tourist travelling on a bus from Kiryat Arba to Jerusalem the day before, the paper said that the passengers (some of whom wore uniforms) attacked passing Arab cars, smashing the windscreens of at least five vehicles and causing them to swerve off the road. The incident occurred outside the Bethlehem military government headquarters, which is on the main road to Hebron. The driver had stopped to report that a stone had been thrown at the bus as it passed the nearby Dheisheh refugee camp. "I've never seen anything like it", the tourist is reported as saying. "They went berserk and were bent on revenge."

A booby-trapped bomb exploded outside a mosque in Hebron on Friday at midday, shortly before worshippers ended their prayers there, the paper reported on 27 February 1983. Two local residents were injured when the device went off under a pile of stones next to the mosque . . . Hebron mayor Mustafa Nebi Natshe said that it was only by chance that more people were not injured since prayers in this particular mosque in the market had been slightly delayed. The paper said, "Two months ago, two boys were injured when a booby-trapped grenade exploded on a soccer field at a Hebron boys' school. A second grenade failed to go off. No one has been detained in the attack."

On 28 February 1983, the shooting already mentioned of five-year old Alia Ja'abari took place as she was watching television in her home. She was shot by settlers celebrating the Jewish feast of Purim.

On 2 March, the *Post* reported that Jewish settlers "chased and detained two youths from the town of Yatta after the settlers had been forced to stop at a roadblock of rocks and burning tires and then were stoned". The paper also reported the detention of two members of the Al Nakam settlement who had allegedly shot at a local Arab and that a dummy bomb had been discovered on Friday alongside a house belonging to Assad Bader opposite Beit Hadassah in the heart of Hebron. It reported that "local settlers who live in Beit Hadassah and some adjacent buildings want to take over the Bader's building which they claim was originally Jewish owned".

On 7 March the uprooting of four high tension pylons for the second time by Kiryat Arba settlers was reported. The first time, as has already been mentioned, was on 6 February 1983. This time the Kiryat Arba Council charged the Mayor of Hebron in the Council's local court with "aiding the setting up of an electricity pylon in the Jewish settlement's area to prevent the development of Kiryat Arba". In fact, the pylons had been there for five years.

On 4 March 1983, the *Jerusalem Post* reported that:

"Yesterday morning, four or five settlers from Carmel, southeast of Hebron, entered a boys' school in Yatta, and reportedly fired into

194

the air and threatened the teachers and students with their weapons after they were stoned as they drove through the large village. They detained two boys and handed them over to the police."

There were many other reports of destruction of property of Palestinians in Hebron by the Jewish settlers. It was reported on 13 May 1983 that a group calling itself "The Defenders' Fist" claimed responsibility for damage to some 60 vehicles. A 15-year-old Kiryat Arba youth was ordered held for eight days, the paper reported on 22 May, on suspicion of slashing car tyres and causing damage to a *falafel** stall in Hebron. It was reported on 1 July 1983 that a bus owned by an Arab company was set on fire on Wednesday night in the village of Al Arub near Hebron. The Israeli radio reported that Jewish settlers claimed responsibility for the arson. Another bus parked in the centre of Hebron near an area sealed off by the Israeli army was destroyed by fire on Saturday night. The paper said that "The police found empty gasoline cans and rags near the scene and have no doubt that the fire was the result of arson".

Arens' Jewish problem

"It is somewhat paradoxical," said an editorial in the *Jerusalem Post* on 5 July 1983, that "the major challenge to Defence Minister Moshe Arens as the new Minister in charge of the territories should be posed not by the local Arab residents but by the Jewish settlers". The editorial referred to several demands which the Jewish settlers in Hebron were making to the new Minister, amongst them the dismissal of Hebron's Mayor Mustafa Natshe. The editorial said that "the Defence Minister has resisted all these demands. To the settlers staging a sit-down strike in front of Hebron's military government headquarters, he said that their demand for Mr. Natshe's dismissal was 'ridiculous'. But it seems that there are Jews in Kiryat Arba and Hebron who are determined to prove to Mr. Arens that unless all the demands are duly met, they will take the law into their own hands to 'discipline' the Arabs."

In an article called "Mohammed Report", written by advocate Elyakin Haetzni of Kiryat Arba, who was one of the strikers in the Hebron Military Governor's Headquarters, and published in June in *Nekuda*, the magazine of the settlements in the West Bank and Gaza,

---

* A Palestinian national dish made from a paste of boiled chick peas.

the settlers' reasons for calling for the dismissal of the mayor of Hebron were laid out. Among the mayor's 'administrative irregularities' and 'criminal offences' that justified his dismissal was the fact that he had petitioned the Israeli High Court of Justice in December 1982 to order the Head of the Civil Administration of the West Bank to order the cessation of building operations in the centre of Hebron. The Mayor was also accused of receiving 'enemy funds' for local development projects.

Mustafa Natshe is the only West Bank mayor who has resorted, while in office, to the Israeli Court. His survival in office in the tense atmosphere of Hebron, when most of the other Arab mayors in the West Bank had been removed from office, was no doubt due to a large extent to his policy of moderation. He exercised great tolerance and he refrained from making extreme statements about the situation that was developing in his town, and he continued to resort to legal channels to express his dissatisfaction at what was taking place.

During his last two weeks in office, Natshe was put to the greatest test during his term. It was evident to him that the settlers were increasing the tension in the area and inciting the local population. He has claimed that the settlers were throwing blank bombs at their own buildings in the settlement in Hebron and claiming that they were being bombed by the Arabs. He sent a complaint to the Minister of Defence against the provocation of the residents in his city by the settlers. When a few days later a Jewish student, Aharon Gross, was stabbed in Hebron, the mayor condemned the act and said: "Such acts create disturbances and instability; violence does not serve the inhabitants, but rather makes life more tense." But Natshe's moderation was not to the liking of the Jewish zealots.

This, however, is not the only reason why the settlers prefer the Arab mayor to be ousted. As long as the municipal council, in its capacity as the local planning council, has jurisdiction over planning matters and the issuing of building licences, the settlers would be better served with an Israeli mayor sympathetic to their cause. An Israeli mayor would be able to withdraw the High Court case and would not restrain their expansionist plans by taking any other legal proceedings.

After waiting for the appropriate moment, the revenge which Rabbi Levinger had announced in the grazing ground in Dahriya during the memorial service of Esther Ohana, came on 7 July 1983.

The Good Samaritan

At noon on Thursday, 7 July 1983, Aharon Gross, aged 19, was standing near the Arab marketplace in the centre of Hebron waiting to hitch a ride from Kiryat Arba settlers. He was armed with an Uzi sub-machine gun. Aharon was a new immigrant to Israel from Staten Island, New York. He was a student at the Shovei Hevron Yeshiva, in the settlement in Hebron. His reason for joining that school was not his belief in the greater land of Israel ideology but because he knew the rabbis who headed it and was looking for a place where there was a close relationship between students and teachers.

At about one o'clock, just as a van with three armed settlers from Kiryat Arba was stopping to pick up Aharon, three Hebron Palestinians attacked the student, stabbed him and took his weapon. The three armed settlers left their wounded colleague and ran after the Palestinians, shooting after them.

There are three army posts in the area. A registered nurse, Mrs. Miriam Levinger, who heard the shooting came out of her house but was told by the soldiers that the wounded person was a Palestinian. She did not go to his rescue. She later justified her failure to assist as being due to her fear of the shooting.

Aharon's body remained on the ground bleeding. Meanwhile, panic had struck the Palestinian shopkeepers in the marketplace, many of whom began closing their shops.

Then Aziz Abu Sneina came to the scene of the attack and saw Aharon lying on the ground in a pool of blood. His glasses and kippa had fallen off. Aziz, an old simple man, examined the victim and thought he was his son. He raised Aharon, dragged him past some soldiers who did not come to his rescue and finally succeeded in transporting him to Alia Hospital, the nearest hospital to the place. There, the doctors examined the wounds and proclaimed Aharon dead. The agony of Aziz Abu Sneina, who believed the victim to be his son, was very great. He took the body to his home and put him on the bed and the family came around to bemoan the tragedy of the death of one whom they believed was their son.

Meanwhile, the three settlers had abandoned their chase and returned to where they left their colleague but found only the glasses, the kippa and blood. The body was not there. They telephoned Alia Hospital but were told that the only stabbing victim was a Palestinian whom they had proclaimed to be dead. After further investigation, the army found the house of Aziz Abu Sneina and took the corpse (which they diagnosed to be still living), to the clinic at the army station. The army arrested Abu Sneina and his son and declared a curfew in Hebron.

The doctors at the army clinic immediately established that Gross was dead. He had no pulse and his pupils were dilated. The doctors concluded that Gross had died between 30 and 45 minutes before he arrived at the military clinic.

After the army declared the curfew on Hebron, the settlers found the chance they had been waiting for. They set fire to the Arab-owned stores and stalls, causing extensive damage. The army did not intervene. The fire raged for two hours, destroying 90% of the market stalls and several stores. No one was detained or questioned in connection with the arson.

But the settlers did not only get the opportunity to destroy a part of the Arab marketplace to make room for the expansion of their settlement in the centre of Hebron. The Minister of Defence, Moshe Arens, conceded to the demand they had been voicing for several months; he dismissed the Palestinian mayor of Hebron and appointed in his place Zamir Shemish, who, for the past 16 years, had been the Custodian of Absentee and State Property in the city of Hebron and had acquired in the course of his office a good knowledge of the status of the immovable properties in the city and of the conditions of their owners.

Moshe Arens, who succeeded Ariel Sharon as Israel's Minister of Defence and remained in that post until September 1984, is as hawkish on the question of the eventual annexation of the occupied territories as the Prime Minister Menaham Begin. He told the striking settlers when he visited them on 23 June that he did not need prodding when it came to restoring and developing Hebron's Jewish quarter.

Whether or not he needed prodding, it is certainly the case that Mr. Arens gave in to all the settlers' demands, including those which only a few weeks before he had called 'ridiculous'. He dismissed the Palestinian mayor of Hebron. Not only that, but the reasons which he gave for dismissing the mayor bear a remarkable resemblance to those given in the article called "Mohammed Report", referred to above. The *Jerusalem Post* editorial on 10 July 1983 posed many questions: it asked:

"Why did the military authorities — with the approval of the Defence Minister — bring up a number of charges against Mr. Natshe and his municipal council, to justify their dismissal although most of these charges were not proved and had nothing to do with the circumstances immediately preceding Thursday's murder? Why was a request by the ousted mayor for an order nisi from the High Court of Justice against the Civil Administration for what he claimed as their aiding the Jewish settlers in destroying buildings in the centre of Hebron and putting up new structures in their place, listed as one of the 'irregularities' in Mr. Natshe's conduct. Why was this particular part of the military authorities' 'background paper' deleted from the official English translation?"

On 9 July, Natshe denied the 'charges' upon which his dismissal was based. He denied that he had boycotted the Civil Administration or refrained from supplying services to the settlers. He said that he did supply water and electricity to the settlers. Palestinian municipalities were not allowed to enter the buildings where the settlers lived to collect garbage for security reasons, he said, and he had refused to supply Beit Romano (where Aharon Gross was a student) with three-phase electricity because three-phase electricity, according to the municipal regulations, is reserved for industrial buildings.

On 10 July, the Labour Party criticised Jewish settlement inside Hebron, saying it would only increase hatred and eventually "exact a fearful price" and will cause a "tragedy for generations". But now (September 1984) that the Labour Party is in power, settlers in Hebron seem to be going on unstopped.

The United States also opposed the rebuilding of the Jewish quarter in Hebron and warned Israel against rebuilding it. But the United States' statement issued on 12 July was mild. It said:

"We do not consider the plan to build settlements in Hebron to be helpful in achieving an atmosphere in the West Bank conducive to the peace process."

On 13 July 1983, the Israeli Minister of Defence, Moshe Arens, said in the Knesset that the government will not be stopped from restoring the Jewish quarter of Hebron, "just as we restored the Jewish quarter in the Old City of Jerusalem . . .".

Now that the stage has been set, it does not take very much to raise passions. On Tuesday, 7 August 1984, several pages from prayerbooks were found discarded by a second-hand dealer in Hebron's flea market. A large crowd of heavily-armed settlers marched through the streets of Hebron. They included Jews from the United States of America, from Yemen, Morocco and Ethiopia. "Many were armed with at least large automatics stuck into their belts, while others had M-16s, Kalachnikovs and Uzi sub-machine guns slung over their shoulders.''*

The 'desecrated' pages were interred in a single earthenware urn covered with a plate of glass. The procession proceeded to the cemetery to bury the urn and to hear Deputy Minister, Dov Shlianski, tell the crowd that "wherever holy texts are desecrated, so will the Jewish people be desecrated. Wherever the Tora is torn and cut, so will throats be cut."

The crowd also heard Member of the Knesset, Rabbi Meir Kahane, who told them: "The Arabs are not to blame. We are, for the primal sin of 1967, when we did not take the God-given opportunity to drive out all the damned from the country."

The Arabs the speakers were referring to were in earshot as the speeches were shouted through a megaphone. Hundreds of soldiers with binoculars and automatic rifles surveyed the area nervously from every high vantage point.

Very speedily, an Ulster-type situation is being created in Hebron, with two communities living in enmity side-by-side. The consequences for the future are not too difficult to imagine.

---

* Reported in the *Jerusalem Post* of 8 August 1984.

References

(1) High Court case no. 302/72 p.d. 27 (2).

(2) The meeting was reported in the *Jerusalem Post* of 25 November 1982, "The U.S. Challenges Reported West Bank Policy Document".

(3) Military Order 5 (Order concerning closed areas) of 6 June 1967. This Order was subsequently replaced by a Military Order concerning closed areas (amendment) of 2 July 1967. Article 70 of Military Proclamation No. 3 (later replaced by Military Order Number 378, Article 90 of 20 April 1970). Under these provisions, large areas in the West Bank are declared closed areas. This is often used to keep away reporters from any areas where action may be taking place which the military government does not wish the media to report on, to isolate an area and prohibit communications between it and the rest of the world, as well as to restrict movement within it — often as a prelude to building a settlement there.

(4) In July 1967, the Jordanian Traffic Law was amended, replacing the former "Traffic Authority" with a "Principal Traffic Authority" which was given the power ot delegating some or all of its authority to the "Traffic Authority" of the areas (i.e. the West Bank). This Order was followed by another in August 1970 which included 173 sections. One of the amendments declared that a person convicted of a security offence shall not be provided with a driving licence nor may his licence (if he already has one) be renewed. A further amendment of September 1981 (by Military Order Number 936) empowers the traffic authority to cancel a driving licence or authorisation if it is proved that the holder has been convicted of a security offence. It also gave the authority discretion to cancel a licence in several cases, including where the conditions existing when the licence was granted have changed. A person aggrieved by the cancellation of his licence or refusal to renew it may appeal within seven days to a special appeal committee composed of military officers.

Another Order of September 1981 declared the establishment of a special committee of military officers to which all applications for licences to drive public vehicles must be forwarded. Among the conditions that must be met before the Committee may issue a licence is the production of a certificate from the Israeli police proving that the applicant has not been convicted of a criminal offence or served a sentence for a criminal offence within the last five years. This was later amended by Order Number 780, making it necessary for the applicant to submit a certificate proving that he has not been convicted of any security offence and prohibiting the driver of a taxi from refusing, without reasonable cause, to accept any passenger who is prepared to pay the fare.

(5) The officer in charge of the judiciary has used his powers which include those vested by Jordanian law in the lawyers' Bar Association, to reduce the period of training of

lawyers and to allow lawyers to carry out part of their training at a judicial department. See Military Orders Numbers 780 of 21 February 1979 and 528 of 7 October 1973. Lawyers in the West Bank require a licence from the officer in charge of the judiciary to practice. See also Military Order Number 745 (Order concerning licensing of medical professionals and their practices) of 4 January 1978, and Order Number 768 (concerning privileges granted by virtue of the law concerning authorised surveyors) of 8 October 1979. See also Military Order 87 (concerning Temporary Tourism law of 19 September 1967) and Order Number 173 (concerning Israeli travel agencies and tour guides) of 28 November 1967.

(6)   The Jordanian Labour Law no. 21 of 1960 has been amended by Military Order Number 825 of 20 March 1980, making it illegal for a person to be elected to the Administration Committee of a trade union unless he is working in the relevant trade or occupation or has been employed by the union. Possible candidates have been restricted by declaring ineligible for nomination: (i) any person who has been found guilty of committing a crime whose sentence exceeds 5 years imprisonment, (ii) any person who has been convicted of a security offence by a court having jurisdiction in the area or in Israel. The person responsible for the purposes of this law is given the following powers:
   — at least 30 days before the election the list of all the nominees must be submitted to him and he may strike off the list the name of any person whom he believes does not comply with the above provisions,
   — he may inform the union that he has annulled the membership of those whom he considers obtained membership illegally or who no longer satisfy the conditions mentioned above. If this happens, he may order the Committee to continue to operate with its reduced number of members,
   — he has the power to issue regulations to ensure that the above provisions are complied with.

(7)   Order Number 65 of 18 August 1967 restricts the right of business people to employ persons from outside the West Bank without first obtaining permission. Order 128 of 27 October 1967 empowers the Military Commander to order the closure of or take possession of any store which violates this Order by not opening up during the normal hours of business. The same Order prohibits the owner from refusing in any unreasonable way to sell his merchandise or provide a service within the normal scope of his business. A store owner is obliged to sell an official publication if so ordered by a Military Commander (Order Number 133 of 25 September 1967). Order Number 1103 prohibits anyone from producing or importing cosmetics without a licence.

(8)   Order Number 361 of 18 December 1969 obliges every garage owner to register the particulars of every car which he services in his garage. Any policeman may at any time enter a garage and inspect the register in which the particulars are written and ascertain the correctness of the information. Failure to keep this register renders a garage owner liable to imprisonment for two years and/or a fine of three thousand Israeli Liras. By an amendment made by Military Order Number 395, the garage owner is required to register the kind of damage that was caused to the car he is repairing, to give an estimation of how he believes it was caused, and to say what kinds of repairs he made to the car.

(9)   Military Order Number 26 concerning the supervision of currency, bills of exchange and gold, of 18 June 1967, and Military Order Number 33, concerning depositing money for security purposes, of 26 June 1967, Order Number 45 of 9 July 1967 vested in the Inspector of banks (who is appointed by the Area Commander) all the powers and functions delegated by the Jordanian banking law to the Jordanian government, the central bank and any other authority or person. An application, therefore, by a local person or authority to open a bank in the area must be made first to obtain permission from the

military appointee, the Inspector of Banks. Order Number 76 of 31 July 1967 declared the Israeli Lira to be the authorised currency, but without the Jordanian dinar ceasing to be legal tender in the area of the West Bank.

(10) In September 1967, all the powers and appointments vested by the Jordanian Insurance Law in the Jordanian government or in any of its ministries, authorities, or other person, were transferred to "the person responsible" appointed by the Area Commander. This was decreed by Military Order Number 93 of 22 August 1967. This Order also made many amendments to the Insurance Law in force at the beginning of the occupation, and placed all insurance activities under the direct supervision of the Israeli Insurance Syndicate.

(11) Military Order Number 50 of July 1967 prohibited the publication or bringing into the West Bank of any publication without the permission of the person responsible who was appointed by the Area Commander.

(12) Military Order Number 25 of June 1967.

(13) Farmers are subject to Military Order Number 47 (concerning the transport of agricultural products) of 9 July 1967; Military Order Number 49 (concerning closed areas – prohibition on transportation of goods) of 11 July 1967; Military Order Number 1010 (concerning the transportation of agricultural products – amendment 3 of 25 July 1982); Military Order Number 818 (concerning regulation of planting decorative plants) of 22 January 1980; Military Order Number 1015 (concerning control of planting fruit trees) of 27 August 1982; Military Order Number 134 (concerning the prohibition of the work of tractors and agricultural equipment from Israel) of 29 September 1967; and Military Order Number 1002 (prohibiting the sale of seedlings without licence and making it a requirement to obtain a licence in order to operate nurseries).

(14) Military Order Number 65 (concerning the prohibition on professions) of 18 August 1967.

(15) By virtue of this Order, the educational institutions in the West Bank are required to obtain permits for all their foreign staff.

(16) Military Order Number 398 (concerning companies) of 19 June 1970.

(17) Military Order Number 172 (concerning Objections Committees) of 22 November 1967.

(18) Military Order Number 952 (concerning the control of currency) of 20 January 1982.

(19) Military Order Number 973 (concerning the importation of money into the area) of 6 September 1982.

(20) According to an amendment of Military Order Number 973, by Order 1070 of 7 July 1983.

(21) Military Order Number 284 (concerning restrictions on training and contacting a hostile organisation outside the area) of 26 July 1968.

(22) Military Order Number 974 (concerning the Fund for the Development of Judea and Samaria) of 9 June 1982.

(23) Military Order Number 998 (concerning control of public institutions) of 11 July 1982.

(24) Income Tax Law No. 25 of 1964, Official Gazette No. 1800, p. 1455 of 16 September 1964.

(25) Military Order Number 28 (concerning Income Tax and Property Tax) of 22 June 1967.

(26) Military Order Number 770 (concerning Income Tax and Property Tax) (amendment 5) of 5 November 1978.

(27) The following principles and procedures are based on the governmental resolution of 11 October 1968:

"Supreme authority in an area administered by Israel is vested in the commander of the

IDF in the areas (hereinafter: the Area Commander).

b) The Area Commander is the exclusive formal authority within the area; he legislates when necessary, he is the executive, he appoints local officials including local judges, when necessary. The Area Commander is the sole address for the local inhabitants.

c) The Area Commander is subordinated to the Defence Minister through the IDF channels of command.

d) The various civil activities in the area will be conducted by the appropriate governmental offices, each office within its authority and budgetary responsibility. The representatives of the ministries shall coordinate their activities with the Area Commander. The representatives of the Ministries will be — as has been the case till now — Staff Officers of the Area Commander.

e) A representative of a ministry will act according to directives given by his minister and the directorate of his office within the framework of the authorised budget. Such activities are subject to coordination with and approval of the Area Commander."

From Singer, Joel, *The Establishment of a Civil Administration in the Areas Administered by Israel,* Israel Yearbook on Human Rights, Vol. 12 (1982), p. 275.

(28)   Benvenisti, op. cit.

(29)   Military Regional Court, Central Region Jurisdiction, file no. 325/82. The decision of the trial has been published but the record of the case has been kept secret. The material included in this section and the direct quotations of the witnesses who testified in the trial are based on the decision as well as on the evidence submitted in the trial, as reported by Israeli journalists who attended the sessions. The trial was reported in the article by Pedhazour, Reven in "A Peep into Pandora's Box," published in the weekly supplement of *Ha'aretz,* an Israeli daily, of 11 March 1983, and from reports in the *Jerusalem Post.*

(30)   Peace Now is an Israeli political grouping of individuals who are concerned with Israel's policy in the Occupied Territories.

(31)   *Jerusalem Post,* 15 October 1982.

(32)   *Jerusalem Post,* 12 November 1982.

(33)   *Jerusalem Post,* 18 February 1983.

(34)   *Ha'aretz* Weekly Supplement, 11 March 1983.

(35)   Such a prison has been established at Al-Fara'a (see *infra*).

(36)   The *Jerusalem Post* reported on 15 April 1983 that "Defence Minister Moshe Arens does not intend to rebuke Chief of Staff Rav-Aluf Rafael Eitan for his remarks on Tuesday about Arab stone-throwers, or to conduct an investigation into the matter". The paper said that the remarks of the Chief of Staff were made in a closed session of the Knesset Foreign Affairs and Defence Committee. Eitan was reported as saying that when 100 settlements are established between Nablus and Jerusalem stones will no longer be thrown at Jews there. "He then reportedly added: 'We shall create facts; the settlements will be established, and then the Arab stone-throwers will scurry about like cockroaches in a bottle.' " This statement was also reported in the *New York Times* on 15 May 1983.

(37)   All the testimonies quoted in this part have been collected by field workers of Law in the Service of Man, the West Bank affiliate of the International Commission of Jurists. They were all signed under oath after giving the signatory the warning required by law for submission of affidavits to a court of law. The original signed copies are all kept at LSM's office in Ramallah and may be examined upon request. About thirty of the affidavits collected in the same way, some of which are also quoted here, have been published by the Commission of the Churches for International Affairs of the World Council of

204

Churches, in 1983, under the title "Human Rights Violations in the West Bank: In Their Own Words."

(38) The *Jerusalem Post* reported on 4 November 1982, that a paratroop officer was found guilty of causing the death of a Palestinian in the village of Sa'ir near Hebron, by negligence.

(39) This information is from a survey conducted by Law in the Service of Man.

(40) Also reported in the *Jerusalem Post*, 29 August 1983.

(41) See Palestine Press Service's list of "Names of Palestinians Wounded, Martyred and Kidnapped", 18 March to 6 May, 1982, P.P.S., P.O. Box 19563, Jerusalem.

(42) Military Proclamation No. 1, dated 7 June 1967, declared the imposition of a general curfew on the West Bank.

(43) On 12 April 1983, the Israeli authorities sealed five houses in Thahriyeh belonging to the families of the five youths who had been brought to trial on the charge of being those youths who had thrown stones, causing the death of an Israeli woman. The sealings left over 40 people homeless.

(44) Since January 1983, curfews have been imposed in the West Bank as follows:
Nablus Old City
January 1, 2, 3, 9, 10, 22 to 25; February 3, 8, 14 to 16, 26 to 28; March 1 to 3, 5, 7, 8, 10, 12, 17, 21, 28 to 31; April 1 to 4, 17 to 19; May 1, 15; June 5, 6.
Dahariya
January 29 to 31; February 1 to 17; March 12 to 31; April 1 to 14.
Dheisheh
February 15 to 21; March 10 to 24, 30; April 3, 18; June 2, 3.
Jalazoun
March 7 to 31; April 5, 25.
Kalandia
February 14; March 11 to 14, 30; June 7, 8.
Al Amari
February 12 to 14; March 11 to 14.
Balata
March 3, 13 to 23, 30; April 2 to 6, 11, 17 to 19, 22, 27 to 31; May 1, 2, 15; June 5, 6.
Arroub
March 10 to 14, (21 to 30); April 4; May 5, 21.
Aida
March 10 to 21; May 13 to 16.
Askar
March 30, 31; April 6, 17 to 19; May 1; June 5, 6.
Ein Beit Elma
February 28; March 10 to 21; April 3 to 6, 17 to 19, 22; May 1; June 5, 6.
Halhoul
March 12 to 26; April 27 (main street closed).
Ramallah
March 6 (4 shops were closed for two weeks).
All dates are inclusive.

(45) Military Order 1071, dated 10 July 1983, amends Military Order 845 concerning increases in fines by augmenting the fine up to 1,500,000 IS (equivalent at that time to $ 25,000).

(46) Military Order 225 concerning rule of responsibility for Crimes, dated 1 March 1968

and Military Order 132 — Rules Concerning Trials of Juveniles, of 24 September 1967. Both these orders state that no person under the age of 12 may be arrested or tried. Military Order 132, article 4, states that a juvenile should be arrested and tried separately from adults, except where the Military Commander orders otherwise in particular circumstances. Article 6A of the Order, as amended, imposes on the parents or guardian of a juvenile between the ages of 12 and 18 the duty to pay the fine of a convicted juvenile. If they fail to pay the fine, they are liable to imprisonment for non-payment.

(47) Military Order 1031, Order Concerning Security Provisions (amendment 40), of 5 December 1982. The relevant section reads as follows:

"47 (a) (ii) Fine must be paid immediately.

"47 (a) (iii) (a) Increment is payable in addition to the fine if the complete fine is not paid within a specified time.

"47 (a) (iii) (b) The increment of 100 percent of the fine or of that part that is unpaid shall be added."

(48) See discussion of identity cards in Part Three.

(49) Law in the Service of Man has interviewed all those who have been placed under town arrest since 1978.

(50) See generally on Al-Fara'a, the press release made by The League for Human and Civil Rights, Tel Aviv, and the collection of Israel Shahak in the Shahak papers entitled: *Concentration camps, tortures and those who fight against them,* which includes also a letter from an army reserve soldier who had served at Al-Fara'a prison.

(51) International Committee of the Red Cross Annual Report, 1978, p. 31.

(52) Detainees in the West Bank have no absolute right to legal representation. Military Order 29, Order Concerning the Operation of Prisons, of 23 June 1967, article 11, states as follows:

"If a prisoner asks to see a lawyer and the Commander is convinced that the application is submitted for the purpose of a legal case pertaining to the prisoner, he must permit the prisoner to meet the lawyer in prison PROVIDED THAT THERE IS NO OBJECTION ON GROUNDS OF SECURITY AND PROVIDED THAT NOTHING IN THE INTERVIEW WOULD AFFECT THE COURSE OF THE INTERROGATION." (emphasis added by this author).

In practice, lawyers are NOT allowed to see clients who are detained except after the interrogation has completely ended (whenever this is) if they are allowed to see the client at all.

(53) Directed by Meron Benvenisti, former deputy mayor of Jerusalem.

(54) Order Number 92.

(55) Military Order 158, Order Amending the Water Supervision Law, of 1 October 1967.

(56) According to LSM figures, 9 homes have been demolished since January 1983, and 29 homes sealed.

(57) Military Order 50, Order Concerning Bringing in of Newspapers and their Distribution, 11 July 1967.

(58) Military Order 101, Order Concerning the Prohibition of Incitement and Adverse Propaganda, 27 August 1967.

(59) Defence (Emergency) Regulations, 1945, Palestine Gazette, 29 March, 937, p. 268.

(60) The military censor has claimed that some of the titles in the list are banned on account of their content, others because of the translation, preface or publisher.

(61) Military Order 107, Order Concerning the Use of Textbooks, 29 August 1967.

(62) See affidavit of Akram Hneiveh, editor of El Shaab newspaper in *Human Rights Violations in the West Bank, In Their Own Words,* Commission of Churches on International

Affairs, World Council of Churches, 1983, p. 51.

(63)   See *Ha'aretz*, 12 March 1982, Amos Elon: The People of the Book; *Ha'aretz*, 7 May 1983, Amos Elon; The Literary Border Guard; *Jerusalem Post*, International Edition, 11-17 April 1982, Benny Morris: IDF Source Tells How and Why Books are Banned. See also Index on Censorship, August 1984, Virgil Falloon: Excessive Secrecy, Lack of Guidelines — A report on military censorship in the West Bank.

(64)   Law in the Service of Man has made a thorough investigation of this practice and interviewed all the students who were affected by it. The report may be obtained from Law in the Service of Man, Box 1413, Ramallah, Via Israel. The International Commission of Jurists issued a press release on 10 January 1984 concerning this subject.

(65)   For a thorough analysis of Military Order 854, the full text of the Order and related orders and laws, see a study by Jonathan Kuttab, published by Law in the Service of Man, 1982.

(66)   Military Order 752, Order Concerning the Law of Administration of Villages, No. 5, of 1954 (amendment 4), 5 March 1978.

(67)   Law of Administration of Villages, no. 5 of 1954, Official Gazette of Jordan, 1169, 1 February 1954.

(68)   The Memorandum of Association of the Village League of Hebron, dated 1978.

(69)   See article on Village Leagues entitled: "Leagues out of their depth", by David Richardson in the Weekend Edition of the *Jerusalem Post*, 19 March 1982. Richardson writes: "With the active support of the military government the league prospered. Funds for village development long withheld or not even dreamed of suddenly became available . . . The assassination of the head of the Ramallah village league, Yusuf Al-Katib, prompted the military government to arm and train at least 200 of the league supporters who are now highly visible bodyguards and are well on the way to becoming a semi-private militia."
       On 20 June 1982, the *Jerusalem Post* wrote: "Israel has been supporting and arming members of the village leagues as a moderate counterweight to nationalist radicals concentrated in the larger cities of the West Bank."

(70)   Order 180, Licences to Carry Arms, 1967, as amended by Order 1080 on 3 October 1983.

(71)   Military Order 947, Order Concerning the Establishment of a Civilian Administration, 8 November 1981.

(72)   Note that pursuant to Military Order 164 (discussed in Part Two) no legal action can be initiated against municipal authorities appointed by the military without the prior written permission of the military government.

(73)   The examples mentioned here are from a press release of the International Commission of Jurists, Geneva, Switzerland, issued 16 February 1983; published in "Human Rights Violations in the West Bank, In Their Own Words", op. cit., p. 54.

(74)   This account was published in "Human Rights Violations in the West Bank, In Their Own Words", op. cit.

(75)   Law in the Service of Man has copies of all the complaints referred to here and later.

Conclusion

This book has described the Israeli solutions for the legal problems encountered in achieving the goal of annexing the West Bank without its inhabitants.

This gradual annexation is Israel's solution to the Palestinian/Israeli problem. It is consistent with the goal which successive governments have been pursuing of establishing a Jewish state throughout Palestine. The task will have been completed when a greater number of Jews come to live in the West Bank and Palestinians have been driven out.

Two questions must be answered here: Will this solution work out? Has an irreversible state of affairs been reached?

In answering the first question, it must be remembered that the Palestinians inhabiting the West Bank do not have the option of leaving and taking refuge in another country. Even if this were not the case, there is a strong feeling amongst the Palestinians in the West Bank that their steadfastness and holding on to the land (referred to as *sumoud*) is a national duty. This being the case then, despite the strong pressures already being exerted, it is highly unlikely that there would be a change in the determination of the Palestinians in the West Bank to stay — whatever the cost.

Those who claim that the changes that have occurred in the West Bank are irreversible suggest that it is in the interests of those Palestinians in the West Bank to call upon Israel to annex the area. In this way, they will become eligible for Israeli citizenship. They would then fight to acquire full civil rights under Israeli law.

Regardless of the fact that it is not likely that Israel will decide to annex the West Bank while a million Palestinians inhabit it, such a demand by Palestinians is highly unlikely. The Palestinians in the West Bank constitute a portion of the entire Palestinian nation. Many of those outside Palestine have been living under difficult conditions as refugees both in and outside refugee camps in different parts of the world. Despite the passage of more than 34 years since their exile, they have not lost their Palestinian identity. Their yearning to return to Palestine is as strong as ever.

The struggle of Palestinians in the West Bank is perceived as a part of the common struggle of all Palestinians for liberation and the establishment of a Palestinian state in Palestine.

As to the suggestion that the situation is irreversible, such a claim is not based on strong grounds. Surely 30,000 Jewish settlers can be dealt with if real intentions to arrive at a compromise peace solution exist? The legal, administrative and physical changes that have been made cease to be relevant if the Israeli government were to pursue a peaceful settlement. The changes described in this book have been made to enable the present situation of annexation of the land without the people to occur. If this position is altered, all the changes made to bring it about become irrelevant.

In fact, what the Israeli government is seeking is to drive home the conclusion that all has been taken care of to achieve the inclusion of the West Bank within Israel and that the expectation that the occupation will some day end is history because the situation has now become irreversible.

It must be remembered that the government of Israel is legally bound by the Camp David agreement to the principle of withdrawal of its military government and the establishment of local autonomy for the Palestinians. These legal obligations continue to be binding despite the fact that the government has not done anything to implement the agreement.

Israel's appreciation of its legal obligation helps explain the government's great rush, since 1979, to acquire and register land in the West Bank in the name of Jews and to complete the legal changes that have been carried out in the area since then and to place the Jewish settlements under Israeli law while reserving for the Palestinian population a separate and different legal status and administration. These changes were carried out in anticipation of the time (which could conceivably come) when Israel's status in the occupied territories will be examined. When such a time comes, Israel wants to be in a position to be able to argue that most of the land in the West Bank is already registered in the names of Jews. So whether or not Israel occupies the area, it owns most of the land there. Those who support annexation argue that the best two guarantees of continued Israeli control are for Jews to acquire legal title to the land and for the number of Jews inhabiting the area to be increased. The first will enable Israel to answer those challenging its legal status and the second protects against the possibility that a future Israeli government may decide to exchange territory for peace.

It must be admitted that the changes that have been carried out in the law are conducive to the achievement of Israel's goal. For the time being, the control of the Palestinians in the West Bank does not put any great risk on the Israeli public. In balance, the occupation is more of an economic benefit than a burden. Palestinians also provide a source of cheap labour for Israel's industry. The continuation of the military government facilitates the implementation of Israel's policies towards the Palestinians. An army is far more efficient in demolishing houses and driving people out of land which has been designated for Jewish settlement than a civilian government would be. It is not likely, therefore, that the occupation will end until the demographic balance has changed in favour of Jews.

In South Africa, where the situation resembles in part that of the West Bank, the black majority enjoyed South African citizenship. Now, the South African government is seeking to deprive all blacks of South African citizenship and to create the so-called independent Bantustans where all blacks who are not needed for South Africa's labour market are being transferred. Even those not transferred are 'allotted' the citizenship of one of the Bantustans.

By proclaiming that Jordan is Palestine, Israel is calling for the same solution for the Palestinians in the West Bank as the government of South Africa is enforcing against the blacks.* But the Palestinians in the West Bank who were born and have lived all their lives there will not go to Jordan, even if they could.

---

* In the first week of November 1984, a twin city agreement was signed between Ariel, a Jewish settlement in the West Bank, and Bisho, capital of the South African homeland Ciskei. The agreement was signed by Ciskeian President Lennox Sebe and Ariel's "mayor" Ya'cov Faitelson. "It provided for tourism and cultural, industrial and scientific exchanges between two towns-in-the-making, which have neither culture, science nor industry to offer." The ceremony was attended by Likud Knesset member Yoram Aridor (a previous Cabinet Minister) who spoke in terms of Israeli-Ciskeian brotherhood and a common struggle against a cruel world of double standards. The Ciskeian President described the occasion as "almost too precious to be scarred by words ... almost too glorious for ordinary men". The basic message of all the speeches, according to an article in the *Jerusalem Post* supplement November 9, 1984 (by Roy Isacovwitz), was that the twinning of Ariel and Bisho was "a mighty blow for freedom; that Africa's premier symbol of man's yearning to be free and independent had finally found a soul mate in the rocky Samarian hills."

Sooner or later, Israel will have to face reality and acknowledge the national existence of the Palestinians and deal with it. The solution cannot be for either the Israelis or the Palestinians to seek the destruction of the other. History has proven that this is just not possible. The real challenge is to find a workable formula for the two groups to co-exist together in the land which both claim as their home.

The greatest obstacle against this is the policy of the United States government. By, in effect, subsidising Israel's settlement programme, the United States is encouraging the illegal Jewish settlement of the occupied territories. It is also preventing Israelis from feeling the full economic consequences of such a policy. It is difficult to believe that any group will have the wisdom and foresight to decide against a policy on moral grounds. It is the economic price to be paid that constitutes the stronger inducement for changing policy.

As long as the United States is footing the bill, the Israeli population is protected against paying any price and, therefore, calling for change.

The situation is akin to that of a rich uncle, who, to the detriment of the future of his nephew, pours money out to him and renders futile all the efforts of the other relatives to make the nephew take responsibility for his actions.

What is at stake, in an area as volatile as the Middle East, is not the future of the nephew or even of the community where he is destined to live. The peace of the world is at stake.